internet
inquiry

internet inquiry

conversations about method

Edited by

Annette N. Markham
University of Wisconsin–Milwaukee

Nancy K. Baym
University of Kansas

Los Angeles • London • New Delhi • Singapore

Copyright © 2009 by SAGE Publications, Inc.

For information:

SAGE Publications, Inc.
2455 Teller Road
Thousand Oaks,
    California 91320
E-mail: order@sagepub.com

SAGE Publications Ltd.
1 Oliver's Yard
55 City Road
London EC1Y 1SP
United Kingdom

SAGE Publications India Pvt. Ltd.
B 1/I 1 Mohan Cooperative
    Industrial Area
Mathura Road, New Delhi 110 044
India

SAGE Publications
    Asia-Pacific Pte. Ltd.
33 Pekin Street #02-01
Far East Square
Singapore 048763

Printed in the United States of America

Library of Congress Cataloging-in-Publication Data

Internet inquiry: conversations about method/edited by Annette N. Markham, Nancy K. Baym.
    p. cm.
Includes bibliographical references and index.
ISBN 978-1-4129-1000-2 (cloth)
ISBN 978-1-4129-1001-9 (pbk.)
    1. Internet research. I. Markham, Annette N. II. Baym, Nancy K.

ZA4228.I57 2009
001.4'202854678—dc22   2008001110

This book is printed on acid-free paper.

08   09   10   11   12   10   9   8   7   6   5   4   3   2   1

Acquisitions Editor:	Todd R. Armstrong
Editorial Assistant:	Aja Baker
Production Editor:	Astrid Virding
Copy Editor:	Gail Naron Chalew
Typesetter:	C&M Digitals (P) Ltd
Proofreader:	Ellen Brink
Indexer:	Nara Wood
Cover Designer:	Gail Buschman
Marketing Manager:	Carmel Schrire

Contents

Introduction

Making Smart Choices on Shifting Ground

Nancy K. Baym and Annette N. Markham

❖   ❖   ❖

Every generation believes it is singular in its experience of rapid and monumental social and technological changes. Ours is no exception. Early in the 21st century, "The Internet" marks our epochal particularity. The internet[1]—with all its capacities, interfaces, uses, and underlying technologies—both epitomizes and enables a seemingly constant barrage of reality-altering, globe-shifting changes. Far from slowing down, the barrage seems to continuously accelerate. Despite studying internet-related social phenomena since the early 1990s, the two of us regularly see new capacities and uses that shift how people make sense of and live their everyday lives and that raise profound challenges for researchers seeking to make sense of the internet's places and roles in this new world.

As qualitative researchers of media-saturated phenomena, we notice how the internet brings into sharp relief previously assumed and invisible epistemologies and practices of inquiry. In fact, challenges of conducting internet research have prompted its researchers to

---

1. "Internet" is often spelled with a capital "I." In keeping with current trends in internet studies, we prefer the lower case "i." Capitalizing suggests that "internet" is a proper noun and implies either that it is a being, like Nancy or Annette, or that it is a specific place, like Madison or Lawrence. Both metaphors lead to granting the internet agency and power that are better granted to those who develop and use it.

confront, head-on, numerous questions that lurk less visibly in traditional research contexts. Consequently, internet researchers have been compelled to reconsider basic principles and practices of qualitative inquiry, with important critiques of a priori methodological certainties. This theme comprises a strong thread throughout the book, discussed in different ways by the authors of this collection.

The internet changes the way we understand and conduct qualitative inquiry. This point is not new to the contributors to this collection, yet its resonance across this volume demonstrates its power. This came as somewhat of a revelation to us as editors. Qualitative scholars that we are, we studied the contributions once we had them in hand, individually and as a group, searching for common themes and patterns of meaning. What a surprise for us to discover that, although the main focus of the book is ostensibly the internet, the most important points contribute to nuanced and new understandings of qualitative inquiry in general.

Why did we put together this collection? Both of us finished our PhDs in Communication Departments in the early 1990s with dissertations that were among the first to focus on the internet as a site for and object of qualitative research. We were naïve enough to think that it would be relatively straightforward to transfer research strategies developed for studying face-to-face contexts to life online. Since those early years, we've witnessed and contributed to critical analyses of this assumption. We've welcomed a small flurry of methodological books on internet research and critical reflections on qualitative internet research and ethnography (well represented by Hall, 2004; Hine, 2005a; Johns, Chen, & Jones, 1999; and Mann & Stewart, 2000). This book contributes to and extends that line of research reflexivity. We aim to make many of the challenges and issues in conducting qualitative internet inquiry explicit so that readers can see how others have worked through them and can thereby heighten their own sensitivity to those concerns.

Qualitative approaches are open ended; the foundational principles of this epistemological category encourage practitioners to engage in dialogue that influences the structure of practice in the field: dialogue about critical decision points, ethical quandaries, and the uniqueness of the internet as a mediating factor in research (or the research site itself). Over the years, we found that our research approaches grew more sophisticated as we engaged in informal conversations with others who had studied similar contexts with different perspectives, or the inverse, with those who studied different contexts with similar perspectives. However, these discussions do not frequently appear in finished research reports or methods textbooks.

Research reports are carefully edited retrospectives, selected among different story lines and options, depending on one's audience and goals. Within these reports, research designs are generally presented as a series of logical and chronologically ordered steps. Seasoned scholars know there's a complex backstage story line and have experienced such complexities themselves. But for novice scholars, it is easy to imagine that the researcher's route was successfully mapped out in advance and that interpretive findings simply emerged from the ground or fell conveniently into the path. Qualitative research requires a tolerance for chaos, ambiguity, and inductive thinking, yet its written accomplishments—particularly those published in chapters and articles rather than monographs—rarely display the researchers' inductive pathways or the decisions that led them down those routes.

This book focuses on those decision-making processes in qualitative research that so often remain private. For this volume, we gathered some of the most accomplished qualitative internet researchers from varied intellectual traditions and asked them to explain how they have negotiated these challenges in their research practices, to make explicit the theoretical frameworks they have used to make decisions, and to offer advice to guide researchers as they confront these questions themselves.

This collection also addresses the broader challenges associated with doing research in this era of media-saturated and ever-shifting sociocultural contexts. Not only are the objects of our research shifting, so too are traditional academic disciplines, which is particularly evident in the interdisciplinary characteristics of internet-related research. The authors in this collection have found themselves grappling with a multiplicity of concerns within and outside their home disciplines. Their success relies on their ability to remain grounded as the research contexts, technologies, and the very nature of their social worlds seem to change, converge, collide, or collapse. We review some of the challenges in this era of research in this introduction, noting that even in these amorphous contexts, quality and rigor emerge from our abilities to comprehend and heed the lessons learned by previous generations of researchers while understanding the need for flexible adaptation, a process of reconsideration without reinvention.

❖ SOCIOCULTURAL CONTEXTS
   IN A MEDIA-SATURATED WORLD

Sociologists such as Bauman (2000), Sennett (1974), Appadurai (1996), and Giddens (1990) are among those who have described major transformations in the social order in the wake of increasingly global and capitalistic infrastructures and flows. The internet is directly implicated in at least four major transformations of our epoch: (1) media convergence, (2) mediated identities, (3) redefinitions of social boundaries, and (4) the transcendence of geographical boundaries. Each of these intertwined cultural contexts inevitably affects the identification of research objects, engagement with research fields, and design and conduct of qualitative inquiry of contemporary social life.

Media are rapidly converging with one another. The (seemingly) neat worlds of face-to-face embodied conversation, public speaking, landline telephones, radio, television, and film have all but collapsed into a tangled web of video clips sent over mobile phones, music played over computers, refrigerators that suggest recipes on built-in computer screens, and sites like YouTube where clips of a broadcast television show sit on the same platform alongside home-made videos. Media are integral to the full range of human social practices. They are appropriated for the everyday conduct of social, occupational, and civic life in ways that bring these fields into new forms of convergence across time and space. Qualitative researchers must grapple more than ever with the problem of how to identify one phenomenon when convergence intertwines them all together. Although the authors advocate throughout this book that quality in research design relies on a good fit among question, phenomenon, and method, these choices are complicated by the cacophony of causal relationships in the field.

The cacophony does not exist simply in the convergence of multiple media and the accompanying swarm of information but also in the shifting subjects of our inquiry. The contemporary self, which used to seem fairly reliably embedded in a human body, must now be seen as constructed with and in response to multiple media. Kenneth Gergen (1991) popularized the concept of "the saturated self," arguing that modern identities are pieced together like quilts from the overwhelming expanses of mediated messages in our environments. As Radhika Gajjala and many of the authors note in this volume, our selves are produced through multiple media.

The sociological subject is powerful, shifting, and, in terms of qualitative research design, confusing. Our research models do not fit the multiphrenic subject very well. For example, when conceptualizing, defining, protecting, interviewing, or observing the subject of inquiry, tradition dictates that the research participant have demographically verifiable characteristics. We are taught as a basic rule of thumb in methods courses to identify and categorize, even if only to protect the rights of our participants, but also to use these categories to help us build our interpretive frameworks. In internet research, this rule of thumb about categorizing has tended to result in researchers juxtaposing what happens online with what happens face-to-face, or to search for the real or authentic. Carried out for various reasons, this research practice simply doesn't fit anymore the multiphrenic or saturated subject. Yet as Shani Orgad discusses in Chapter 2, the question of how to treat data collected from online discussion forums and interviews relative to that collected in physically co-present interviews raises issues that go to the heart of how core concepts such as "authentic" or "trustworthy" are to be understood when experience and identity are saturated by so many communication media.

The internet also highlights the contemporary disruption of social boundaries, as exemplified by the shifting nature of private and public, concepts that were never as simple as they might have appeared. On the internet's open forums people share their medication regimes, heartaches, and sexual preferences. Genres such as reality television, talk shows, and internet video sharing thrive on the willingness of private citizens to bare the most personal and private elements of their lives to mass audiences. As researchers Malin Sveningsson Elm, Elizabeth Buchanan, and Susannah Stern argue in Chapter 3, this inversion of public and private has profound implications for how researchers must approach the ethics of data collection in "public" internet sites, and also for how the very concept of "privacy" is constructed even in domains we thought we understood. In Chapter 4, Lori Kendall, Jenny Sundén, and John Edward Campbell further push us to consider what researchers might be losing when we omit our "private" feelings and desires from our scholarly analyses rather than allowing them into the process and public record.

Convergence, mediated selves, and shifts in social boundaries are situated within and create contexts in which geographical and temporal boundaries must be reconsidered. When people can have speedy and regular contact across distances using a variety of mediated means for as many purposes as there are conversations, shared or traditionally conceptually geographic and temporal space is less forceful than ever before in bounding our identities, relationships, collaborators, information sources, entertainment, or financial dealings. Instead, the temporal and spatial boundaries influencing social interaction and structures are shifting, ad hoc. For the qualitative researcher, trained in methods of studying a physically grounded site, this raises questions of how to frame the boundaries of a study when any practice is bounded in many ways through space and time, as Christine Hine, Lori Kendall, and danah boyd examine in Chapter 1.

The changes in global communication infrastructures in recent times also shift the traditional grounds and audiences for our research. A researcher's work is liable to be read in contexts it never would have been in years past, which, as the contributors to Chapter 5 (Annette Markham, Elaine Lally, and Ramesh Srinivasan) discuss, creates both methodological and rhetorical challenges in constructing and presenting our work.

❖ CHOICES WITHIN THE RUBRIC OF QUALITATIVE RESEARCH

Anyone who wants to use qualitative methods to study the internet must comprehend and select from a dizzying array of choices, depending on what region and/or discipline he or she is approaching the internet from, what advice is received from friends or mentors, and what books are randomly picked off the shelves to assist in developing the study. While there are models and general rubrics to guide one's choices, qualitative internet research is still novel enough to make those decisions difficult.

In common definition and traditional application, qualitative methods have been associated with close analysis and interpretation by the researcher, trained in various specific methods of information collection (e.g., interviewing, participant observation in the field, and notation or collection of such things as written texts, transcripts of conversations, documents, and artifacts) and in even more specific methods of data analysis within one's school of thought (e.g., conversation analysis, grounded theory, deconstruction, rhetorical criticism, network analysis, phenomenology, and so forth).

Each of these methods (and others not mentioned here) of data collection, analysis, interpretation, and writing exists within cultural, historical, and political frameworks that delimit one's activities as a researcher. Each of these procedures has also been deconstructed in the wake of postmodernism. Qualitative approaches look decidedly different from country to country, even within disciplines. Alternately, qualitative approaches seem easily lumped together. Subtle distinctions in epistemological grounding can make a big difference in one's approach, but it may be difficult to comprehend this effect when the labels seem similar. This is particularly challenging for newcomers unfamiliar with the historical evolution of a method or longstanding methodological debates. We cannot answer the question, "What is qualitative method?" but the complexity of the question must be noted. As Hine aptly notes

(2005b), the phrase "qualitative method" itself may be inappropriate because it cannot adequately encapsulate the practices said to be housed under its roof.

Let's face it: Everything appears to be up for grabs in this era of research, internet or no. Studies and study results emerge in different forms and venues, with different standards of quality, based on an unimaginably broad range of perspectives and methods. We are undoubtedly not the only ones to notice this phenomenon, but because our object of research, the internet, both contributes to and is entangled in this shifting ground, we feel the impact.

❖ THE CHANGING ROLE OF DISCIPLINARITY

How then do we grapple with the choices? Do we cling to tradition because it has steadier grounding? Or do we continually experiment? People from many disciplines are drawn to study the internet for many reasons. Some want to use the technologies to conduct traditional research within their disciplinary groundings, others to be freed from the shackles of traditional disciplinary practices. Some want to understand something about particular technologies, but have little training in the methods for studying them. Others know a lot about the methods of social research but little about the technologically mediated context they're studying.

Many are drawn to the internet as a research topic because its self-replenishing novelty always holds out the promise for unique intellectual spaces. Research in this area tends to chase new technologies. Related, more current, or cutting-edge research is often valued more highly than what are seen as its out-of-date, old-fashioned counterparts. New kinds of interactions emerge so rapidly that the opportunities to contribute something original to an area by incorporating the internet into research are endlessly open. But novel research terrain brings with it novel difficulties. It is hard to know how well older theoretical and methodological frameworks can be applied to understand contemporary social formations. Can we still draw on theories that were developed in an earlier epoch to frame our inquiry and explain our findings? How do we apply procedural models to a study when these models do not seem to fit anymore? How can we move beyond documenting the new to saying things of lasting value about phenomena that change so rapidly?

In the context of this mixed allure and challenge, few people who study the internet are trained by a person, let alone a program, that gave them specialized guidance on how to do it well. Quality in academia is a discipline-specific assessment, and the arbiters tend to be those flagship journals, each of which aligns with editorial divisions of publishing houses that publish our research, host the conferences where we present our work, and provide institutional homes. While most disciplines have awakened to an understanding of the importance of the internet in their fields, most do not have a richly developed core of scholars who agree on methodological approaches or standards. This absence of disciplinary boundaries keeps internet studies both desirable and frustrating.

Layered atop this, the global nature of the internet exposes many cultural differences in assumptions, approaches, and interpretations, as many of the authors discuss in this volume. This exposure is not a bad thing, in that it forces internet researchers to continually evaluate their own work in light of contrasting perspectives. Internet researchers push the boundaries of disciplinary belonging in ways that exemplify what all academic researchers would do well to problematize.

Because disciplinary journals, editorial boards, and reviewers may have lacked expertise in internet research (a situation that is changing now, of course), the quality of published qualitative research of the internet varies widely. Although certain scholars can cite hallmark exemplars (as illustrated by the recommended reading authors chose to include in this volume) or name current key journals (such as *new media & society, Information Society, Journal of Computer-Mediated Communication*, and *Information Community & Society*), these provide interesting illustrations of potential rather than guides for new researchers in the field. This absence of canonical texts indicates a markedly undisciplined field for inquiry and offers much potential for creative research endeavors. Quality must be evaluated at the individual rather than institutional level, a challenge that forces researchers to strive to understand a broad array of theories and methods from multiple disciplines.

Those who turn to the internet as a new topic of study may find it easy to forget that we are not the first people to live through times of technological, cultural, or disciplinary change. Even those on the cutting edge need to know what remains continuous across these changes and what history has to teach us. If the lack of obvious and singular cultural, methodological, or disciplinary context is taken to mean that there is nothing to be learned from disciplinary traditions or studies of earlier media, the result is liable to be weak work. One of this book's central messages is the importance of historical understanding in making sense of novel research topics. Chasing the new in an academic context is in many ways a lost cause: There is no way to keep ahead of the ever-shifting postmodern subject living in interwoven political, economic, and social contexts that are media saturated. One makes lasting contributions and manages the challenges by grounding research. This, of course, is a complicated goal, not achieved solely by reading the literature in one's own field, but certainly aided by a clear understanding of the tools one is using and a keen reflexivity about the situatedness of the self, one's discipline, and the object and context of research.

❖ RECONSIDERING WITHOUT REINVENTING

What qualitative internet researchers need is thus an exaggerated form of what all qualitative researchers require—a way to navigate the novelty of the contemporary landscape while drawing on and contributing to the accumulated methodological and topical wisdom of relevant pasts. The particular novelty and multiple contextualities of internet research increase the need to be able to articulate and defend the processes of decision making during research. The authors in this collection are all drawn to studying the novel, but they share a commitment to making sense of the new by understanding their research processes' and objects' continuity with the past.

This book comes out of the belief that credible research is driven by clearly defined questions and adaptability in answering them. As Sally Jackson (1986) aptly reminds us, method is not a recipe for success, but a means of argument. The procedures we learn and teach are not a means of ensuring truth, but of anticipating possible counter-arguments. Procedures are designed in order to raise broader issues, as Stern notes in Chapter 3, and we need to consider those broader issues in making wise methodological choices. The "steps taken" to solve a "problem" constitute method, but these steps are loaded with assumptions and premises before the process even begins. To understand and apply the appropriate method, one must also examine the guiding assumptions. Then, one must match the most appropriate method to the question, retaining consistency among one's ontological, epistemological, and methodological premises.

❖ THE FORMAT OF THE BOOK

The reader will note that unlike most edited collections, each chapter in this book is titled as a question. We developed these questions to provoke explicit consideration of key issues. We narrowed them down to six, which are by no means exhaustive, but which we have found especially salient in conducting, reading, and teaching qualitative internet inquiry:

1. How can qualitative internet researchers define the boundaries of their projects?

2. How can researchers make sense of the issues involved in collecting and interpreting online and offline data?

3. How do various notions of privacy influence decisions in qualitative internet research?

4. How do issues of gender and sexuality influence the structures and processes of qualitative internet research?

5. How can qualitative researchers produce work that is meaningful across time, location, and culture?

6. What constitutes quality in qualitative internet research?

We asked scholars whose work exemplifies how to handle these issues well to explain how they think through these questions, in general and in practice. At the end of each chapter, after the first author has offered his or her essay addressing the question and provided some key reading references, responses are provided by additional authors. The resulting range of perspectives offers conceptual, theoretical, and practical guidance while demonstrating that there are many defensible directions in which any research project could go. Rather than making the decisions that lead to one right answer, research must make strong, context-sensitive choices that lead to insightful answers.

In the first chapter, sociologist Christine Hine, whose research focuses on the sociology of science and technology, including ethnographic studies of scientific culture, looks at how to define the boundaries of a research project, both its starting and stopping points. Responses are offered by sociologist Lori Kendall, who uses symbolic interactionism and feminist approaches to study information technologies and culture, including online community and identity, and danah boyd, an information studies scholar with a background in computer science, who studies emergent social practices in networked publics.

In the second chapter, media and communication scholar Shani Orgad, whose research uses constructivist and narrative approaches to explore communicative processes in mediated contexts, offers her analysis of how to grapple with the issue of online versus offline in collecting information and making sense of it in qualitative internet analysis. The respondents are audience/media scholar Maria Bakardjieva, who uses phenomenological sociology to examine how users mobilize and appropriate the internet in a variety of social contexts including the home, educational settings, and online and local communities; and Radhika Gajjala, a feminist, postcolonialist media scholar who studies the intersections of culture and technology.

In the third chapter, the question of the extent to which privacy or perceived privacy is an issue for qualitative internet researchers is taken on by Malin Sveningsson Elm, a media and communication studies scholar who studies social interaction online, particularly the presentation of self in online communities and relationships. Responses are offered by Elizabeth Buchanan, an information studies and education researcher, who examines ethical practices and regulations associated with information science and internet research from a social constructivist perspective; and Susannah Stern, a mass communications scholar who uses critical methods to study uses and effects of electronic media, with a special interest in children and youth.

In the fourth chapter, Lori Kendall returns with a provocative analysis of how issues of gender and sexuality influenced structures and processes of qualitative internet research in her work on masculinity in an online discussion group. Responses are offered by Jenny Sundén, a researcher of media technology and communication studies who has studied online embodiment and cyberfeminist politics, and John Edward Campbell, a communications scholar who studies masculinity in gay spaces on the internet.

In the fifth chapter, Annette Markham considers the question of how to produce work that is meaningful across time and location, given that internet technologies change radically and are used in very different ways across contexts. Elaine Lally, a cultural studies and anthropology scholar who studies information and communication technologies as forms of material culture, and Ramesh Srinivasan, an information scientist conducting research on culture and globalism, respond.

In the final chapter, Nancy Baym argues that the concept of dialectics can help frame the issue of quality in qualitative internet research. She draws on the chapters included here, her own research experience, and what others have written about standards in qualitative research to offer guidelines on what constitutes quality. Annette Markham responds.

The result of our collaboration is not a "how-to" guide. It is, rather, an exploration and explanation of vantage points, a project meant to stimulate thinking.

❖ CROSS-CUTTING CONCLUSIONS

In closing the introduction to this collection, we want to identify six cross-cutting issues raised by the authors in this collection—issues that are fundamental to all qualitative research, not just internet-related research, and that reverberate throughout all of the essays included here.

First, *research design is always ongoing*. Theory and method inform one another so that the study is continuously reframed throughout the research process. Different questions occur at different stages of a research process, and the same questions reappear at different points.

Second, *the constitution of data is the result of a series of decisions* at critical junctures in the design and conduct of a study. The endless and jumbled network of links that comprise our research sites and subjects create endless sources of information that could be used as data in a project. We must constantly and thoroughly evaluate what will count as data and how we are distinguishing side issues from key sources of information. Reflexivity may enable us to minimize or at least acknowledge the ways in which our culturally embedded rationalities influence what is eventually labeled "data."

Third, *ethical treatment of human subjects is inductive and context-sensitive*. As almost all the authors in this collection discuss, ethical issues are neither simple nor universal. The context-specific uses of the internet highlight many of the complications associated with determining moral or legal parameters for protecting the participants of research projects. Given the complex ways in which people adapt and appropriate technologies for interaction, researchers must reconsider carefully the frameworks that delimit concepts such as trust, authenticity, privacy, and consent. Although one might wish for clear guidelines, navigating these issues in the contexts of specific projects must be inductive rather than rule driven.

Fourth, *the role of the self in research is a subject for reflexive inquiry*. The often ostensibly disembodied internet calls into question the nature and place of the self in research at a level different from the related postmodern questions of the self as part of the research process. The internet highlights the extent to which researchers co-create the fields of study. Our choices, because they occur in contexts that have no standard rules for research design and practice, seem more poignant and meaningful. What decisions are we making to seek consent; what counts as an authentic self-representation? How are we conceptualizing the embodied persons we study? How are we framing our own embodied sensibilities? Do we approach what we are studying as traces left in public spaces or as embodied activities by people situated in rich offline contexts? We must consider how to interpret other people's selves and how to represent ourselves to the people we study, especially when we may not be meeting them in person. The connection of researcher and researched is a phenomenon heightened by the often invisible bodies of the researcher and researched in internet contexts. The researchers in this collection make powerful arguments for embracing the challenge of understanding how we are connected in multiple and complex ways to the contexts we create, study, and report.

Fifth, *research practices are situated*. An awareness of our emotional, bodily, institutional, economic, and social situations inevitably has an impact on all the choices we make in the field, including choices about how we approach the field, collect and interpret data, and represent our work. As research contexts and publishing venues become more globally accessible, we become more accountable for taking this situatedness into consideration. Crafting work that speaks to people in other places and future times requires attention to the situated nature of our methods and the products of our inquiry.

Finally, *research requires the ongoing balance of dialectical tensions*. The authors in these chapters point to a number of dialectics—messiness vs. neatness, depth vs. breadth, local vs. global—and one could identify others. These dialectics pull researchers in opposing directions, and a step toward either side entails some sacrifice of insights that the other side would offer. Researchers must be able to identify, articulate, and make reasoned comparisons regarding what might be gained and lost with each research option they might follow.

These six cross-cutting issues relate to any qualitative inquiry and are not internet specific. Yet the particularities of internet contexts highlight these issues as important markers for reflection and attention.

In sum, although the internet has made more data available to researchers than ever before and created seemingly infinite, alluring research opportunities, the process of conducting qualitative internet research—indeed all qualitative research, and arguably all research—is more complex than ever before. We hope that the insights gathered in the chapters that follow serve as exemplars and sources of advice to help readers manage these challenges with rigor in their own research.

QUESTION ONE

How Can Qualitative Internet Researchers Define the Boundaries of Their Projects?

Christine Hine

❖   ❖   ❖

The notion of immersion implies that the "field" that ethnogra-phers enter exists as an independently bounded set of relationships and activities that is autonomous of the fieldwork through which it is discovered. Yet in a world of infinite interconnections and over-lapping contexts, the ethnographic field cannot simply exist, await-ing discovery. It has to be laboriously constructed, pulled apart from all the other possibilities for contextualization to which its constituent relationships and connections could also be referred. (Amit, 2000b, p. 6)

This chapter reflects on how a study of the internet might be defined in terms of the places one chooses to begin and the deci-sions one makes about avenues to pursue. In addressing this ques-tion I have in mind my own experiences as an ethnographer working in the broad area of the sociology of science and technology and try-ing specifically to contribute to an understanding of the role that information and communications technologies play in contemporary society.

Responding essays by Lori Kendall (pp. 21–25) and danah boyd (pp. 26–32).

I first describe the analytic approach that informs how I think about the internet and helps me decide which kind of internet inquiry to undertake. Science and technology studies is the disciplinary place from which my internet research projects begin. This starting point decides, to some extent, what will count as interesting places for me to explore. My analytic approach is also shaped by an interest in the status of ethnography as a method for understanding contemporary society; ethnography too gives fuel for reflection on the boundaries of projects. I therefore turn next to some strands of thinking in ethnographic scholarship from anthropology and sociology more broadly, which help show that internet studies are not alone in having dilemmas about where projects start and stop. Finally, I illustrate these points by describing some recent projects, including one of my own, that took unconventional approaches to defining their field sites.

I hope to show that deciding where to start and when to stop can be an intrinsic part of the ethnographer's attempts to ensure that his or her research questions are both coherently addressed and adapted to the cultural landscape that emerges. When the research is internet research (and I would suggest that most ethnographies of contemporary society could usefully incorporate some internet research), the possible connections to pursue multiply, and the occasions for making decisions on the shape of the project and for learning about it in the process multiply as well. Internet research proves to be a rich arena for thinking about how contemporary culture is constituted, and a powerful way to do that thinking is to reflect on the boundaries of individual projects and, at the same time, to explore the boundaries of what it means to do ethnography.

❖ SCIENCE AND TECHNOLOGY
   STUDIES AND THE INTERNET

While the question of this chapter is ostensibly about methodological choices, it has an essential link to theory. Working out methodologically where to start and stop a study is bound up with where one feels a study should travel analytically. The problem is determining what would count as an adequate response to a research question, which can only really be decided within the parameters of a given disciplinary approach or theoretical framework. As Cooper (2001) explains, theories give us particular ways of viewing the world that can shape ideas about how to go about empirical research.[1] Each theoretical perspective has an angle on what is interesting about social situations and, hence, how we should go about studying them. It is important, then, to start out by explaining the theoretical framework that shapes the way I think about adequate responses to internet research questions. This framework, from science and technology studies, gives some clear pointers about ways to take a sociological interest in technologies, and in particular it provides some stimulating food for thought in connection with boundaries.

The sensibilities of science and technology studies shape my approach to the internet in two key ways. The first is a distinctive concern with the development of technologies as a social process. Science is often represented (mistakenly according to the sociology of scientific knowledge) as a form of knowledge independent of particular social contexts of production. In a similar style, technologies are often thought of as produced straightforwardly, and asocially, by the application of scientific and engineering knowledge and economic rationales. Instead of accepting this view of an inevitable technology arising independently of social and cultural influence, science and technology studies suggests that we should look for the social dynamics at the heart of new technologies. It becomes interesting to look at the assumptions that designers work with, the factors that influence judgments about whether a technology is effective or marketable, and the way that commercial organizations market and disseminate new technologies. Science and technology studies has advocated that researchers aim to open up the black box of technology to find out how it comes to be that way (Latour, 1987).

Science and technology studies is also useful for thinking about the internet in·its approach to the contingency and variability of technologies in use. Instead of having effects on society, technologies have been portrayed by the constructivist sociology of technology as intrinsically social. What might be thought of as "effects" of technologies are, instead, to be thought of as emergent qualities dependent on particular sets of local dynamics. Technologies have an "interpretative flexibility" (Pinch & Bijker, 1987), which means that different social groups might view them quite differently. One interesting research focus is to explore how people come to grips with new technologies, what informs their ideas about how to use them, and how social boundaries form and transform around them in a dynamic process not determined by the technology as an independent agent (Oudshoorn & Pinch, 2003). The social dynamics of production and use carve out boundaries between users and producers, create and sustain power relations and hierarchies, and define the sanctioned uses of technologies (Grint & Woolgar, 1997). What technologies are and what they can do can therefore become topics for social research.

Both areas of interest—technology development and technology appropriation—are well suited to ethnographic approaches. This kind of methodology, with its focus on being true to lived experience and on examining how mundane realities come to be, is well suited for such skeptical examination of technologies and has a key place in the history of science and technology studies (Hess, 2001). There are some dilemmas, however, in determining exactly where such a study should go. While an ethnographer might routinely expect to find a context of technology use and go to study it, or negotiate access into a company designing new technologies and document the work that goes on there, not all field sites are as readily identified. Recently, science and technology studies has stressed that one should not accept taken-for-granted sets of boundaries in accounting for the form of technologies and their apparent impacts on social life, and this approach has implications for the design of ethnographic studies (Hess, 2001).

The problem in defining appropriate field sites is that it is not always possible to identify in advance where the relevant social dynamics for understanding a particular technology are going on. This constraint implies that a useful way to study technologies in all their social complexity may be to try and trace their histories and connections and the social groups that are identified around them while remaining ambivalent about the identity of the object being studied. One iconic example of this approach is the Zimbabwe bush pump, as described by de Laet and Mol (2000):

> The Pump is a mechanical object, it is a hydraulic system, but it is also a device installed by the community, a health promoter and a nation-building apparatus. It has each of these identities—and each comes with its own different boundaries. (p. 252)

The description that de Laet and Mol offer of the bush pump shows how it is flexibly and variably defined and how assessing even whether it is working successfully or not is a highly contextual judgment. The identity of the technology, and thus where to start and stop in studying it, cannot be decided in advance. Indeed, it is by following a trail that led them to places they could not have defined beforehand that de Laet and Mol arrived at their argument about the particular quality of the bush pump, its fluidity, which accounted for its success. Had they set out with a defined idea of what the technology was, they would not have found out what they did. Their advice is to suspend judgment on the appropriateness of various forms of boundaries and instead engage with the situations that are found. This idea of technologies with inherently multiple identities clearly resonates with Markham's (1998) observation that the internet was viewed variously by its users as a tool, a place, and a way of being.

The argument for flexible approaches to methodology is taken further by John Law in a book provocatively titled *After Method* (Law,

2004). Law starts from the proposition that methods in social science are constitutive of, rather than reflective of social reality (Law & Urry, 2004). Rather than simply portraying the way that things are in the social world, methods thus shape the ways in which it is possible for us to think about society. In *After Method* Law (2004) argues that the world is an inherently messy and complex place and that any attempt to superimpose the methodological stances of social science on that situation will inevitably do injustices to some features of the situation. Our methodological instincts are to clean up complexity and tell straightforward linear stories, and thus we tend to exclude descriptions that are faithful to experiences of mess, ambivalence, elusiveness, and multiplicity. Law argues that we need to examine our methods for the directions that they push us in and consider whether their biases and exclusions are desirable ones. He suggests that we face up to the selective nature of methods and try to develop alternative forms that select for different qualities than linearity and order, focusing in on the researcher's agency as a constructor of reality and not hiding behind portrayals of method as mere technique. Applied to technologies, this stance means accepting that there are many versions of what a given technology is and how it is bounded and that we need to address some of this complexity with our methodological approaches.

The theoretical perspectives and methodological predilections of science and technology studies therefore inform the way that I think about ethnography of the internet; they inevitably shape my decisions on the appropriate places to start and stop projects. Sensitized by the emphasis in science and technology studies on opening up black boxes, I am predisposed not to accept taken-for-granted ideas about what technologies can do and how they come about. I expect to find social processes at the heart of the development of internet technologies, shaping the form that these technologies take. I am predisposed to find variations in what people do with the internet and how they experience what they do. The internet will often not be experienced as a single entity and will have many different social meanings. I expect, then, to find that I will be in doubt for much of the time about what the technology is that I am focusing on, and whether the issue that I am examining at the time is relevant or not. Law's writings on method provide the inspiration to explore the texture of social life as lived without expecting that there will be clear patterns or boundaries. When a technology appears to offer up a clearly defined field site—maybe a newsgroup, maybe a multi-player online gaming site, maybe a cybercafé—these sensibilities suggest that one should become suspicious.

The added value of the science and technology studies approach lies in its ability to question the taken-for-granted aspects of technologies, and that includes judgments about what is and is not relevant to answering the question at hand. The focus has to be on working across the immediately apparent boundaries, exploring connections, making tentative forays that are then turned into defensible decisions, and retrofitting research questions to emergent field sites. In a later section of this chapter, to flesh out these assertions, I describe a research project I have recently undertaken. First, however, there is more to discuss about ethnography, particularly about recent work on how ethnography can be fitted to the conditions of everyday life in complex societies.

❖   ETHNOGRAPHY IN COMPLEX SOCIETIES

Thus far much of my discussion could apply to qualitative methods in general as much as to ethnography in particular. All qualitative studies have to be designed with particular ideas in mind about where would be interesting to go or whom to interview to study a particular topic. While we might adhere to some form of grounded approach[2] to build theory out of qualitative data, our prior commitments help shape what we will count as being data in the first place. Deciding what to study and what to exclude is thus as pertinent to qualitative interviewing, for example, as it is to ethnography. However, within ethnography the commitment to ongoing methodological flexibility and to the adaptation of methods to the circumstances in which ethnographers find themselves produces a particular consciousness that research design is an ongoing concern and that what counts as data has constantly to be re-evaluated. In what follows I focus specifically on the organization of ethnographic fieldwork and on the design of multi-sited studies; in the conclusion I return to qualitative inquiry more broadly to consider how far the issues raised here apply.

Ethnography has a reputation as an approach that allows researchers to study social situations on their own terms. The key idea is that the researcher should become immersed in the social situation being studied and should use that experience to try to learn how life is lived there, rather than coming in with a particular pre-formed research question or assumptions about the issues that will be of interest. Ethnography is thought of as the most open of research approaches, which adapts itself to the social situations that it finds. This does not mean, however, that ethnographers just wander around aimlessly or that simply by being in a situation they will soak up data. Ethnography might be adaptive, but it is still purposive. As Hammersley and Atkinson (1995, p. 24) argue, rather than research design becoming irrelevant, it "should be a reflexive process which operates throughout every stage of a project." Ethnographers begin with a set of foreshadowed problems that give them a sense of what will be interesting to study, but these preliminary thoughts are to be constantly re-evaluated in the face of field experiences.

Classically, an ethnographer is often thought of as going out into a chosen field site, undertaking research into the culture encountered there, and coming back to write about the experience. This caricature does not do justice to the complexities of the process, and most pertinently for the discussion here it ignores the problems in working out what exactly would count as an appropriate field site. The question of where to begin and end an ethnography, and where to go in between, has to be one of the main sources of anxiety for a contemporary ethnographer. Many of the people who might form subjects of ethnographic inquiry live media-saturated lives, connected to diverse others across the globe by travel and migration, by media representation, and by telephone and internet communications. The world is a complicated place, and ethnography as a methodological stance has had to struggle with the consequent difficulty of defining field sites. On this topic one can tap into exciting currents of writing in contemporary anthropology and cultural studies for inspiration on how field sites might be defined for internet research.

Let us begin with the idea of complex societies and the problem of adjusting methods to suit, about which Ulf Hannerz (1992) has some interesting provocations. He suggests that ethnography, narrowly construed as the study of a particular bounded field site, does an injustice to cultural complexity. Culture cannot, in Hannerz's view, be adequately described by a patchwork of place-based ethnographies. This patchwork would yield uneven and arbitrary coverage and fail to address the varying connections between places and the ways in which place itself is constituted:

> As collective systems of meaning, cultures belong primarily to social relationships, and to networks of such relationships. Only indirectly, and without logical necessity, do they belong to places. The less people stay put in one place, and also the less dependent their communications are on face-to-face contacts, the more attenuated does the link between culture and territory become. (Hannerz, 1992, p. 39)

Hannerz's recipe for the study of cultural complexity focuses instead on "the interfaces, the affinities, the confrontations, the interpenetrations and the flow-through, between clusters of meaning and ways of managing meaning" (Hannerz, 1992, p. 22). The significance of various forms of connection for defining contemporary cultural life has suffused recent anthropology and cultural studies. In sociology, Urry (2000) has taken a lead in suggesting that mobilities, networks, and flows increasingly place in doubt the idea of a society construed as a coherent bounded unit. Appadurai (1996) uses the notion of "scapes" to capture the heterogeneous territories mapped out by diverse forms of connection: We have thus not just landscapes but also ethnoscapes, mediascapes, technoscapes, and financescapes. Rosenau (2003) talks of "distant proximities" through which local and global are constituted, and he suggests that distance and proximity can only usefully be assessed on experiential grounds, rather than as geographic concepts.

The terminology varies, but the commitment to finding out about contemporary culture as simultaneously bounded and connected, and of using fieldwork as a way to explore its dynamics, remains constant. Fieldwork, however, is not always instantly recognizable, and attempts to explore cultural complexities sometimes push it to its limits. Amit (2000a) assembles a collection of papers that reflect on the problems in defining "the field" as a domain separate from everyday life, particularly when anthropologists study close to home or in spheres that touch upon their own personal lives as well as their professional activities.

Concerns about ethnography as an appropriate medium to address cultural complexity and multi-sited cultural formations have been prominent in recent years. Ethnographers have of course never been dumb victims of narrowly defined field sites, and their theoretical sensitivities position them to see the local in terms of global phenomena; see, for example, the collection of papers edited by Miller (1995). However, despite portrayals of ethnography as inherently a method for seeing the global in, and constituted by, the local, there has been continued concern that place-based studies might not be the best way to represent complex connections. Marcus (1995) has proposed a specifically multi-sited ethnography as a way of addressing trans-local connections, even while acknowledging that ethnography had always to some extent been multi-sited. Burawoy and colleagues in their collection of globally oriented ethnographies redefine the work of ethnography as being "to study others 'in their space and time'" (Burawoy et al., 2000, p. 4), leaving it effectively up to the subjects of the ethnography to decide whether the study be about a particular bounded place or about networks of diverse connections. Ethnography thus becomes increasingly construed as the exploration and description of the practices of locating, connecting, siting, and bounding through which culture is constituted. Ethnographers taking this approach will need to be sensitive to heterogeneous practices and resources, drawing on a variety of media and forms of interaction and representation.

Much of this writing about ethnography is tied to the particular project of anthropology, construed as a multi-faceted study of the constitution of cultures. While I hope to illuminate aspects of contemporary culture, I do not share a commitment to the overall disciplinary project of anthropology. Inevitably, then, some of my methodological choices will be different from those of anthropology. For some studies I will want to study particular places, and in some internet studies I will focus on a particular online space, either as an interesting phenomenon in its own right or as an insight into the local constitution of a broader phenomenon in which I am interested. For example, I have studied the discursive practices of one newsgroup in order to explore a specific question about the ways in which laboratory practices transferred to online spaces (Hine, 2002). I have also interviewed various web site developers within an organization to explore the cultural dynamics that underpin web design practices (Hine, 2001). Neither study was explicitly framed as ethnographic. Each project left several questions dangling that could have benefited from an ethnographic engagement, but would have required broader conceptions of field site if I were to explore them in depth. While these were qualitative studies, I did not develop the level of immersion in the settings that ethnographic inquiry would be expected to have, and I focused on narrower research questions than an ethnography would usually employ at the outset. In the next section I describe some studies that illustrate the purchase offered by being open about the constitution and evolution of research questions and the field sites in which to study them.

❖ MULTI-SITED ETHNOGRAPHY AND THE INTERNET

The debate about ethnography and cultural complexity can provoke thinking about how to design studies in, through, and around the internet. If we are interested in the internet as a cultural phenomenon, it does not make sense to assume that it is always a place that one goes to and that this place is in turn a field site to be studied ethnographically. As Markham (1998) argues, the internet can be seen as tool, place, and way of being, and these different aspects offer different methodological choices. I have argued previously (Hine, 2000) that ethnography was important in establishing that the internet could function as a cultural context, meaning that culturally interesting and sociologically relevant things were happening there. Having established this point, and yet having reached a stage where the internet is increasingly seen as a part of everyday life rather than as a separate and automatically virtual sphere (Howard & Jones, 2004; Miller & Slater, 2000; Wellman & Haythornthwaite, 2002), it would be a shame to become restricted methodologically by notions of internet as place. It may indeed sometimes be a place, but taking note of anthropological debates about the significance of place is one way of making sure that we do not miss out on representing cultural complexity at the same time.

There have been some intriguing methodological responses to the internet that have made bold attempts to both address the cultural complexities that its use occasions and to cut across the pictures drawn by more conventional approaches. I can only include here a brief and incomplete roll call. Beaulieu (2004) offers a more systematic review of forms of ethnographic engagement with the internet, looking specifically at epistemological issues. She argues that while virtual ethnographies have been self-consciously innovative, evoking many anxieties about the adequacies of method as a result, there is much continuity between them and more conventional notions about what ethnography should be and that the adjustments to fundamental ethnographic principles have, in practice, been slight. I therefore present here some examples of innovative studies without making particular claims that they either conform to or transform ethnographic principles. The key point is that they illustrate different ways of starting to design a study that engages with the internet (or some aspect of it), and they demonstrate the kinds of decisions that arise regarding where to go and what to do there.

Nicola Green (1999) has conducted a multi-sited ethnography of a virtual technology. Her work on virtual reality in design and use shows how a study of these technologies can grapple with uncertainty and track the various objects, people, and stories involved. She builds an approach based on feminist poststructuralism and science and technology studies to argue that virtual reality technologies are best studied through a flexible approach that follows people and objects and the stories about them. More specifically, she progressively defines her study and finds herself involved within sites where virtual reality technologies are produced, using them herself, and also focusing on the workers who make virtual reality systems available for members of the public to use. Each perspective adds another layer that further illuminates virtual reality as a complex phenomenon produced through diverse forms of labor. Green (1999) shows that virtual reality requires various forms of social investment for it to be realized as a practical achievement, casting a rather different light on stories of virtual reality as an instance of inevitable technological progress.

T. L. Taylor (1999) focuses her attention on virtual worlds and explores some of the challenges that this form of research involves, not least the challenge of distributed and multiple presence for ethnographers. If a researcher feels the need to engage with producers, understand the experience of users, and be appropriately present within online settings too, then considerable flexibility and attention to appropriate forms of engagement for each setting are going to be required. Ethnographers in virtual fields have also to consider how active to be in relation to the particular technologies that they study.

While it might be appealing simply to lurk and observe ongoing activities in a virtual field site, there are some interesting opportunities to be exploited by a move into more active engagement. Max Forte (2005) conducted an ethnographic study of resurgence in aboriginal identity in the Caribbean. Part of his engagement with the subjects of his study was to volunteer to develop web sites explaining their cause. This web site production became a way of deepening his engagement with fieldwork and also of creating a field through his interactions with web site visitors. He argues that his approach allows him to understand "the social and cultural 'constructedness' of web sites, that is to say the patterns and processes of cultural practice that bring together individuals into online groups of producers, promoters and information consumers" (Forte, 2005, p. 93).

Ethnography of the internet can, then, usefully be about mobility between contexts of production and use, and between online and offline, and it can creatively deploy forms of engagement to look at how these sites are socially constructed and at the same time are social conduits. The internet also provides some intriguing possibilities for ethnographers to exploit based on the many traces of social activities that it preserves, in the form of web sites, message boards, hyperlinks, etc. These online traces can be used in various ways to help the researcher shape an appropriate field site and explore the varied social textures of that field. Philip Howard (2002) deploys an interesting combination of social network analysis and ethnography in an attempt to get to the heart of new organizational dynamics revolving around digital technologies. He uses social network analysis of online data as a sensitizing device for a more conventional organizational ethnography. In a very different approach, Anne Beaulieu (2005) uses hyperlinks as a way of moving around a field site, but also reflects on how hyperlinks come to be created and used. She set out to study practices of scientific data sharing and argues that hyperlinks form a way of moving around that field, but need to be thoroughly contextualized in terms of what they mean to their producers and users.

Online traces then provide one way of moving around a field site. It is possible both to follow links and to reflect on what these links mean for those involved. More conventional ways of moving around are, however, still relevant even for internet researchers. Nina Wakeford and Katrina Jungnickel carried out an ethnographic study of the role of place in the consumption of digital information using a bus journey to provide the spatial parameters of the study and to guide their engagement with the urban environment. The bus journey became a way to explore the placing of digital technologies, which in turn provided a means to discuss with designers the potential for new technologies to build on practices observed on the bus (Wakeford, 2003). The accompanying web site and blog (http://www.73urbanjourneys .com) creatively interweave technology to expand the boundaries of the ethnography and use place-based (or transport-based) ethnography to critically engage with the ideas of mobility, ubiquity, and virtuality that permeate the technology.

Each of these studies, for me, demonstrates the strength of approaches that engage deeply with technologies and with the people designing and using them and that also push against traditional definitions of appropriate field sites. The results are studies that illuminate the social dynamics at the heart of the technologies concerned. The key to this insight is immersion, not necessarily through being in a particular field site, but by engaging in relevant practices wherever they might be found. In the next section I focus on a study that I carried out in order to reflect further on the question of boundaries in ethnographies of the internet and the particular problem of what counts as relevant. The outcomes of the study are described at length in Hine (2008). Here I focus specifically on the decisions I made about where to go and where not to go, thereby further highlighting the ongoing reflexive shaping of the field and emphasizing that the result is a combination of theoretically oriented artifact and upshot of practical constraints.

❖ STUDYING E-SCIENCE ETHNOGRAPHICALLY

Thus far I have discussed some theoretical approaches that shape how I think about the internet, as well as some ways of deciding where might be interesting to go to study it. It should be clear that, while the internet can be an interesting place to go to conduct a study, it can be productive to define a study in very different ways. Here, for purposes of illustration it seems most apt to describe a study that crossed the boundaries between online and offline in wanton fashion to pursue its topic, aiming to explore cultural constructions in a field without assuming its boundaries in advance.

This field (and I carefully call it field and not field site, for it is diffuse and only occasionally constituted as a whole and certainly not a place) is the biological discipline of systematics, or taxonomy, and specifically the ways in which it has in recent years come to see the internet as a suitable place to conduct its activities. I wanted to explore how the current situation had come about and what practices enabled it and were facilitated by it. One key rationale for conducting this study was the desire to contribute to the ongoing interest in e-science and cyberinfrastructure (Hey & Trefethen, 2002). These concepts have acted as foci for increasing amounts of policy attention that hope to make science more efficient and enable it to address larger and more complex questions. I anticipated that studying systematics would give some insight into how far these hopes were sustainable. There was, then, an application domain for the study, although I was also keen to pursue it as a study of contemporary scientific culture in its own right.

Rather than going to one particular site, I hoped to carry out a multi-sited study that would encompass diverse aspects of the discipline and its relationship to the internet. I identified sites to visit and people to interview by a mixture of sources, online and offline. One of the first pieces of data that I explored in depth was a report produced in the United Kingdom by the Select Committee on Science and Technology of the House of Lords (2002). This report set out to explore the state of systematics in Britain, in the context of commitments made under the Convention on Biological Diversity. It provided me with rich data on the way that expectations about the role of digital technology were being embedded into the practices of systematics, as the internet was presented almost universally as the hope and destiny of systematics. In addition to its status as qualitative data, this report also provided me with a provisional "map" of the field, via the individuals and institutions that gave evidence to the committee. This testimony gave me a starting point for web sites to visit, institutions to explore, and individuals to approach for interviews. I progressively identified new sites to include, and of course made many pragmatic decisions about places I could practically include and those that had to be left out. I restricted myself in the offline sphere to Northern Europe, but ranged farther afield online in the hope of finding out how far local developments fitted in with those elsewhere. Pursuing the links that I found relevant to understanding what was going on took me into online spaces in various forms, into the material and literary culture of the discipline, into policy documents, and into institutional environments; this pursuit led me, in the end, to an argument that these were domains that really ought to be addressed if one were aiming at an adequate account of the relationship between systematics and the internet.

The key guiding principle in my study was to proceed by asking myself why activities that I encountered might be happening and what kind of sense they made to those involved. I read, I interviewed, I lurked, I questioned, I linked, and I searched, all of the time making tentative connections and engaging in an overall project of making sense of what was going on. The project proceeded, then, as an alternation between exploration and reining in, making tentative steps and testing their relevance for the job at hand, while trying also to remain open to redefining the job. I had in mind as a model Heath et al.'s (1999) study of the networked and interlinking locations in which scientific work is done. The process that I undertook was one of co-constructing the tool and the job (Clarke & Fujimura, 1992), so that the right ethnographic approach for the task was, I hoped, the final outcome, but neither tool nor job was wholly foreseeable from the outset.

In looking for relevant ways to frame my study, I was inspired by science and technology studies to question whether the boundaries of the technology are as they at first appear. The search has, perforce, taken me to technologies other than the internet, since it became clear that current uses of the internet had their roots in quite different technologies that had previously been deployed by those involved, and that those prior involvements shaped what could and should be done in diverse ways. Looking at "the Internet" thus turned out not to be the most useful way of bounding the current study. I found that looking at existing databases that institutions held, detailing their specimen holdings, told me a lot that helped make the distributed databases that were later available on the internet make sense. Taxonomy works with very long time horizons and with an expectation that its resources need to be maintained indefinitely for potential future use. The provision of online databases is in line with a culture that expects specimens themselves to be maintained not because someone will consult them imminently, but because someone might eventually. Online specimen databases that somebody may one day want to use make sense within that cultural context. In short, then, it was not appropriate to stay with distributed databases on the internet as the object of study.

As a further insight into online databases it was also useful to look at the ways in which information about them circulated and where they were represented, advocated, and funded. One online forum offered access to debates around the role and construction of online databases and acted as a venue for database providers to promote their work. As an ethnographer I treated this discussion group as rich data, but was concerned to check my stance, analytically and ethically. I wanted to make sure both that my analysis of the data was not wildly out of kilter with the way that the participants viewed it and also that my use of the data did not offend sensibilities. I therefore introduced myself to the group owner, and subsequently to the entire group, and asked some questions about what the discussions meant to participants. By asking questions of the group, I once more extended the boundaries of the ethnography, identifying myself as an ethnographer to a large audience and inviting the many silent readers of the group to respond to me and thus make themselves present within the ethnographic purview. I found that many other participants were using the list to monitor hot topics in the discipline and keep in touch with current trends, just as I often was. They were, however, quite critical readers who reflected on how what they read in the group made sense within their other experiences of the discipline. Systematics has been a highly reflexive discipline, prone to examinations of its status and practices, and this online group provided a new and immediate venue for this kind of reflection.

Another way in which the study moved beyond a narrow version of the relevant technologies was its engagement with material culture. It became increasingly important, as I found out more about the institutions and individuals behind online systematics, to go to these institutions and to find out more about the collections of specimens that the online databases described. Accordingly, I visited museums, botanical gardens, and herbaria, touring collections of animals preserved in bottles of spirit, plants pressed on sheets of paper, dried fungi in paper packets, arrays of insects pinned out in drawers, and vials of fungal cultures in fridges. By exploring material collections I was able to understand many more aspects of online resources. I found out about practices of loaning and visiting collections and explored beliefs about how objects were owned, how they should be stored and ordered, and the qualities that objects must have if they were to be useful to systematics. Understanding this material culture turned out to be a vital path to making sense of the virtual culture. The two were not separate, but thoroughly intertwined.

While engaged in these explorations I found a complex landscape both online and offline, comprised of institutions, initiatives, and individuals. Web sites in particular gave me insight into the way that initiatives in the field were branded and promoted, and they revealed a highly complex network of interconnections. I also benefited hugely from an open culture that encouraged posting of meetings reports, minutes, and project participant lists. I still, however, felt the need for some way of grasping the connections among the virtual entities. There were some appealing candidates: Dodge and Kitchin (2001) show the fascinating variety of different ways to map cyberspace. Web sphere analysis, as developed by Schneider and Foot (2004, 2005) offers a way of archiving and exploring the complex fields that emerge on the web around a topic. Rogers and Marres' (2000) Issue Crawler explores the networks that arise in the hyperlinks between sites related to a topic.

Social network analysis and hyperlink analysis offer ways to explore the spatiality of the web (Park & Thelwall, 2003). For my purposes, however, I sought something a little more quick and dirty, something more dynamic. I wanted to be able to "see" connections on the web, but not to be seduced by any one particular representation as the way the field really is. I settled on use of the TouchGraph Google Browser (http://www .touchgraph.com/TGGoogleBrowser.html), which offers visualizations of site networks using the Google facility to track down related sites.

An example of a visualization provided by the TouchGraph Google Browser is shown in Figure 1.1. The diagram is generated in real time and can be extended outward: Clicking on a node retrieves its related sites, and clicking on any of those sites extends the network once again. Nodes can be pulled into position using the mouse to move overlapping nodes apart. The representation is, then, appealingly dynamic. I found that I was readily able to use these representations as tools for exploration rather than static figures. I was also able, using this means, to check more straightforwardly that my own less systematic ways of mapping the field had not missed key players. I was able to explore the ways in which institutions and initiatives were varyingly visible across the field, both online and offline. Building and comparing these visualizations, and placing them alongside interview data in various projects, gave me insight into the ways that identities were forged in this field, as well as the various faces presented by projects and institutions.

Note that there is a strong autobiographical element to the research that I undertook. I was positioned to conduct research on the contemporary situation by research I had conducted many years earlier, as part of my doctoral research. In particular, I had acted as an ethnographer on a pioneering taxonomic database project in the late 1980s and early 1990s (Hine, 1995), and this experience gave me a starting insight into some pertinent issues, access into relevant networks, and some understanding of the technical issues at hand. I also have to confess to an earlier autobiographical connection: As an undergraduate I studied botany, and as a postgraduate I took a Masters in Biological Computation and conducted my doctoral research into the problem of taxonomic instability. I was therefore once a participant, at a humble level, in this field and lived through some of the transformations that have brought the discipline to its current state. That experience inevitably shaped the places that I went and my interpretations of them.

I chose not to study the field by undertaking a conventional ethnography within a particular institution carrying out taxonomic work. I regret the loss of textural detail about the way that work in contemporary systematics is experienced that such an ethnography would have provided. It would have been interesting, indeed, to have worked alongside systematists on a sustained basis, and this very different kind of study might have told me much about the way in which systematics, the discipline, comes into being through the practices of systematists working on a local scale. Nonetheless, for the study I wanted to do, and particularly for exploring the varied experiences of systematics as enacted both in local places and through diverse technologies and forms of connection, it seemed right to move around. The study was bounded, then, both in reach and depth. I set limits on it when I decided not to pursue a particular set of connections outward, as well as when I opted not to drill down in a particular place to more depth. Decisions to stop entailed feelings of doubt and loss, stronger in some cases than others. These decisions were always made as trade-offs to enable me to work in more detail somewhere else more promising.

The project that I carried out combined face-to-face interviews, visits to physical sites, autobiographical experiences, historical documents, web sites, searches and surfing, participation in online groups, simple structured analyses of messages, e-mail interactions, and dynamic visualizations of web-based networks. Without subscribing to the notion that there was a separate online sphere of systematics, I remained open to the idea that culturally significant things might be happening online and that they might not be fully reflected in things that I could find offline. In the end, though, I am not sure that the result would be characterized as an ethnography. I was inspired by the principles of ethnography and in particular felt that I held true to its commitment to adaptive studies of meaning-making in social life and to a notion of learning through immersion. At the same time, the resulting study is quite different from the conventional image of ethnography as the upshot of a long period of immersion within a field site.

❖ CONCLUSION: THE BOUNDARIES OF ETHNOGRAPHY

Many of the issues that I have explored in this chapter relate to qualitative methods more broadly. As Hammersley and Atkinson describe, it is difficult to make an absolute distinction between ethnography and other forms of social research: "There is a sense in which all social researchers are participant observers, and, as a result, the boundaries around ethnography are necessarily unclear" (1995, p. 1). Specific issues that are pertinent for a broader range of methodological approaches include the question of where to focus a study: Qualitative studies will all be shaped by ideas about where interesting phenomena are to be studied, and when studying the internet it can be very useful to think creatively about that issue. To return to the perspectives from science and technology studies introduced at the beginning of this chapter, it is important not to assume that we know in advance what the internet is. Some studies of the internet might confine themselves to a particular online or offline setting, but in other cases we may define a topic of interest that requires us to cross between online and offline and reflect on the differences we encounter in different sites. Social phenomena are not uniquely confined to online or offline sites, and it would be a mistake to allow these notions automatically to provide boundaries for our studies.

The approaches that I described in this chapter rely on the idea of the construction of project boundaries as a social process, which is linked more explicitly to ethnography in particular as an adaptive methodological approach. The decision about when to start and stop, and where to go in between, is for ethnographers not made independently of the field, but is an intrinsic part of the relationship to it. A set of fieldwork boundaries is the outcome of a project, rather than its precursor. The decision about what to study is made collaboratively with research encounters, but it is also inevitably shaped by other factors, such as supervisory input, ideas about what is defensible within one's disciplinary context, and responsibilities to funding bodies for whom the study has to be recognizably the one that they paid for. All studies will be bounded, to some extent, by what the researcher can practically achieve. Even though the internet extends the potential spatial remit of our studies, we can still only engage with so many people in depth, conduct so many interviews, or analyze so many web sites. Qualitative research and, in particular, ethnography with its emphasis on immersion, require depth and engagement in the attempt to understand how social and cultural life is organized, and realizing that potential places a practical boundary on a project.

More innovative ethnographies may push against methodological boundaries such that it becomes debatable whether they are still defensibly ethnographic. Specifically, studies in which the ethnographer moves around, is only intermittently present, or fails to carve out a consistent version of "the field" can seem to threaten the notion of ethnography as founded on immersion and leave lingering doubts about the status of the study (see papers collected by Amit [2000a]). The boundaries of methodologies themselves can be fluid and negotiated, rather than fixed (Gubrium & Holstein, 1999). Just as some people argue that mobile ethnographies are just ethnography dressed up, so others will doubt that they are ethnography at all. In this situation the key recourse has to be the dialogues in which the study is able to engage: If we can do studies of the internet that say something interesting and that advance debate, whether in policy circles, in the theoretical resources of academic disciplines, or in informing practical action, then our studies will have some claim to adequacy.

❖ RECOMMENDED READING

For introductions to the science and technology studies approach see Bruno Latour's (1987) book *Science in Action: How to Follow Scientists and Engineers through Society* and Wiebe Bijker's (1995) *Of Bicycles, Bakelites and Bulbs*. John Law's (2004) *After Method: Mess in Social Science Research* is an interesting reflection on the reasons for challenging methodological orthodoxy, grounded in science and technology studies.

An accessible introduction to various forms of ethnography is provided by Martyn Hammersley and Paul Atkinson's *Ethnography: Principles in Practice* (1995). John Brewer's *Ethnography* (2000) reflects on the current role of ethnography within social research and offers practical advice. Some interesting perspectives on ethnography's ability to explore complex cultural connections are provided by George Marcus in *Ethnography through Thick and Thin* (1998) and, in relation to computing culture more specifically, David Hakken's (1999) *Cyborgs@Cyberspace*. Emily Martin's (1995) *Flexible Bodies: The Role of Immunity in American Culture from the Days of Polio to the Age of AIDS* is a classic example of a multi-sited ethnography of contemporary culture.

Texts that talk specifically about the internet as a field site, and about different ways of thinking of the internet as a conduit of culture, are Annette Markham's (1998) *Life Online: Researching Real Experience in Virtual Space* and Christine Hine's (2000) *Virtual Ethnography*. Daniel Miller and Don Slater in *The Internet: An Ethnographic Approach* (2000) offer a useful account of an ethnography of the internet that does not assume that the internet contains a distinctive virtual culture.

❖ NOTES

1. Cooper uses two contrasting examples to illustrate this point: Goffman's social interactionist perspective might encourage a researcher to focus on the detail of social interactions and the way people manage the impressions they give off; Foucault's distinctive understanding of the operations of power offers a stimulus to developing critical perspectives on aspects of contemporary social life that might otherwise be taken for granted.

2. The term has acquired many different interpretations since its inception, but originates from Glaser and Strauss (1967) and connotes an attempt to develop theory grounded in the data, rather than imposing prior conceptualizations on data.

Figure 1.1 TouchGraph Google Browser visualization of sites related to the Natural History Museum, London

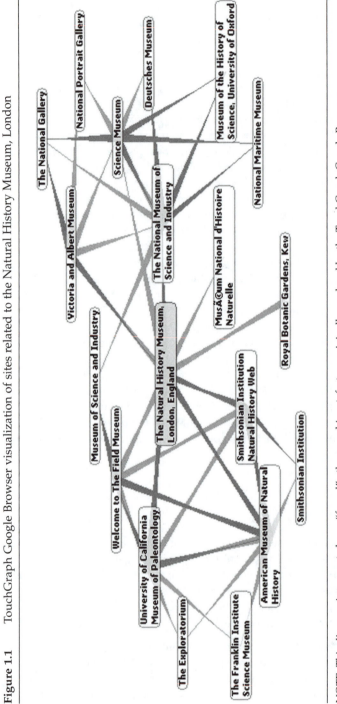

NOTE: This diagram is presented as a "found" ethnographic artefact, as originally rendered by the TouchGraph Google Browser.

A Response to Christine Hine

Lori Kendall

❖ ❖ ❖

Hine provides a wonderfully detailed consideration of internet project boundaries and ways to proceed in constructing an internet research project. I find two of her insights particularly important. First, project boundaries might not be set within a particular location, as field sites have sometimes traditionally been conceived. This insight is exemplified by her statement that "internet research proves to be a rich arena for thinking about how contemporary culture is constituted, and a powerful way to do that is to reflect on boundaries of individual projects" (p. 2). The internet, or people's use of it, provides a starting point from which to acquire a rich view of culture. As Hine points out, this approach to internet studies requires immersion "by engaging in relevant practices wherever they might be found" (p. 12).

Second, the definitions of the research objects are emergent rather than predetermined. As Hine puts it, "The identity of the technology, and thus where to start and stop in studying it cannot be decided in advance" (p. 4). Here again, as her example of de Laet and Mol's research demonstrates, the meaning of particular technologies varies within particular cultural contexts. The researcher must allow these meanings to emerge through engagement with the cultural context and the people within it.

Hine's primary focus is on a type of boundary that, for lack of a better term, I'll call spatial. This is exemplified by her use of spatial metaphors embodied in the word "where," as in phrases like "where to start and stop a study" (p. 2) and "where to go and where not to go" (p. 12). Hine recognizes these as metaphors, and her consideration of

21

project boundaries is deeper than merely spatial concerns such as physical or virtual locations. Hine's focus on spatiality gives me the opportunity to focus in turn on other kinds of boundaries contained and implied in her account. In doing so, I discuss the underlying motivations or logics for setting project boundaries. Here also, Hine focuses on one particular sphere of influence, but hints at others. Her focus is primarily on theory and on the connection between theory and methodological choices, including boundary decisions.

I briefly consider three different kinds of boundaries and three different spheres of influence on boundary choices. I am calling the three types of boundaries spatial, temporal, and relational and the three spheres of influence analytical, ethical, and personal. Spatial boundaries refer to questions of where, who, and what to study. Temporal boundaries refer to questions of time spent and the issues of beginning and ending research. Relational boundaries refer primarily to relationships between researchers and the people they study (although other relationships are also pertinent to research projects, such as relationships between researchers and their audience for written reports). The analytical sphere of influence refers to theoretical and analytical decisions regarding project boundaries. The ethical sphere of influence refers to boundary decisions made for ethical reasons, especially those made to protect participants. The personal sphere of influence refers to various aspects of the researcher's background that might influence the choice of project boundaries, such as personal proclivities, skills, or history.

These categories of boundaries and their motivational spheres of influence blur and overlap. For instance, much of what I highlight as temporal boundaries is bound up with questions of spatial boundaries and as such is covered in Hine's discussion. My aim in applying these labels is not to identify actual discrete categories, but rather to highlight particular aspects of boundary decisions. The metaphor I would use is that of the research project as a translucent faceted gem. One can turn the gem so as to focus on a single facet, but through that facet also see the other facets. Given Hine's detailed consideration of spatial boundaries chosen through analytical considerations, I briefly focus on the other two types of boundaries and spheres of influence.

Hine points out that choosing boundaries for a project involves "when to start and stop" as well as "where to go in between" (p. 7). These temporal considerations, like spatial ones, are often influenced by analytical considerations, as well as by practical ones. (Practical considerations constitute a fourth "sphere of influence" that I am mostly ignoring for purposes of this discussion. However it is important to remember that, as Hine says, "All studies will be bounded, to some extent, by what the researcher can practically achieve" [p. 18].) Temporal considerations, perhaps more than spatial ones, are also influenced by ethical and personal issues.

For instance, in the approximately three years of ethnographic research for my book, *Hanging Out in the Virtual Pub* (discussed further in Chapter 4 of this book), I formed relationships with the people I studied, participants in an online forum I called BlueSky. At one point during the study, a participant asked me point-blank if I intended to maintain those relationships after I completed my study. In short, that participant wanted to know whether I was merely using the people I studied to further my academic career or whether the relationships I had formed had meaning to me apart from my research interests. Ethnographic research projects and often other forms of qualitative research (such as projects involving in-depth interviews) involve lengthy association with participants. These relationships complicate ethical considerations of the research, which in turn can affect decisions about temporal boundaries.

In my case, I did maintain my relationships with the BlueSky participants, and continued to hang out online with them for several years following the completion of the research on which my book was based. In fact, these ongoing relationships complicated the "end date" of my research, and I would be hard pressed to give an exact date for its completion. Participants read my dissertation and provided feedback on it. Both this feedback and the insights provided through my continued participation on BlueSky informed the rewrite for publication.

This experience points also to the influence of the personal dimension on qualitative research. Hine identifies this as the "autobiographical element" (p. 16). Our own proclivities as researchers, connected perhaps to our past interests or relationships, influence the choices we make in starting and stopping projects and in choosing where to go in pursuing those projects.

Ethical and personal considerations also influence what I am calling the "relational" boundary of qualitative research. In addition to considering where to go and who to talk to, as well as how long the project should be, we also must consider what kinds of relationships we will have with participants. This is not of course something that is completely within our control. Which is to say, relational boundaries will not be determined solely by the personal sphere of influence. Our participants' desires or antipathies may encourage or preclude certain kinds of relationships. Our own choices may also be influenced by analytical concerns, such as how much we need to know about our participants. And they may be influenced by ethical concerns; the closer our personal relationships, the greater the vulnerability of both our participants and ourselves.

In my own experience, all of these different boundaries, and all of the various motivations for determining those boundaries, overlap and blur. This was particularly true when I began a new research project that overlapped in significant ways with the BlueSky project. Several BlueSky participants began using an online blogging system. I followed them to that system and began a research project there. This created a tangled web of spatial, temporal, and relational boundaries between the two projects. This entanglement seemed analytically useful to me, in that one of my aims was to compare chat and blogging as different sorts of systems for computer-mediated communication. The personal dimension—my continued friendship with several BlueSky participants—also influenced project boundaries. Meanwhile, ethical issues became particularly complex, as *Hanging Out in the Virtual Pub* was published during the blogging study. Given the BlueSky participants' interest in discussing the book, both on BlueSky and in their blogs, and given that my network of contacts through blogging had expanded beyond just BlueSky participants, it became difficult to maintain their confidentiality. I found that I needed to curtail my blog participation somewhat to reduce potential exposure of BlueSky participant identities.

Hine's discussion presents a relatively traditional way of looking at the boundaries of research projects. In her depiction, the researcher is primarily motivated by theoretical concerns, with other issues such as ethical and practical matters mainly providing limits on what is possible. I have no argument with her account, but hope to have broadened the types of boundaries considered and the reasons for considering them. However, in this short space, I can only scratch the surface. I point the reader toward the list of recommended reading that follows for consideration of other approaches to even more research boundaries.

❖ RECOMMENDED READING

Brown, Karen McCarthy. 1991. *Mama Lola*. Berkeley: University of California Press.

Brown's book pushes the conceptual envelope of ethnography. Her immersion into the world of Haitian Vodou included her own initiation into Vodou practice, highlighting conventional boundaries between researcher and participants. In addition to more traditional forms of ethnographic study and reporting, Brown includes several fictional chapters reflecting family stories told to her by informants. Her book thus additionally breaches the usual boundaries between research and writing and between fiction and nonfiction. Although I do not provide similar fictional excerpts in my work, Brown's creative approach has had a significant influence on my ethnographic writing.

Markham, Annette N. 1998. *Life Online.* Walnut Creek, CA: AltaMira Press.

Markham's account provides a detailed look at all kinds of boundaries involved in qualitative research: between personal and professional life, online and offline reality, self and other, and body and self, among others.

Nippert-Eng, Christena E. 1995. *Home and Work.* Chicago: University of Chicago Press.

From the emerging field of cognitive sociology, Nippert-Eng's work addresses the issue of boundaries themselves and how we understand and create them. Of particular interest is a chapter that includes lengthy excerpts from two interviews, with minimal editing or analytical interventions. This provides an example of an unusual decision concerning the boundary between researcher and reader. For researchers, this chapter also provides a useful model of interviewing techniques.

Stacey, Judith. 1990. *Brave New Families.* New York: Basic Books.

Stacey's study of families in Silicon Valley illustrates the great depth that is possible through qualitative studies and the ways in which even a small number of cases can illuminate larger social structures and issues. Stacey explicitly discusses several boundary issues with regard to her personal life and her research. In an interesting attempt to compensate for the power differences between the researcher and the researched, she provides an epilogue that includes extensive comments by one of her respondents regarding her reaction to her analysis.

A Response to Christine Hine

danah boyd

❖   ❖   ❖

As an undergraduate, I once (foolishly) asked my professor how long the assigned paper had to be. "Long enough to touch the ground" was what he told me. Needless to say, this response did not satisfy my desire to know the "correct" answer that would confirm that I was being a "good" student. Yet, his answer altered my worldview. I began to appreciate that the boundaries of an essay should be determined by the point being made, not by the page count. (It took me many more years to learn that brevity is an art.)

In a graduate school qualitative methods course, I asked my advisor how I would know when I was finished collecting data. He offered the same Dumbledore smile as the previous professor before responding, "When you stop learning new things without expanding the scope of your question." Once again, I asked a question of the wise and received a koan in response. While I have not reached methodological enlightenment, I have begun to appreciate the brilliance of these answers.

Having grown up with the internet, I've always had a paradoxical relationship to it. Rather than seeing the internet simply as either a "cultural artifact" *or* as a place "where culture is formed and reformed" (Hine, 2000, p. 9), I've always accepted both naturally. The internet is increasingly entwined in people's lives; it is both an imagined space and an architected place. Things happen on it, through it, because of it. While all cultures change over time, what makes the internet so confounding for research is that the fundamental architecture (Lessig, 1999) also changes rapidly. Innovations have always radically altered the world—could you imagine society without light or gas? While tangible innovations have restructured society immensely, the pace of innovation and dissemination today is unparalleled. This, of course, complicates internet research.

Networked technologies have completely disrupted any simple construction of a field site. Traditionally, ethnographers sought out a physical site and focused on the culture, peoples, practices, and artifacts present in a geographically bounded context. This approach made sense because early anthropologists studied populations with limited mobility. Furthermore, there was a collective understanding that culture and people were contained by place. Mobility complicated matters (resulting in excellent ethnographies of diaspora populations), but mediated technologies changed the rules entirely. In a networked society, we cannot take for granted the idea that culture is about collocated peoples. It is not a question of mobility but of access to a hypertextual world. Geography can no longer be the defining framework of culture; people are part of many cultures including those defined by tastes, worldview, language, religion, social networks, practices, etc. Of course, as Hine rightfully points out, we should not simply reject what anthropologists learned by studying places, but instead recognize that what they learned is not the complete story.

When ethnography first went digital, early internet researchers tended to focus on the place-driven metaphors that framed the internet. This was logical, considering the emphasis on "rooms" invoked in early social software like chat rooms and MUDs/MOOs. Architectural features appeared to provide meaningful boundaries but, as Hine notes, "one should not accept taken-for-granted sets of boundaries" (p. 4). Sure enough, when Deja News appeared in 1995, the walls that separated Usenet groups collapsed, scripts devastated the boundaries of MUDs and MOOs, and search has continued to collapse all place-driven web contexts ever since.

Early internet culture focused heavily on social groups gathering around topic or activity. More recent social technologies like blogs and social network sites have altered that dynamic. In these more recent technologies, "community" is an egocentric notion where individuals construct their social world through links and attention. Rather than relying on interests or structure-based boundaries, current social groups are defined through relationships. Each participant's view is framed by her or his connections to others and the behaviors of those people. The difficulty with this egocentric network view is that there's no overarching set of norms or practices; instead, each node reveals an entirely different set of assumptions. This issue is quite noticeable when researchers (including myself) have foolishly tried to discuss the blogosphere or MySpace as a continuous cultural environment only to be challenged by other blind researchers looking at the elephant's trunk or ear.

To try to balance the view, I've approached my latest project on MySpace from numerous disconnected angles. Every day, I look at random MySpace profiles (it is possible to do this because profiles are numerically generated). I interview teens from different cultural backgrounds. I talk with parents, the site's creators, and adults who use the site. I read commentary about MySpace on blogs and in the news; I listen to people talking about MySpace on the bus and at malls throughout the United States. Through my blog, others know that I'm researching MySpace; strangers send me data on a daily basis. In this way, I've begun this project in the widest way I could possibly imagine. All the same, I've found that there are behaviors or groups that I can track more easily, and so I've chosen to narrow my focus so that I can concentrate more deeply on understanding the dynamics between smaller, connected groups. In contemporary networked life, culture is socially proximate not geographically defined; creating boundaries by medium or genre only confuses matters. Thus, it makes far more sense to find a sample population and try to flush out who they know and the culture that forms among them. During the course of my study, for a selection of people, I try to spiral out to understand their worldview and compare it to other worldviews that I see within the broader system.

Given that networked technologies complicate research, what does it mean to do ethnographic internet research? How do we work through boundary issues? Hine's essay provides critical insight into how ethnography is "an adaptive methodological approach (p. 18). By discussing different ethnographic projects, she reveals the diversity of approaches that researchers take in undergoing an ethnographic study. Furthermore, she highlights the disciplinary roots and reflexive considerations that ethnographers must consider. In constructing her essay, Hine highlights the most critical feature of ethnography as a method: It is not prescriptive. There is no genie that will come and grant boundaries for a researcher. Learning to do ethnography is a lifelong process and we are all learning as we go. While I cannot offer a box of solutions, I can draw from my own work as well as a rich history of ethnographic practice to offer some guidelines that have helped me.

1. *Read ethnographies.* Read to make sense of what it is that ethnographers do and how they do it; do not focus on deconstruction. Read voraciously and then re-read what you've read. Get inside the heads of

other ethnographers—hear their struggles, understand their choices, make sense of their reflexive considerations, try to see what they are doing from their points of view. Read theoretical literature to properly situate research in prior work, but do not forget to read other ethnographies. *The voices of other ethnographers have helped me understand how to approach questions, how to think about the practice. Keeping those voices in mind when I'm in the field allows me to better "see."*

2. *Begin by focusing on a culture.* What defines that culture? Its practices? Its identity? Who are the relevant social groups? What are the relevant social dynamics? What boundaries are applicable? Unlike other methodologies, ethnographers do not begin with rigid, narrow questions; they begin with cultures. Questions are important because they provide guidelines for observation, but researchers must be prepared for observations and data to reveal new questions. Be bound by culture, not by questions. *When I started studying Friendster, I decided to focus on the early adopters—self-identified geeks, freaks, and queers. I wanted to see how these groups overlapped and complicated each other's participation even though the site's popularity had spread far beyond that.*

3. *Get into the field, hang out, observe, document, question, analyze.* Ethnography is about participant observation or deep hanging out; to observe a culture, you must build rapport, be present, and participate. Everything that is observed should be documented; thick description (drawing on Geertz, 1973) is key. Observations provoke hypotheses, and early analysis provokes new questions. Document everything. Ethnography is "writing culture" and it is important to try to document and make sense of everything available. Thus, it's critical to hang out across numerous spaces to see the relevant culture from different angles. *This is why I spend time in schools, at malls, in people's homes, online, and in a variety of public spaces. By hanging out in different mediated and unmediated contexts, I can see practices from different angles.*

4. *Never get too comfortable.* Always work to make the familiar strange; do not fetishize anything. When you start seeing patterns, try looking at what you're observing from a new angle. Try to make sense of practices in terms of the practitioner and the observer. Be reflexive of your own biases, and question any and all biases that you have. Question your own questioning. Try not to get too recursive, although ethnography really is turtles all the way down (Geertz, 1973, p. 29). *For me, the best part about having a background in computer science is knowing how the systems that I study work; they are never magic to me. It is trickier to not love the populations who adopt them so whenever I start sharing an affinity*

with a particular group, I try to find and make sense of others whose motiva-
tions initially bother me. For example, I spent a month tracking down neo-
Nazis and cocaine distributors on Friendster just to understand how they
viewed the network differently from other participants.

5. *Understand that boundary construction is a social process.* The reflexivity and questioning inherent in ethnography are antithetical to boundary construction. As Hine aptly notes, "The focus has to be on working across the immediately apparent boundaries, exploring connections, making tentative forays which are then turned into defensible decisions, and retrofitting research questions to emergent field sites" (p. 6). In other words, the boundaries of a project emerge when the ethnographer decides which questions to focus on based on patterns in data and observations. By placing observations and interpretations into an "intelligible frame" (Geertz, 1973, p. 26), the scope of a project often emerges. While there are always an infinite number of paths to follow, one will learn to recognize when data, theory, and questions come into a collective focus.

6. *Understand that making meaning is an interpretive process.* Never lose touch of the goal of ethnography: to make meaning of culture. Interpretations should be situated and they must be questioned. Ethnographers should always be reflexive about their interpretations, biases, and limitations.

These rules of thumb are not unique to internet ethnographies, but they are just as critical to internet ethnographies as to those that take place in unmediated contexts. What makes studying digital cultures distinctive is not the mindset, but how the architecture affects our practice. There are four key architectural properties of mediated sociality to keep in mind: persistence, searchability, replicability, and invisible audiences (boyd, 2007). When people speak online, their words are not ephemeral. Search engines make text, media, and people findable at the flick of a few keys. Hearsay is one thing, but online, you often can't distinguish the original from the duplicate; likewise, it's difficult to tell if the author is *really* the author. Finally, aside from the people who sneak around your back and hide behind trees whenever you turn around, most people have a sense of who can hear or see them when they navigate everyday life; online, no one knows when a dog might be looking. These properties collapse social contexts and change the rules about how people can and do behave.

My research centers on these properties precisely because they reveal how critical context is to human behavior. At the same time, these properties alter the context in which we are doing research, and thus, it is just as critical for researchers to learn how to operate with them in mind as it is for teens who are trying to find a space of their own on social network sites. For example, just because people's expressions on the internet are *public* in the sense that they can be viewed by anyone does not mean that people are behaving as though their audience consists of billions of people across all space and all time. How we act in a park with our children is different from how we act in a pub with our friends; just because these are both public places does not mean that there is a uniform context. When we look to understand people's practices online, we must understand the context within which the individuals think they are operating. This imagined context provides one mechanism for bounding our research. For example, in my own research, I'm only interested in the online spaces that teens perceive to be meant for them to congregate with their friends and peers.

In studying new media, internet researchers may inaccurately bound their view by idealizing the possibilities of the internet rather than recognizing and working within the actualities of practice. Just because people can theoretically use the internet to broadcast their expressions, reach out to diverse populations across the world, or free themselves of their offline identity does not mean that this is what people do or see themselves as doing. People's worldviews—and their neuroses—leak from the offline to the online. To fulfill their goals and desires, people envision structure within the wide-open spaces available online. Internet ethnography is not about the technology—it is about the people, their practices, and the cultures they form. In an unstable technological environment, it is essential to be continuously reflexive about our own views and values concerning emerging technologies.

The internet provides fascinating fodder for observing people and their practices, but ethnographies of internet life must work to acknowledge and then let go of the underlying technology. Discovering the boundaries of such work has nothing to do with the technology and everything to do with the cultures being considered.

❖ RECOMMENDED READING

Clifford Geertz's (1973) *The Interpretation of Cultures* is what helped me understand ethnography as a method and a state of mind. Whenever I feel lost in what I am doing, I return to this text. Two books have given me valuable insight into thinking about how to do ethnography in mediated spaces: Christine Hine's (2000) *Virtual Ethnography* and Daniel Miller and Don Slater's (2000) *The Internet: An Ethnographic Approach.*

Fundamentally, I believe that learning ethnography requires reading ethnographies. Since ethnography is about "writing culture," it's extremely valuable to read how others have written culture. Several ethnographies are listed in the reference list. Each of these different ethnographies draws on different traditions and exhibits a unique style and voice. While these are some of my favorite ethnographies, other ethnographers will have their own lists. Reading a diversity of ethnographies, even if the topic is not particularly relevant, will give one a sense of how ethnographers explain culture.

To help ground the conduct of ethnography of internet culture, it is important to read texts that help explain different aspects of it. For example, Lawrence Lessig's (1999) *Code and Other Laws of Cyberspace* helps elucidate how code is a form of architecture; understanding this, one can see how different relevant players have tried to influence the internet's development. Judith Donath's (1999) essay, "Identity and Deception in the Virtual Community," reflects how people's signaling practices must change because of different limitations online, whereas Jenny Sundén's (2003) *Material Virtualities* looks at shifts in embodiment as people "type themselves into being." These are only a few examples of a wide array of literature studying internet culture; familiarizing oneself with this literature will help one recognize different practices that emerge.

QUESTION TWO

How Can Researchers Make Sense of the Issues Involved in Collecting and Interpreting Online and Offline Data?

Shani Orgad

❖   ❖   ❖

Before addressing the question that is the subject of this chapter, I want to introduce two working definitions of "qualitative internet research" and "online and offline data," which, without being in any way prescriptive, reflect my personal understanding of these concepts. This understanding has been significantly influenced by my own research experience. After a brief discussion of these concepts, I move on to explain why I think consideration of both online and offline data is important in thinking through our research projects. Next, I explore critical junctures in the research process when these issues might arise and become a problem. I put forward possible justifications for doing research that combines online and offline data. I also discuss the implications of deciding not to obtain and analyze offline and online data, but rather relying on one kind of data only. The chapter concludes with some thoughts about online and offline data in future qualitative internet research in light of current technological trends that are increasingly blurring the line

---

Responding essays by Maria Bakardjieva (pp. 54–60) and Radhika Gajjala (pp. 61–68).

between online and offline communication and of recent debates about the nature of the research field site in internet studies.

❖ WORKING DEFINITIONS

Qualitative Internet Research

Departing from the definition of qualitative research as that which uses the internet to facilitate data collection or data analysis, we can define this concept as a qualitative inquiry into internet phenomena (Markham, 2003). More specifically, by the term "qualitative internet research" I refer to the study of the multiple meanings and experiences that emerge around the internet in a particular context. These meanings and experiences can relate to contexts of use (by individuals, organizations, networks, etc.) and/or to contexts of design and production processes. The task of a researcher involved in a qualitative internet research project is to inquire into those meanings and experiences and explore their significance.

The question underlying a qualitative internet research project would be this: What does "the internet" stand for in a particular context, for particular agents? Clearly, "the internet" is not a monolithic thing. Part of any qualitative exploration would have to be the articulation of what research arenas "the internet" comprises and how they shape, as well as are shaped by, participants' and producers' experiences of use. For example, my study, *Storytelling Online: Talking Breast Cancer on the Internet* (Orgad, 2005b), began by mapping the landscape of breast cancer patients' online communication, a process of describing the kinds of online spaces and environments in which participants engaged. This "landscape" defined the arenas of focus for the research, which included cancer-related message boards, personal diaries, and e-mail.

Equally, "qualitative" does not map onto one single thing. While I acknowledge the difficulty, if not impossibility, of reaching a clear definition of "online qualitative research" (see also Denzin, 2004), my own perspective leans toward the interpretative as opposed to the more positivist and naturalistic conception of human experience and its analysis. More specifically, "qualitative" implies to me a commitment to an interpretive understanding of people's experiences of the internet and of the texts (in the broad sense) they create online and offline. Crucially, as Denzin (2004, p. 7) usefully points out, "online interpretative work provide(s) the foundations for social criticism and social action." For instance, in my own study a qualitative approach meant not just documenting and describing patients' practices of telling their personal stories online—though this was a substantial part of the work—but fundamentally also thinking about these practices critically: whether, how, and to what extent women's online storytelling transforms their experiences and the cultural and social environments in which their experiences are embedded.

Online Data and Offline Data

As with any research, to investigate the above question and inquire about a specific internet phenomenon, the researcher must obtain data. The data can be obtained from two main types of sources: online and offline. They can include *texts* such as online postings and textual elements such as threads or links, face-to-face interview accounts, or ethnographers' field notes; *images* such as pictures from web sites or photos of spaces that are related to users' experience of the internet; and *sound*, for example online clips. In short, "data" refer to all the information derived from employing qualitative research procedures. *Online data* are materials obtained using what have been often described as virtual methodologies: methods implemented by and through the internet. These include, for instance, participant observation in online spaces (such as the early studies of MUDs or MOOs); see, for example, Baym's study of an online community of soap opera fans (Baym, 2000); Kendall's study of BlueSky (Kendall, 2002); and Schaap's online ethnography of a role-playing MUD called New Carthage (Schaap, 2002). The ethnographic material that researchers reap from their online ethnography constitutes what I refer to here as "online data." Another type of online data is texts of interviews with research participants that are conducted online. Kivits (2005) is one of many researchers who have conducted interviews with internet users via e-mail, in this case specifically to explore their use of the internet for seeking health information. She analyzed the online data she obtained, namely the e-mail transcripts of the online interviews, to account for users' information-seeking practices on the internet and how they made sense of this information.

The other kind of data is obtained using methodologies in offline settings. Here, to study internet-related phenomena, the researcher employs methodological procedures in offline contexts, which generate *offline data*. For example, in studying the integration of the internet in the everyday lives of users, researchers such as Bakardjieva and Smith (2001) and Mackay (2005) conducted ethnographic visits to and interviews in the domestic settings of internet users. Influenced by studies of television audiences, research of this kind is based on offline data that consist of users' accounts obtained through interviews, participant observation in users' households, and, in the case of Mackay, users' diaries recording their media use.

Why Is It Important to Consider the Question of Online/Offline Data in Thinking Through Our Research Projects?

A distinction between online and offline has never been made in research of older communication media. For instance, researchers do not discuss the use of television data versus offline data, or telephone data versus everyday data. More generally, beyond the methodological context, we do not tend to talk about the "television world" versus the "offline world" or about "radio contexts" versus "offline contexts" in the same way as we refer to "online" and "offline" in relation to the internet. The distinction between the online and the offline, and consequently between online and offline data in the research context, is rooted in an interrelated distinction that has specifically characterized common thinking about the internet. Hine (2000) usefully describes this distinction as that between the view of the internet as a "cultural artifact" and as a "culture."

On the one hand, the internet, like other communication media, has been seen as a medium. Researchers working within this premise have explored how it is used as a means of communication within our social lives. As with studies of other communication technologies, they have studied the internet within specific bounded social settings, for example, in the home. The focus therefore has been on offline contexts, and thus research has relied on *offline data*. On the other hand, the internet has been commonly viewed as a communicative social space in its own right. Unlike other media such as the television or the telephone, internet spaces have often been seen as distinct and separate from offline, or "real" social life, encompassing relations and practices of their own. In research terms, this view established cyberspace as a plausible research field site (Hine, 2000) and advanced investigations of online social spaces independently of offline social relations. Such studies rested on the assumption that online sociality has an inherent cultural coherence that is internally meaningful and understandable in its own terms (Slater, 2002). Consequently, study of these online contexts relied mainly, and often exclusively, on *online data*.

The distinction between the online and offline has been constitutive of the understanding of the internet from the earliest days of internet research. Methodologically, the distinction has led to a large extent to a separation between the use of offline and online data. Large-scale surveys of internet use such as those conducted by the Pew

Internet & American Life Project base their analyses of online life mainly on offline data such as information elicited by phone surveys or tracking surveys of internet activities (see, for example, Howard, Rainie, & Jones, 2001). Other researchers, such as Bakardjieva and Smith (2001), though working from a different perspective in their study of internet use, also rely predominantly on offline data, including interviews with domestic users, a tour of the computer and internet-related spaces in respondents' homes, and a group interview with respondents' family members.[1]

In contrast there have been numerous studies, especially in the early days of internet research, drawing exclusively on online data. For example, Donath's (1999) study of identity deception in an online community, Reid's (1999) exploration of social control in MUDs, and Danet, Ruedenberg-Wright, and Rosenbaum-Tamari's (1997) study of language use in computer media all relied on the analysis of online texts and interactions.

More recently, however, this separation is being increasingly deconstructed. It has become clear that the separation between the online and offline cannot be sustained. Researchers have consistently argued for the need to frame the online both in its own right and in relation to other contexts and realities. This recognition clearly undermines, as Haythornthwaite and Wellman point out, the assumption "that only things that happen on the internet were relevant to understanding the internet" (2002, p. 5).

Recognition of the complex relationship between online and offline has profound methodological implications. In particular, two key questions in relation to online and offline data arise at two critical junctures of the research. The first question arises at the stage of designing an empirical study: Do we need offline data to make sense of online phenomena? Do we necessarily need offline information to be able to adequately account for online meanings and experiences? Or can we produce high-quality, persuasive, and grounded qualitative research of an internet phenomenon that draws merely on online data? What claims can a study relying only on data retrieved online make? The opposite question is as intriguing: If the internet is treated as simply a means of communication that is used in an everyday social context, can it therefore be studied as such—that is, merely by using methodological procedures in offline contexts, without any online data?

The second key question arises at the stage of data analysis and concerns the interpretation of online and/or offline data: Are offline and online data comparable? Can they be integrated, and if so, how? If a decision has been made to rely on only online *or* offline data, researchers

must confront questions regarding the adequacy, validity, and limitations of the analysis. Of course, these questions also arise for researchers
who use *both* online and offline data.

I turn to the two questions in more detail below, discussing each in
the context of the particular research junctures at which it may arise
and highlighting possible ways of tackling each. Crucially, my intention is not to provide prescriptive answers, but rather to demonstrate
what I regard as useful, sensible, ethical, and context-sensitive approaches
to these questions.

❖ IS OBTAINING OFFLINE AND ONLINE DATA NECESSARY? IF SO, WHEN? IF NOT, WHY?

As mentioned earlier, the question of, and thus the decision about,
whether it is necessary to obtain both online and offline data arises at
the very early stages of designing the empirical research. The answer
to the question seems simple: "It depends on the question you ask and
on the context you study." However, in what follows I unpack this
seemingly straightforward answer by pointing to particular considerations that might be involved and by grounding the discussion in
specific examples from my own study and that of others.

In their study of young people's cultural life and social resistance,
Wilson and Atkinson (2005) ask, "What is the relationship between
young people's online (activist) activities and offline social action?"
The emphasis in the question is on understanding this group's culture
and the ways online and offline contexts inform and enable each other.
The theoretical concern about the relationship between online and
offline contexts, in terms of a specific group's activities and practices,
informs a methodology that would aim at capturing the online, the
offline, and the connections between them. Thus, Wilson and Atkinson's
study was based on an analysis of the contents of 28 web pages (online
data), in-depth face-to-face interviews with web site producers and
organizers, fieldwork that involved attending events organized by the
groups involved, and a study of the media coverage of the groups'
events (offline data).

Similarly, in my research into the online communication of women
suffering from breast cancer (Orgad, 2005b), obtaining both online and
offline data regarding the participants' experiences was crucial for
making sense of the meanings of online communication for women
with breast cancer. Patients' online participation and their use of the
internet are deeply embedded in their everyday experience of chronic

illness. Therefore, if we are to understand patients' online contexts, we clearly have to have knowledge of their offline contexts; that is, of the everyday life aspects of their coping with breast cancer. By the same token, to make sense of patients' experience of breast cancer (offline), it is necessary to come to grips with their online engagement, which is a significant part of their experience of coping with their illness. So as early as at the stage of designing an empirical study I made a decision to obtain both online and offline data, on the basis of which I would build my analysis.

In both of these examples the decision to obtain online and offline data is situated in the context of the specific research goals. It might seem more sensible and context-sensitive to seek access to both online and offline data. However, this is not necessarily the case. Eichhorn's (2001) study demonstrates how the researcher's decision to rely primarily on online data and deliberately avoid the study of participants in their offline environments was an informed context-sensitive decision, stemming from a careful understanding of the phenomenon being studied. In her study of girls' textual online community ("zines"), which was carried out primarily online, it was unlikely that the tactics and practices that Eichhorn aimed to examine would have been rendered visible had she opted to study them within an offline environment, such as a school or a classroom.

More generally, Eichhorn (2001) challenges the assumption that ethnographic research of an online-based phenomenon necessarily depends on face-to-face relationships with the study's participants. In her work, participating in informants' everyday lives did not necessarily mean accessing their offline environments. On the contrary, Eichhorn insists that "understanding people's lives, particularly in the technologically driven Western world, may sometimes require ethnographers to do what the people they seek to study do, even if it necessitates staying at home" (p. 566).

A related argument against the use of offline data is that, in seeking to combine online and offline data, particularly when the data relate to participants' lives and activities, researchers run the risk of implying that online data are not as authentic as offline data. That being said, employing procedures to study participants in their offline environments could be a fruitful way of contextualizing and adding authenticity to the findings obtained online (Hine, 2000). Turkle (1996), for example, in her notable study *Life on the Screen*, reflects on the significance of conducting face-to-face in-depth interviews with her online informants as a way to further "explore an individual's life history and tease out the roles technology has played" (p. 324). She goes so far as only to include findings on those online informants whom she also met in person, a methodological decision she justifies with her concern with the relationship between users' experiences in online reality and real life.

In my study, the transition from e-mail correspondence with my informants to face-to-face meetings proved extremely significant for understanding the experience of breast cancer patients' online engagement. I consider this transition to have been a key turning point in my understanding of the relationship between patients' lives and their online experience. In hindsight, I realize that so long as I only had access to participants' construction of their online experience through their e-mail accounts, the relationship between patients' lives and their online experience seemed fairly palpable and straightforward. In most of the e-mail accounts I initially received from patients, "the internet" is described in a fairly idealized way: either as a "dazzling" and "empowering" "miracle" (reproducing popular emancipatory constructions of the internet) or in a reductive way, as being nothing but another source of information about cancer. The offline data that I obtained later through face-to-face interviews revealed much more complex connections between patients' online and offline experiences. These accounts were primarily personal narratives about how they coped with their illness. Rather than foregrounding the experience of using the internet (as in the e-mail accounts), in the face-to-face accounts this experience was embedded in their stories.

The face-to-face interviews also enabled respondents to move away from utopian or dystopian discourses and clichés about "the internet." Instead, in their face-to-face accounts, "the internet" was usually disaggregated into its different components, in the particular contexts where it played a role in their coping. While in the e-mail accounts "the internet" appeared to be a pretty much singular "thing," the face-to-face interviews revealed its various facets and situated contexts.

Even Eichhorn (2001), who persuasively explains why conducting research relationships both online and offline is not always appropriate and may not necessarily fit the research context and goals, reflects on the invaluable significance of the only face-to-face meeting she had with one of the participants of the online community she studied. She describes this meeting as an important turning point in her understanding of this community and as presenting an opportunity to ask questions she had previously failed to recognize as being relevant to her research (p. 571).

Crucially, however, in all the examples I have mentioned, the researchers do not treat the offline data on participants' lives and experiences as more "truthful" or "authentic" than the data obtained online. Rather than validating the veracity of the data obtained online, the rationale for deciding to gather offline data is based in a perceived need to add context, to enhance information, and to yield insights into aspects that would otherwise remain invisible, but that may be consequential to the research. More generally, rather than being led by some general rules of inquiry, what guided the researchers in the above examples were the particular research contexts and the demands of their research goals.

The question of whether there is a need to enhance online data with offline data can arise at later stages of the research project. Rutter and Smith (2005), for instance, sought to discover how sociability is discursively constructed in the "RumCom" newsgroup online. The major component of data used in their study was the messages that were published on this online space. However, this kind of data did not seem on its own to be sufficient. They wrote, "We also wanted to add some depth beyond what we could discover through the analysis of messages. We felt that our online ethnography had to do more than merely observe and collect textual data" (p. 87). They therefore complemented the online data that they had initially obtained with a series of phone and face-to-face interviews with some of their online informants. This offline data allowed them to inquire into the ways in which online participants became involved in the RumCom newsgroup and what they got out of it, information that had remained obscure as long as they obtained only online data.

I have so far discussed the relationship between online and offline data only in one direction; that is, as the research moves from online to offline. One can, however, picture a research situation that starts offline and then moves to obtaining online data. The rationale for such a move might be similar to what I described in relation to the move in the opposite direction: the need to add depth to the phenomenon being studied, to contextualize and enhance the offline data.

Bakardjieva and Smith (2001) designed a quasi-ethnographic study that aimed to explore computer networking from the standpoint of the domestic user. They sought to devise a methodology that would allow them to investigate "both the real-life contexts and actions of our [their] subjects *and* their exploits in cyberspace" (p. 69). Influenced by studies of the domestication of media and technology in people's everyday lives, the researchers deliberately focused on the offline environment of users' homes as the sites in which they studied domestic practices of internet use. The offline data they obtained included interviews with domestic users, a tour of the computer and internet-related spaces in respondents' homes, and a group interview with respondents' family members. These data were complemented by one component of online data, which they describe as a tour of users' "computer space"; that is, the traces of internet use that were saved in respondents' computers or in their accounts on the provider's server (p. 70). Arguably, a more elaborate use of online data, such as, for example, the ethnography of the actual internet spaces in which these users participated, could have further augmented the researchers' understanding of the ways in which the internet is integrated into users' everyday life situations and tied in to specific social-biographical situations.

In this context, Sanders' (2005) research is quite illuminating, as it uses a multi-layered research design consisting of both online and offline components. In studying the sex work community in Britain, Sanders started her ethnography offline, observing indoor sex markets and street prostitution for ten months. She later found it necessary to explore the impact of computer-mediated communication (CMC) on the organization of sex economies, to which end she turned to the internet to collect online data, mainly through instances of lurking. Observing forums such as message boards and live chat sessions where sex workers and clients interact (textually) gave Sanders insights into how commercial sex was advertised, discussed, selected, and negotiated online between clients, sex workers, and owners of establishments. The researcher then realized that to fully understand the role of the internet in sustaining the identities of sex workers, she needed to move back offline: to recruit online participants for face-to-face interviews. "In the same way that sex workers and clients inevitably transfer their relationship from online to real encounters," she reflects, "questions relating risks and management strategies led me to move beyond the screen to face-to-face relationships" (p. 71).

Sanders' study reveals other important considerations that need to be taken into account when making decisions about the use of online and offline data, particularly when the latter involves moving the relationship with participants from online to offline, and even more particularly when sensitive or high-risk groups are concerned. The nature of these considerations can be ethical, involving questions of the researcher's trustworthiness and rapport with her informants. One of the lessons Sanders and other researchers (e.g., Kendall, 2002; Mann & Stewart, 2000; Orgad, 2005a) learned is that it is highly problematic, if not impossible, to move from online to offline with informants without establishing bona fide status, trust, and rapport. However, in some cases, offline information on online participants could simply prove infeasible, particularly where hard-to-reach populations, such as sex workers, are concerned.

Another aspect that the researcher has to consider is the sample of respondents. As long as we rely on online methodologies our access is limited only to those who actively participate (e.g., those who post messages) and therefore are visible. However, many online participants are only lurkers, but their participation and practices can be extremely significant and highly consequential for understanding an internet-related context. Yet from a discursive point of view, the "silent" are difficult to incorporate into the analysis, as they leave no observable traces (Hine, 2000, p. 25).

Let me give an example from my study of breast cancer patients' online communication. A breast cancer patient writes the following to her fellow sufferers' mailing list:

> [I]f you want to . . . post as much as you want . . . even a lot in one day. If you want to, stay silent and get support without posting. If you want to, stay away for a while and come back. We have some members who come and go. AND wow, some of our members "graduate" and feel they are not in need of support . . . if those members want to come back . . . they are always welcome.

Staying in the background—only reading messages, as the patient cited above describes it—can play a significant role in how patients cope with their illness. Lurking enables patients to learn about others' experiences and to relate their own situation to that of others without having to necessarily expose themselves and their feelings. Similarly, another patient reflects on the valuable therapeutic effect of putting her experience into text by typing it—before actually interacting online:

> Probably the best part of the internet is that you need to type your question or feeling before you can share it and sometimes just writing it down is a therapy of its own.[2]

To be able to inquire into these highly meaningful practices, such as lurking or simply typing out one's experience (without necessarily publishing it online), I had to go beyond the screen to gain access to those participants and their activities, which would have otherwise remained invisible. Relying only on the observable representational level of online activities (i.e., texts) was not sufficient on its own to explain the significance and capture the complexity of these activities.

But how do you do this? How do you access the invisible? To tackle this task, I recruited some interviewees by snowballing offline. I exploited initial contacts with women whom I met online in order to recruit their acquaintances who participated online, but not necessarily actively and visibly. I thus gained access to an appropriate range of participants engaged in different levels of involvement, in different kinds of online activities in relation to their illness.

Researchers may also be interested in studying those who are not online—those who "fail" or refuse to engage online. This can be an interesting phenomenon to study in itself (and speaks to some of the boundary discussions in the first chapter). Studying this group can also shed light on internet use and online participation. For example, in my study one of the interviewees was a patient who initially visited breast cancer patients' forums; however, after a short time, she became very critical of these sites and stopped participating in them. Nor did she reply to my online request for women willing to participate in the study. "You would have never found me online," she told me in our face-to-face interview. Indeed, I recruited her through snowballing (another patient referred me to her), rather than online, where I found the majority of the interviewees.

Though my research focused on the experience of women who participated online in the context of their illness, rather than nonparticipants, the experience of this woman and other nonusers I met proved invaluable. They illuminated some of the significant constraints of the spaces in which patients were actively participating and helped me think critically about the phenomenon I studied: To what extent are these online spaces inclusive, allowing "people from all walks of life" (as one forum describes its mission) to share their experience?

Clearly, if we wish to study those who are not online, relying on online data is not sufficient. We need to gain access to informants' offline contexts and retrieve offline data. Indeed, driven primarily by the digital divide agenda, researchers have recently recognized that studying those who are not online can be a significant aspect of understanding internet phenomena (e.g., Lenhart, 2001, based on a telephone survey). I suggest that exploring participants who are excluded from certain CMC contexts, or have "failed" to engage in CMC, can be very fruitful for qualitative studies of internet phenomena, and not just in relation to the digital divide. For instance, two of my interviewees, despite having the technical capacity and competence needed to engage in CMC, found the breast cancer internet sites they encountered inappropriate and unsatisfactory. Their experience of rejecting the internet as a communicative space in coping with their illness was extremely telling—not only in terms of the specificity of their experience but also in the light it threw on the majority of the "successful" cases. These two patients were looking for a forum that would allow a critical and rational discussion on breast cancer, whereas the majority of the forums they found online focused on patients' emotional and confessional stories. This distinction helped me understand the centrality of the subjective, experiential, and confessional discourse that governs many patients' internet spaces, and in particular the significance of storytelling as a key social activity in which breast cancer patients engage online (see Orgad, 2005b).

Whereas I started online and then moved offline with my research participants, Eichhorn (2001) decided to locate her research almost exclusively in an online site, relying primarily on online data. Situating her research online, rather than in an offline setting such as a school or classroom, enabled her to examine a group of young women not always visible in the school system. As she reflects,

> Significantly, many of these young women wrote about feeling either invisible or even at risk in the school environment. . . . In contrast with the lack of visibility many of these young women experienced in their schools, the textual community of 'zines was a space in which these young women, many not "out" in their local communities, could have their identities and experiences recognized and validated. (p. 574)

Eichhorn's decision to locate her research in an online site, relying primarily on online data, opened up the possibility of studying "this often unaccounted for group of young people" (Eichhorn, 2001, p. 574). Whatever decision is made, the crucial point is that it should be sensitive to the context being studied and be situated within the demands of the research question.

❖ HOW CAN WE USE AND ANALYZE ONLINE AND OFFLINE DATA?

The other critical juncture at which the issue of online and offline data arises is the stage of analysis and interpretation of the data. How can we integrate the two sets of data? Are the two sets of data comparable and, if so, how?

Such questions become particularly crucial if the rationale for obtaining both online and offline data was to break down the online/offline distinction conceptually. In regarding the data as two sets of distinctively different and separate data, we run the risk of reproducing the very idea that we aimed to challenge; that is, that the online and the offline are two separate distinguished realms.

An attempt to break down the distinction between online and offline cannot be pursued only in theory; it is a project substantially implicated in methodology and, in this context, particularly in the way the data are treated. In what follows I try to demonstrate some of the implications of breaking down this distinction by reflecting on the data analysis in my research on breast cancer patients' online communication.

My data analysis involved three different types of texts: (1) e-mail accounts, (2) online texts from breast cancer web sites, and (3) face-to-face interviews. Crucially, no hierarchy was implied among the different texts; the three types were treated equally in terms of their contribution to the data analysis. In addition, rather than organizing the analytical discussion by kinds of data and the information elicited from each, I organized it along three thematic dimensions that characterized what I described as participants' "storytelling online," namely, emplotment, exchange, and the negotiation of public and private. I coded the different kinds of data (12 face-to-face interviews, 28 e-mail accounts and one letter, and various texts from breast cancer web sites) according to the three dimensions.

When analyzing the data, my aim was to identify participants' understandings of their online experience in relation to each of the three thematic categories. I looked for the different manifestations, as well as absences, of each of the three aspects in patients' accounts (e-mail and face-to-face) and in texts on breast cancer web sites (e.g., a web site's instructions for how to post a message). In reading the various texts, I asked myself these questions: What do women's narratives say is significant about the exchanges? What do they emphasize and what do they omit or understate? What is surprising about what they say about their online interactions? What is problematic? In light of these questions, I examined differences and similarities among the different sets of data and tried to make sense of them.

I used discourse analysis of the web site texts to contextualize patients' accounts (both e-mail and face-to-face) of their illness and online experience, and vice versa; I used patients' accounts of their illness experience and internet use to make sense of breast cancer web sites' texts. For example, a common feature of the face-to-face interviews was that participants understated or even denied their participation in exchanging personal stories online, whereas examination of their e-mail accounts and observation of the web sites they visited showed that often they were quite actively engaged. Also, the face-to-face and e-mail accounts were produced for me, the researcher: They were the stories of these patients' online experience in relation to their illness. The online texts taken from breast cancer web sites, on the other hand, were stories about the experience of illness and coping with it, produced by patients and posted for their online fellow sufferers. The significantly different audiences had crucial implications for the content and form of these texts, an issue I took up in analyzing the data.

Another difference between the data obtained online and that gleaned from face-to-face interviews derived from their timing: The online accounts that women posted on web sites were often created when they were going through the illness and undergoing treatment. The e-mail accounts they wrote for me were often still temporally close to their actual experience (since I recruited interviewees from the web sites where they posted their stories, usually near the time of posting). The face-to-face interviews, however, were mostly conducted at least a year later. Naturally, at that time, women often had a very different perspective of their experience of illness and, inextricably, of internet use. For all those reasons, it appeared crucial to integrate the different kinds of accounts and perspectives from the different sets of data into an understanding of the communicative context that I studied.

Fundamentally, in reading and analyzing women's accounts, my aim was not to evaluate whether they were "truthful" or not. Rather, the aim was to obtain an enhanced understanding of women's experiences of using the internet in relation to their illness. So, for example, a woman told me in a face-to-face interview that the internet played a very limited role, if any, in her experience of coping with breast cancer. However, this statement was contradicted by the online data I gathered, which included her various postings and revealed her rather active participation. There was also an online account she wrote me two years earlier in reply to the recruitment message I posted on one of the breast cancer boards, in which she recounted her use of the internet and its significance as a tool for information seeking and a space for support. How do you reconcile such differences between the same person's accounts? The principle that guided me is rooted in the interpretative approach to life stories (Plummer, 2001): All autobiographical memory is true. When people talk about their lives they inevitably forget, select, exaggerate, become confused, and sometimes lie. It is the interpreter's task to identify these gaps and discern their meaning. My interpretation of the case cited above was that the face-to-face interview, which took place a year after this woman was already cured, was part of her attempt to construct herself as a healthy person. She associated her online participation in breast cancer forums with her illness, a chapter she wanted to forget and put behind. She therefore tended to marginalize and almost dismiss the significance of this chapter, and the internet's part in it, in her life.[3]

The more general point I wish to draw from this example is that, in their analyses, researchers should try to use the different kinds of data as mutually contextualizing each other. There is a tendency, as Slater (2002) observes, to treat the offline "as that which makes sense of, or explains, the online" (p. 544). However, the offline does not explain the online, nor does the online explain the offline. Therefore, greater advantage is gained when examining the ways in which each configures the other.

Yet, a qualitative research project may aim to compare online and offline manifestations of a certain context. In this case, to fit the method and the analysis to the research question, it appears most sensible to treat the online and offline data in a comparative fashion, analyzing one against the other. Early CMC research focusing on the "cues-filtered-out" approach employed experimental studies of small groups to compare face-to-face and computer-mediated group behavior (for a review of these studies, see Baym, 2002). Discourse and linguistic analysis have often been used to compare CMC discourses and offline discourses, oral or written (e.g., Baron, 2003). The assumption underlying these comparisons has often been that CMC is a constrained version of face-to-face embodied interaction. However, this is a highly problematic view. Theoretically, it fails to recognize CMC's unique and varied qualities or to understand how users draw on their existing communicative capabilities to construct social meaning within the challenges and the opportunities posed by the online medium (Baym, 2002, p. 66). Consequently, an analysis that takes the face-to-face as its starting point is unable to explain the specificity of the online phenomenon it aims to study; it can explain what is going on online only in terms of face-to-face qualities.

Normatively, regarding online communication as a constrained version of face-to-face communication implies that online communication is "less" than face-to-face communication: less authentic, less real, less close, and less truthful. Methodologically, treating the online as a constrained version of the offline limits the tools and practices that researchers use to those that they can apply to the offline. It does not allow researchers to develop methods that are sensitive and specific to what happens online. In my study, for example, if I were guided by a need to compare the online to the offline I would have probably been unable to analyze and account for the significance of discursive forms such as threads—which do not have straightforward face-to-face parallels.

This is not to say that comparing online and offline data cannot yield interesting and important observations about the qualities of CMC. However, one needs to carefully account for the underlying theoretical and conceptual framework that invites such comparative treatment of the data in the first place.

Whether online and offline data are used in the analysis in an integrative fashion or in a comparative way, a key practice to be wary of is making judgments about the authenticity of the data. There is often a tendency to imply, explicitly or implicitly, that the information the researcher has garnered from online sources (e.g., web sites, CMC interactions) is not as authentic as that generated from offline ones. In treating online and offline data, we should be informed by recognition of the distinct character of online and offline contexts and interactions and of their consequent texts, while at the same time accounting for the inextricable connections, similarities, and continuities between the two.

❖ HOW CAN WE PRESENT OUR INTERPRETATIONS?

Lastly, an important issue of concern in the construction of our analysis is the presentation of the data. Do we differentiate online from offline data, or do we present both as one coherent set of data? This may seem a technical and rather marginal issue, but it constitutes a significant feature of the treatment of data. In reporting my study, I used different fonts to reflect the different sources from which I was quoting: (1) academic or any other published text that was not a direct part of the ethnographic material; (2) extracts from face-to-face interviews used to build my analysis; and (3) extracts from online texts, whether e-mail accounts from participants or texts posted in public online forums. One reader challenged this approach by arguing that in identifying the different online and offline sources by different fonts I was not acting in line with what I was advocating—that the online and the offline should be seen and treated as interwoven rather than significantly separate. While I do not think that either point of view is right or wrong, I do think that whatever decision researchers make about differentiation should reflect its possible implications. In my case, my decision to use different fonts was made to help the reader identify the different sources of the quotes (especially given the prevalence of quotes in my analysis). In so doing, my intention was certainly not to imply that the online and the offline should be or were being treated as two separate or isolated realms (see also Markham, 2004a, for further discussion of issues of presentation).

Our responsibility to reflexively interrogate our methods carries through all stages of research design, analysis, interpretation, and presentation of findings and applies whether researchers are relying on offline data, online data, or both. Pitts (2004), for example, demonstrates a level of reflexivity in her study of personal web pages of women with breast cancer. Unlike my study, Pitts analyzed only online data, namely the texts of 50 personal web sites of individual breast cancer survivors. In presenting her analysis of these data she reflects on their limits:

> I can make no claims about the off-line identities of the authors who wrote the web sites, and I do not assume that cybersubjects' on-line identities are necessarily identical to their off-line identities. . . . I operate under the assumption that the web pages are in some sense "truthful," in that their authors do indeed have breast cancer or know someone with breast cancer. . . . That this assumption is not empirically verified must be considered a limitation of this research. (p. 40)

While researchers should be encouraged to reflexively interrogate their methods and analyses, I think that Pitts actually falls into the trap that I discussed earlier; that is, of treating online data as less authentic or truthful than offline data. Pitts seems to work with some absolute notion of offline data as inherently more "truthful" or "verified" than online data; hence, she judges the online data on which she bases her analysis as limited and probably less authentic than their offline counterparts. Rather, standards of authenticity should be seen as situationally negotiated and sustained (Hine, 2000). In this sense, Pitts' later reflection on her decision not to look for offline data on her informants seems more context-sensitive and sensible. It demonstrates an understanding of the perceptions of her informants and the judgments *they* made about the online spaces in which they participate:

> I believe that this would go against the spirit of personal web pages, which are intended to be public but also to afford varying levels of anonymity and a choice about making personal disclosures, such as one's real name, location, appearance and so on, to readers. (p. 41)

In short, whether the analysis is based on both online and offline data or on only one kind of data, the question of the authenticity, validity, and adequacy of the analysis is one that the researcher has to face, critically and reflexively.

❖ CONCLUSIONS: REVISITING THE ONLINE/OFFLINE DISTINCTION

The key argument in this chapter is that, in thinking through their own research projects or evaluating those of others, researchers need to critically consider the data that they obtain and interpret. It is not enough to recognize the complex nature of the relationship between the online and the offline at a conceptual level while ignoring its methodological implications. I find it striking that researchers make claims about the immersion of users' experiences and practices in their everyday lives, while the data they rely upon provide them with very limited grounds to adequately understand the relationship between their participants' online and offline worlds. This does not, as I have stressed, mean that it is only through offline data that researchers can make sense of respondents' everyday lives. The key point is that the data on which researchers build their analyses, whether these are online, offline, or both, should be of high quality. The data should be collected and generated after solid preparation based on a clear rationale; should fit with the question and the context; should convincingly support the claims being made; should be used reflexively and be context-sensitive; and, finally, should be ethically grounded.

Throughout the course of the research project, researchers must ask themselves such questions as the following: Does obtaining online and offline data fit the questions I'm asking and the context I'm studying? Would offline data reveal something significant about the context being studied that could not be obtained from online data? In what ways might the offline data enhance the interpretation of the online data?

It must also be borne in mind, as I have argued, that combining online and offline data is not always an appropriate decision. Doing so might be insensitive to the context being studied, might involve problematic ethical consequences, or might simply be impractical. Thus, here are two equally important questions: Can I make a persuasive case with only one of the two kinds of data? What might possibly be lost or risked in obtaining the two kinds of data? Moving research relationships from online to offline and, more generally, pursuing offline data to complement online data can certainly open up research paths, but could equally be counterproductive and close off research routes.

Perhaps we should revisit the distinction between online and offline data and reconsider its usefulness.[4] As the space of media and communication becomes more hybrid, and with the increasing trend toward the convergence of technology, the lines between online and offline communication are blurring (Herring, 2004; Orgad, 2007). The term "online" itself does not map consistently into a single media technology. The mediascape becomes more hybrid and multi-layered, and "virtuality" is not restricted to being online, but can embrace and link several media including what we would once have considered as "offline media," for instance the telephone. Furthermore, traditional modes of CMC are increasingly being used to establish face-to-face contacts (Herring, 2004).

These changes challenge the methodological distinction between online and offline data, with which I opened this chapter, in significant ways. What are the implications for our research and our analysis, as the data become even messier and less stable? This line of questioning connects to a recent discussion on the need to move beyond the concept of place-bounded ethnography and thereby to redefine the field and its boundaries (Eichhorn, 2001; Hine, 2000; Leander & McKim, 2003). Influenced by ideas such as Marcus's (1995) "multi-sited ethnography" and Olwig and Hastrup's (1997) view of the field as being a "field of relations," qualitative internet researchers are looking for ways to move beyond bounded sites, to follow connections made meaningful from a specific setting (Hine, 2000). For example, in their discussion of methodological approaches to the analysis of adolescents' internet literacy practices, Leander and McKim (2003) propose replacing the notion of users' everyday "sites" by that of "sitings."[5] They emphasize the need to develop methodologies that follow participants' practices of moving and traveling between online and offline and within a far wider and hybrid mediascape.

However, even if the line between online data and offline data is blurring, the issues discussed in this chapter still have relevance for any researcher who is thinking through a qualitative internet project or evaluating that of another. For example, in a study (Baron et al., 2005) of how away messages in instant messaging are used by American college students to help manage their social spheres, one set of data collected by the researchers consisted of 190 away messages. The other kind of data the researchers used was traditional "offline data," derived from interviews and a focus group with users. Although the distinction between online and offline data does not fully apply to this research, some of the key issues that I discussed in this chapter may still arise and be relevant, namely, the question of triangulating different sets of data; using the face-to-face interviews with participants to contextualize their instant messaging practices; and vice versa, using the data of the instant messaging to make sense of what respondents said in their interviews.

"Online social worlds are accessible to researchers in ways that few other worlds are. If we want to understand them, we need to look with rigor and detail" (Baym, 2000, p. 198). Looking with rigor and detail may mean adopting very different methodological strategies and taking very different decisions in the course of the research project. In this chapter I have sought to discuss some of the questions, dilemmas, strategies, and decisions that may be involved in grappling with aspects of online and offline data in qualitative internet research. While there are no right or wrong answers to any of the issues and the questions discussed, what is important is that the decisions made should be grounded in the particular context being studied and the specific questions being asked.

❖ RECOMMENDED READING

For a collection of case studies and reviews that explore methodological solutions to understanding the social interactions mediated by information and communications technologies, see Hine's (2005b) edited book, *Virtual Methods: Issues in Social Research on the Internet*. For particular discussions on the question of online and offline data see chapters by Mackay, Sanders, Orgad, and Rutter and Smith.

For a critical review of key epistemological, conceptual, and methodological aspects related to the relationship between online and offline, see Slater's chapter, "Social Relationships and Identity Online and Offline," in L. Lievrouw and S. Livingstone (2002), *The Handbook of New Media*.

For an ethnographic study of the internet that offers a sophisticated analysis of the online/offline relationship in a situated context (Trinidad), and draws on rich ethnographic online and offline material, see Miller and Slater's (2000) *The Internet: An Ethnographic Approach*.

For a collection of reflexive reports and short essays on researchers' experiences of doing qualitative internet research, including some discussions of issues of online and offline data, see Johns, Chen, and Hall's (2004) book, *Online Social Research: Methods, Issues, & Ethics*.

❖ NOTES

1. As I mention later in the chapter, Bakardjieva and Smith's (2001) study included only one component of online data, which they describe as a tour of users' "computer space."

2. An extract from an e-mail account of one of my research participants.

3. Marginalizing the role the internet played in coping with the illness was a recurring phenomenon in women's accounts. When asked to reflect on the place of the internet in the experience of their illness, interviewees often depicted their online experience as insignificant.

4. For an extended critique of the two-realm approach that governs thinking about the internet and a discussion of how to enhance understanding of the intensity of the interrelationship between online and offline, see Orgad (2007).

5. In making this proposal, Leander and McKim (2003) are particularly inspired by the work of Olwig and Hastrup (1997).

A Response to Shani Orgad

Maria Bakardjieva

❖ ❖ ❖

Most of my work has approached the internet from the direction of everyday life; that is, from the side of the living person typing away on the keyboard with the messy desk around her or the laptop humming in her lap. My research questions, in very general terms, focus on what brings this person to this keyboard and screen and what she might bring back from the screen to her immediate environment in terms of action, meanings, and relationships. From this perspective, the online and offline look so entwined that it hardly makes any sense to talk about them as separate sources of data. After all, the internet is exactly that place where the online and the offline meet. To study it would mean to hold both sides in view at the same time, especially because every so often the internet is only a bridge between one offline and another. With that said, it is also true that the internet is many different things, and its research is an incredibly diverse enterprise. To find our way in the maze, it is useful to coin taxonomies and rely on them when trying to construct meaningful and feasible research projects. So, I accept the invitation to explore the utility of the dichotomy between online and offline data.

To begin, I recontextualize the title question of this chapter itself by asking, Why is the issue of grappling with online and offline data important, or is it? What other research design questions are related to it and may in fact need to be addressed before the online/offline data issue arises?

❖ STUDYING THE CONTEXT OF WHAT?

At many places in her essay Shani Orgad mentions the importance of us being attentive to the "context that we are studying." My argument here is that before we can start inspecting the context, we have to answer the "of what" question: What is our research object, and surely, what do we want to learn about it? The "research object" comprises the phenomenon that we ask our research question about. Indisputably, in social research we do not deal with naturally existing objects that we literally stumble upon and become curious about. Indeed, it is often argued that natural scientists may be running out of such objects as well, if they have ever had them (see Hacking, 1999).

In qualitative social research, our objects are, admittedly and unapologetically, constructed (see, for example, Crotty, 1998). As much as the internet may be teeming with mailing lists or discussion forums on which people post their messages, the online or virtual communities of soap opera fans or women with breast cancer are certainly "phenomena," seen as such and defined by researchers. Numerous teenagers log onto the internet every day or, for that matter, never log off, but the phenomenon of teenagers' internet use is isolated and constructed as an object to be investigated for its properties, peculiarities, favorable and unfavorable conditions, applications, and effects by researchers. This construction, we must realize, places tremendous power and responsibility in our hands. Our power stems from the fact that we can choose how to label, slice, turn, expand, or trim down our object (see, for example, Chapter 1, this volume; Markham, 2005c). And our responsibility, of course, compels us to do this in a way that respects the efforts and achievements of those who have tackled the same or similar research objects before us, and to endeavor to say something useful to the others who might want to learn about our object down the road. Very importantly, the theory we espouse will play a central role in how we see and isolate our research object from the stream of social life.

Once a researcher has defined her object, she should try to decide what she wants to know about that object. Say for example you have stumbled on a phenomenon that others speak about as "blogging." You are ready to accept that label and feel excited about studying it. Here, then, is the place to ask yourself what your definition of blogging is and what you are curious to find out about it. Leaving the definitional part of this process aside (because the definitions of blogging vary greatly), I would be most interested in learning why people (or a particular category of them to make things manageable) blog, what meaning they ascribe to their blogs, what relationships they form in the process of blogging, and how the activity and its associated experiences affect their lives. You may notice that I have shifted the research object enough to probably warrant a change of label. My research object may be more accurately called "bloggers." You, on your part, might prefer to stick with blogs as a particular kind of content appearing on the internet and wish to know how blogs are similar and different in style and dynamic from other online texts or what categories of blogs could be identified in the growing tide of blogging. Our different curiosities, then, may lead us to wade through texts on the internet (more likely you) or meet with people in homes, classrooms, and cafes (most definitely me), or both (of which Shani Orgad's study [2005b] is an excellent example). The reflexive monitoring of how good a job we are doing involves not so much wondering if we should collect data online or off, but rather making sure that we are thoroughly and comprehensively engaging with our chosen research object in pursuit of answers to the questions we have raised.

❖   ON-PAGE, ON-SCREEN, ON-LINE, AND OFF

Those of us who come to internet research from the route of Media Studies may agree that as a discipline Media Studies stands on three legs: the study of content (print, audio, and video), the study of production organizations and processes, and the study of reception and audiences, as can be easily recognized in McQuail's (2000) influential *Mass Communication Theory.* There is a very clear analogy here with the online/offline distinction in internet research that Orgad discusses. That is why I find it hard to accept her claim that such a distinction has "never been made in qualitative research concerning different communication media." We may not have talked about these earlier studies in the same way, but it takes only a brief look into the scholarly journals devoted to "traditional" media to discover that the studies reported there orient themselves to one or more of the three dimensions pointed out above. Think about research on images of women in the media, or racism in the media, or the representation of different political or health issues in the media. All such studies are based decisively on on-page, on-screen, and on-radiowave data. In contrast, studies of reception focus on the experiences and responses of audiences and collect extensive or in-depth off-page and off-screen data (some of the classic examples here would be Lull, 1991; Morley, 1986; Radway, 1984; and Silverstone,

1994). Then, there are studies that combine the analysis of on-media texts with off-page and off-screen interviews and observations (Morley, 1980; Philo & Berry, 2004).

All pre-internet media—the press, film, radio, and television—have been interpreted and researched as cultural artifacts and as culture, to reiterate Hine's (2000) distinction of approaches to studying the internet. I insist on us noticing this continuity so that we can learn from the achievements of earlier scholarship. Such research can teach us vital lessons about how to delimit our objects of inquiry as well as what questions might be interesting to ask about them. Pre-internet media scholarship demonstrates that excellent studies can be conducted on either content or audiences alone, as well as on the interaction between the two. I tend to think about these approaches as user-centered versus medium-centered and believe the same distinction can be applied to internet studies.

Arguably, it is in the best interest of our collective knowledge that the work done on these different aspects of the media-in-society nexus be balanced out in the overall body of scholarly production. Otherwise, we may get collectively lost in on-media content without users or, equally harmful, neglect the importance of on-media images and events as part of the social world of users. This need for balance, however, does not mean that each and every study should attempt to straddle both sides of the on/off slash. It all depends on how you carve and delimit your research object and questions.

In one of my projects (Bakardjieva, 2005), I was interested in studying the internet's integration into the everyday life of the home. I visited and interviewed users in their homes or, as Orgad would put it, in "traditional research contexts." Note, however, that at the time I was collecting my data, there was nothing traditional in a living room or basement with a connected computer pitched in the middle of it. I "toured" the interior of users' computers, examining the content of their bookmarks and e-mails, hoping to tap into the meaning that those electronic artifacts had for users. In most cases this material was all the evidence there was about my respondents' life online simply because the majority of them did not participate in online groups and had not created their own web sites. Thus, to try to collect data from online spaces would have been unreasonable and impractical in the framework of that particular study. As Slater (2002) has observed, "Virtuality is one possible, but not necessary, emergent feature of people's assimilation of the new medium and has to be established empirically in any given case" (p. 540).

At the same time, I became very curious about the online community related experiences that a few of my informants had reported. Later,

I carried out a different study that took as its object the supportive cultures attained by some online groups and that asked these questions: What contributed to the emergence of such cultures? What held these communities together? How did they manage their affairs day in and day out? With such a research object and set of questions in hand, my main observations had to be conducted online, not necessarily as an ethnography, but as an analysis of the interactive texts in which community life materialized. Yet, to make sense of these texts, I felt I should engage community members in e-mail interviews as well. In the interviews I asked members about the broader experiences that shaped and were transformed by their online participation. Despite the fact that those were computer-mediated interviews, they generated valuable insights into the ways in which people's online and offline worlds were intertwined (see Bakardjieva & Feenberg, 2001; and Feenberg & Bakardjieva, 2004).

❖ E-MAIL AND OTHER ROWDY HYBRIDS

After having studied the internet for ten years, I would be the last person to argue that there is only continuity between the internet and previous media. However, the major breakthrough does not lie in the "discovery" of the distinction between online and offline by internet researchers. On the contrary: in the case of the internet, communication forms and activities flow through the online/offline divide as never before. Consequently, medium, content and users cannot be easily separated. Take for example the most prolific of internet species, e-mail. E-mails are neither online content alone nor the offline behavior of audiences. To me, it is quite obvious that they are both. The same applies to instant messaging, voice-over IP uses, videoconferencing, chatting, and many other internet-facilitated activities. In projects focusing on these internet applications, I fully agree with Orgad that the distinction between online and offline data would be, or more precisely, has always been significantly blurred. That is why this dichotomy should be revisited and possibly replaced by other more useful distinctions, such as user-centered versus medium-centered approaches (as suggested above), naturally occurring data versus researcher-elicited data, participant versus nonparticipant observation, interview data versus computer-captured and compiled data, and possibly many other typologies that would better inform and guide our research design choices.

The awkwardness of the online/offline data distinction becomes obvious in Orgad's categorization of the e-mail interview as a source of online data. Even though accounts solicited via e-mail may have reached the researcher over an internet protocol and wire, are they not a data type that is significantly different from the postings that cancer patients had made spontaneously on their discussion boards? If those interviews had been carried out by phone, would that have put them in an entirely different class of data? There are of course specific differences between what an online interview can achieve compared to its face-to-face or phone-mediated counterpart. But the subtleties of these different versions of the interview method are not at all elucidated by the online/offline distinction. Thus the e-mail interview is another rowdy hybrid that has to be understood along several dimensions, in parallel and contrast with a number of other alternative approaches, instead of being forced on one side of the online/offline hedge.

To take another example: If a researcher asks his participants to record their media use in blogs or e-mail messages instead of paper diaries, will that automatically turn their entries into online data? And if so, what would be the significant difference? In my view, this would be another technical incarnation of the diary method, which may bring about more convenience and regularity of entry-making, more effective communication between subjects and researchers, etc., but it does not constitute an essentially new type of "online data" different from the paper (offline?) version.

❖ IN CONCLUSION

My advice to those who prepare for qualitative internet research, therefore, starts with a perhaps familiar incantation: Define your research object and formulate your question first. Decide what the data necessary for studying your research object may look like and where you can find them. Doing so will likely involve consideration of what sides of your object are made up of online texts and interactions and what you could learn about it through offline or online interviews and observations. What will be your entry point/s? Then proceed as with any other study—specify your methods and how to go about applying them.

At the end of the day, qualitative internet research is like the qualitative research into any other area of mediated social life. It involves looking at people, their hustle and bustle, their conversations, and their artifacts and texts produced in and through different media. It requires careful planning, ethical choices, and imaginative decision making. And I am ready to bet that, as we move into the future, research on most areas of social life will be internet-related research. Thus online and offline data will routinely be collected and used for what they are—complementary records of events unfolding within the same social world and not as specimens from two different planets.

❖ RECOMMENDED READING

For a discussion of the continuity and differences between methodologies used to study the content of traditional media and the internet, see Clive Seale (2005), "New Directions for Critical Internet Health Studies: Representing Cancer Experience on the Web."

For a study of internet use combining quantitative and qualitative methods in a systematic way, see the 2005 article by Selwyn, Gorard, and Furlong, "Whose Internet is It Anyway? Exploring Adults' (Non)use of the Internet in Everyday Life."

For a productive ethnographic approach to internet adoption and integration into the life of a small Irish town, see the study by Katie Ward (2003), "An Ethnographic Study of Internet Consumption in Ireland: Between Domesticity and the Public Participation."

For an effective analysis of qualitative interviews in the course of a project examining the gendering of domestic internet practices, see Van Zoonen (2002), "Gendering the Internet: Claims, Controversies and Cultures."

For a "child-centered" study navigating the offline and online with interesting results, see Livingstone (2006), "Children's Privacy Online: Experimenting with Boundaries Within and Beyond the Family."

Response to Shani Orgad

Radhika Gajjala

❖   ❖   ❖

In her essay, Shani Orgad does a wonderful job of articulating what it means to do qualitative research with the internet as the site for research. She points to the necessity of examining both online and offline phenomena. I agree with what she has written. However, most internet research (and not just in reference to Shani Orgad's essay) is based on the assumption that "online" and "offline" are physical states of being and that they are implicitly treated as somehow distinct and mutually exclusive. When we actually scrutinize what it means to be online and to be offline, we see that they are not separable states of being in actuality—for when we are online we are simultaneously somewhere else physically as well—but we are definitely not disembodied (i.e., without body). Neither are we not online or not connected when we are offline, since we are simultaneously connected physically, hands typing, eyes reading, mouth speaking, and engaged with activities in the wider physical space surrounding us as well. We cannot really separate our being online from being offline, because online and offline are not discrete entities. In a sense, using this vocabulary, Orgad is trying to emphasize the simultaneity of being online and offline, and she does it well. But the vocabulary itself limits our ability to study practices of everyday life in relation to internet communication.

We need to examine the binary distinction between online and offline as well as the assumptions behind it by asking what it means to shift to the examination of practices of everyday life. Unpacking notions of being online vs. being offline is indeed more difficult than we realize, since this vocabulary itself is such a part of our everyday life. Although we have already established that online is "real," we continue to perpetuate the distinction between online and offline as if they can be mutually exclusive in our daily practice. I myself struggle with this binary articulation as I continue my teaching and research in this area. I continually attempt to design assignments in class to make students understand how their everyday lives are affected by internet-mediated social activities.

While I first encountered the internet as a graduate student in 1992, it is only since 1995 that I actually have been "living" online, performing identities in various online contexts. This living online has taken various forms. I had "homes" on MOOs (multi-user domains, object oriented) such as Lambda MOO, PMC MOO, Media MOO, and LinguaMOO.[1] I was an active participant on several e-mail lists and also a founder, owner, and moderator of some lists (the women-writing-culture list, the Third-World-women list, the postcolonial list, and the sa-cyborgs list). I was a "lurker" (i.e., someone who only reads but does not post) on Usenet bulletin boards. I also built a web site, where I experimented with various software through which I would try to represent myself in a variety of ways using text, image, and even sound.

This living online became my methodology for studying cyberspace and virtual community, which I term "cyberethnography." I first studied a South Asian women's e-mail list (SAWnet) using this methodology. My book *Cyberselves: Feminist Ethnographies of South Asian Women* (2004) describes these research efforts in detail. Thus my collection of "data" occurred through what I learned about myself online and about those with whom I interacted online—ethnographically and autoethnographically.

My efforts researching the internet are closely linked to my teaching pedagogy, through which I focus on trying to make my students understand the interrelationship between meaning-making in their everyday lives and in online settings. I design class assignments to guide students to understand the production of raced/classed identities through online/offline intersections. This examination is layered and multi-modal. In my classes, graduate and undergraduate students are asked to interact within online sociocultural networks. Note that these assignments follow much of what Shani Orgad suggests in her essay about qualitative internet research—we examine both online and offline data. At the point at which we "become the interface," I attempt to articulate how offline and online interweave.

In one assignment involving LinguaMOO (LinguaMOO is now offline; see http://en.wikipedia.org/wiki/MOO for information about this now-classic online community), most of the students who were asked to explore that environment were unfamiliar with it (with the exception of a few students who had been cybernauts before the world-wide web and graphic user interfaces took over the internet). This unfamiliarity itself worked to produce an encounter with the interface that revealed interesting insights. In the case of MySpace, note that only a few of the students exploring that environment were comfortable being at the same online site at which those who were being studied were producing selves—the rest were more comfortable doing textual analyses—while drawing their understanding of online praxis through their experience of being on a similar but separate social networking environment, Facebook. This assignment allowed them to understand, through doing, the limitations of the form and the nature of the online conditions for the production of selves as we examined text produced by those we were studying.

The students' attempts to understand the offline conditions of existence had to be limited to observation and interviews over a two-month period. Textual analyses about the particular online environment being studied were supplemented with oral histories and interviews offline to produce a multi-dimensional understanding of how the offline and online interact in producing online raced and classed subjects. In placing our bodies within and in relation to cyber "space" and by "putting stuff"[2] in cyberspace, we produce interactional performative interfaces. As we produce selves at the interface, we become the interface with which others interact.

Becoming the interface might suggest to some a "leaving behind" of the body. However, since becoming the interface happens via a recoding of the self through an interplay of online and offline practices of meaning-making, we can never really leave the body behind. Practices that form an integral part of who we are online come from embodied, material everyday practices that are shaped by and in turn shape how we move through the world as raced, gendered, classed beings. Thus, at the online/offline intersection, I produce myself through acts of knowledge, memory, and everyday habit—reaching for conversations and sites that recognize my presence. Physicality of the body is expressed through everyday material practices, even when those practices involve the online production of self. The practice of *engaging* such a technological environment produces the subject/agent. Meaning, therefore, is made through doing—doing in this case is coding, programming, typing oneself into existence, and building objects.

Jennifer Daryl Slack (1989, p. 339, italics mine) writes as follows:

> Technology is not simply an object connected in various ways to the institutional and organizational structures from within which it emerges to be reconnected in a new context, but . . . it is *always an articulated*

moment of interconnections among the range of social practices, discursive
statements, ideological positions, social forces, and social groups within which
the object moves.

How are these articulated moments of interconnections manifested
in relation to the internet? Could it be that the vocabulary and binaries
generated (such as online and offline, virtual and real, and so on) actually shape social practices and discursive statements through specific
ideological positions and power dynamics? Such scholars as Marvin
(1988), Slack (1989), and Sterne (2000) have pointed out how social ideological struggles are negotiated in relation to technologies and how
various practices produce hierarchies around the use, consumption,
production, design, reproduction, and circulation of such technologies.
How does this negotiation affect our view of qualitative inquiry into
internet-mediated environments? Is internet mediation simply situated
at the intersection of online and offline (where the binary online/
offline remains uninterrogated)? If we are to take ideological struggles
and material-discursive hierarchies into consideration as we approach
the study of the internet through critical lenses, we would have to draw
on particular kinds of ethnographic encounters in which the researcher
lives both online and offline and in relation to the digital technologies
that allow her to produce her cyborg selves. Thus, the production of
cyberselves through the experience of doing—where the practices of
being simultaneously online and offline, here and there in her everyday negotiations of society and culture—becomes integral to the study
of these environments. Ethnography thus conducted is situated,
immersive, and critical—not distant and "objective."

Material practices within and in relation to digitally mediated environments provide arenas "for negotiating issues crucial to the conduct
of social life; among them, who is inside and outside, who may speak,
who may not, and who has authority and may be believed" (Marvin,
1988, p. 4). Through a focus on examining practices of production of
selves in and around digital technologies and digitally mediated spaces
methodologically, we begin to observe more than just how the technology works, thus getting beyond the fascination with its "newness."
Therefore, on the one hand, as Marvin (1988, pp. 4–5) states,

The focus of communication is shifted from the instrument to the
drama in which existing groups perpetually negotiate power, authority,
representation, and knowledge with whatever resources are available.
New media intrude on these negotiations by providing new platforms on
which old groups are projected onto new technologies that alter, or

seem to alter, critical social distances. New media may change the perceived effectiveness of one group's surveillance of another, the permissible familiarity of exchange, the frequency and intensity of contact, and the efficiency of customary tests for truth and deception. . . . New practices do not so much flow directly from technologies that inspire them as they are improvised out of old practices that no longer work in new settings.

On the other hand, as Jenny Sundén (2003) notes, a distance—both spatial/physical and between the mind/body—is created between the typist/programmer and subject typed into existence in encounters with digital interfaces such as computers. Writing about the production of selves within online text-based environments known as MOOs, Sundén (2003, p. 4) writes,

This distance is on one level introduced in text-based online worlds through the act of typing, and further reinforced by the mediating computer technology itself. By actively having to type oneself into being, a certain gap in this construction is at the same time created. The mediation between different realms, the very creation of texts by the means of computers, makes the interspace that always exists between myself and the understanding of this self particularly clear. Following the idea of a subject that can never have a direct and unmediated access to herself, that the I writing and the I written about can never be seen as one, cyber subjects are always at least double.

The action of *producing oneself* in such an environment is enacted through typing. However, the particular participant's agency is produced both through the act of typing and the programming that results, as well as through her or his embodied negotiations of sociocultural literacies, memories, histories, patterns, and negotiations in relation to the "old groups" that Marvin (1988) mentions.

So how do we go about researching in this framework? What literally are the steps I would suggest that someone follow to understand the acts of producing one's self in relation to computer-mediated environments? Now that I have laid out a case for examining practices at the online/offline intersection and urged that we examine the practices people use to produce selves in multiple online/offline intersections, what kind of investigation and exploration of contexts is needed to study or understand that intersection?

Actually, the basic approach is very simple and straightforward: You observe and describe in great detail. It is important that you note every detail—these will be your basic notes. For instance, suppose you wanted to understand the social networking practices of Mexican American teens in the northwestern part of the state of Ohio. You get in touch with a group that meets that description. You find out how they engage in the practice of social networking using computers and the internet in a general way, by talking to them and to others around them (maybe parents, community leaders, siblings, and so on) while also observing the environment in which they use computers. You observe how the technical infrastructure is made accessible to them and the physical, material conditions under which they access the internet. What kinds of computers and software are they using? Are they using computers in a public space such as a community center? What artifacts surround their environment as they use the computer? What conversations do they seem to engage in as they sit around near the computers? You make detailed notes and take pictures and videos if you have permission and human subject review board approval to do so. Sometimes you will be able to take pictures and videos under the condition that you do not use such material for public presentation. That is fine because having the pictures and/or video on hand for viewing later is useful to your analysis anyway.

The next step is to ask members of the group to make notes regarding their experience and their perceptions about the environment and to keep a journal for you if they are agreeable; then you interview a few members in depth. Tape record interviews when possible, but also have a research partner take detailed notes and observations while you interview the group member. Later, certain parts of your own research notes will become a focus for more detailed analysis, since they offer particular insights into why someone is at this particular online/offline intersection and how he or she negotiates the particular socio-technical environment. You will begin to build theory from the basic narratives you have recorded by connecting them to existing frameworks in the discipline and elsewhere, thereby articulating a framework for understanding the particular practices you observed.

As you are following the steps laid out above, also explore the online context in which these interviewees are social networking. Thus if they are using MySpace.com, you need to explore that network both as an outside viewer just reading the web sites and as a user who begins to use the network. You begin to live in the networks that your interviewees are living in—with their permission of course. You will then be able to describe the social networking environment and experience as you see it and in detail.

Alongside all the above activity, you will need to contextualize the users that you are studying. To do this, you will need to research the history of migration of Mexican Americans to northwest Ohio and also talk to various members of the community about their individual stories of travel and life in the community. These oral histories and literature reviews will contribute further to your understanding and analysis of the online/offline intersection. In contextualizing, it is also necessary to view media representations of the community within which you are examining the online/offline intersection in order to contextualize how the online presences may be read by a mainstream audience.

From what I have just laid out, one can see that to study "qualitatively" the online/offline intersections through a cyberethnographic focus on "epistemologies of doing," the researcher has to conduct a multi-layered investigation of self and others while also collecting statistical and other kinds of data as are relevant to the particular context being examined (Gajjala, Rybas, & Altman, 2007).

❖ RECOMMENDED READING

Regarding epistemology and knowledge, I recommend V. Dalmiya and L. Alcoff's chapter, "Are Old Wives' Tales Justified?" in the edited collection *Feminist Epistemologies* (1993). This chapter explains the philosophical basis for the concept of "epistemologies of doing."

To help illustrate how technologies are a part of our everyday lives, I recommend C. Marvin's *When Old Technologies Were New* (1988) and S. R. Munt's *Technospaces: Inside the New Media* (2001). I also recommend the three articles by Slack listed in the references (1981; Slack & Allor, 1983; Slack & Wise, 2005). These readings contribute to the basis for my refusal of the mutually exclusive binaries of "online" vs. "offline" and "virtual" vs. "real."

❖ NOTES

1. You can do a search on Google for each of these MOOs and see if they are still around and try them out.

2. One of my undergraduate students, during a discussion of the notion of space, said space is "somewhere we put stuff." Thought of in this manner, various newer cyberenvironments such as Facebook and MySpace and older ones such as MOOs and MUDs are where people "put stuff"—collections that contribute to the performativity of online identities within context of race, class, geography, ethnicity, religion, and gender.

QUESTION THREE

How Do Various Notions of Privacy Influence Decisions in Qualitative Internet Research?

Malin Sveningsson Elm

❖   ❖   ❖

During the last two decades, a new area of research has emerged— one that focuses on social and cultural aspects of the environments we find on the internet. These environments have come to pose a number of questions and challenges for social researchers; one area that has been much discussed is the issue of privacy, and the need to safeguard individuals' right to privacy online.

Privacy is a notion that concerns, among other things, the individual's integrity and right to self-determination. The basic idea is that each and all individuals should have the right to decide for themselves what and how much others get to know about them. It is only the information that they choose to reveal that should be known to others. Examining this idea in the context of culture, it follows that the meaning of privacy may change with different cultural contexts. Specifically, the type of information people want to keep for themselves differs from culture to culture. In some countries, citizens may be extremely concerned about keeping information about personal data for themselves. One country that fits into this category is the United States. There, the issue of privacy has been very much discussed, but discussion has

---

Responding essays by Elizabeth Buchanan (pp. 88–92) and Susannah Stern (pp. 94–98).

mainly focused on information about people's personal lives, and, not surprisingly, information that may lead to the loss of property. In other countries, citizens may not care so much about what information others get about their family or property, but it may instead be crucial to safeguard information about their political activities or sexual orientations and relationships. In this category, we find dictatorships in which political opposition is forbidden or countries that forbid sexual practices other than heterosexuality—and in some countries, even more narrowly, within marriage. Still, there may be other countries in which citizens do not experience a need to keep many secrets at all, or in which other information and activities are seen as more important to hide than the ones named above. Of course, we must also allow that, for each cultural context, there is a great variation in perceptions among citizens.

The issue of privacy is central not only for ordinary people but also for researchers. In the research arena, privacy can be seen as safeguarding the research subjects' right to integrity and self-determination—to decide for themselves what kind of information to share with the researcher and under what conditions. In this way, privacy is closely related to one of the most basic requirements of research ethics; namely, what is commonly referred to as informed consent—the principle that states that all research subjects should give their knowledgeable consent to being studied. It is this aspect of privacy that this chapter discusses. Taking as its point of departure existing ethical guidelines, this chapter looks at the principle of informed consent and under which conditions it needs to be sought. As is discussed later, research may sometimes be done without informed consent if the environment that is studied is public. The question posed in this article is thus, How can we as researchers make sense of the variables "private" and "public" to better judge the appropriateness and ethical soundness of our studies?

First, we look at some of the ethical guidelines that exist today— both for offline and online settings—to see what they have to say about informed consent. Then follows a discussion of the concepts of public and private and what we really mean when we use those terms. Third, we look at various kinds of research contexts, both on- and offline, to examine what factors can and perhaps should frame these contexts as public and/or private. We then look at what degree of privacy can be expected in various kinds of places (i.e., whether or not informed consent should be required). Most research that has been done to date has stopped at this point. It has often been seen as enough that the research subjects give their consent for the research to be seen as ethically sound. However, in addition to examining place, we should also take content into account, both on- and offline, because if the material is of a sensitive nature, other considerations become relevant and necessary. The last part of the chapter thus discusses to what degree different kinds of content should be seen as private or public and, consequently, what kind of content can be studied without informed consent.

❖ ETHICAL GUIDELINES

Different countries have different policies guiding research ethics; the kinds of organizations that ensure compliance with guidelines also differ. Despite differences in organization, however, these guidelines generally concern the same matters. Regardless of country, obtaining informed consent is a central aspect of most existing guidelines for research ethics. Along with hiding the true identity of research subjects, getting informed consent is often seen as a guarantee of sorts that the research is really ethically sound; that is, if research subjects have given their consent, researchers often feel no need to think more about ethical aspects of their research. However, things may not always be this straightforward. Sometimes, research may be unethical even though performed with informed consent, and as this chapter claims, some- times research may not be unethical even though performed without informed consent. Ethical guidelines were created to cover a wide range of situations, but particularly in inductive social research the principles do not always match what we encounter when we go out into the field. In those cases, we may instead have to look beyond the guidelines to see what lies behind them, and to examine what kind of values we are seek- ing to protect by adhering to them. Sometimes, these values may be pro- tected without necessarily adhering to all predefined rules.

In the ethical guidelines of the Swedish Research Council, the prin- ciple of informed consent is covered by two requirements: (1) the infor- mational requirement, stating that the researcher shall, at least in sensitive situations, inform those affected about his or her activity, and (2) the requirement of consent, stating that the participants should have the right to decide whether, for how long, and under what condi- tions they will take part (HSFR, 1990/1999). Other countries, such as Norway, have agreed on similar ethical guidelines (NESH, 1999).

Most of these ethical principles were worked out before the advent of the internet. However, the internet has not only changed our ways of looking at social life but has also made us reconsider questions of how social life is to be studied when it takes place online. Although some principles and methods of qualitative research as we have traditionally conceptualized them transfer to these new environments, others require rethinking and revising. This is especially obvious in research ethics.

When studying online environments, it may often be difficult to obtain informed consent. As I found in previous research (Sveningsson, 2001, 2003), in many internet environments, far too many participants are online simultaneously to allow researchers to inform them individually. Take chat rooms, for example. New participants can log on and off rapidly, affording impossibly small windows of opportunity for informing and gaining consent for research. If researchers were to post public messages asking for consent every time a new individual logs on, the rest of the users would probably classify the researchers as spammers, get annoyed, and treat them the way spammers are generally treated—by filtering them out or harassing them to make them leave (Sveningsson, 2001). As a last resort, the users themselves might leave the chat room. In all these scenarios, the research situation would be seriously compromised or even destroyed, as this is not what natural chat room discourse would look like. Further, if researchers take the time to write and send private messages to all new participants, most likely there will be very little time left for them to actually observe the online interaction.

In other types of internet environments, it may be impossible for researchers to even contact the users whose contributions they are analyzing. This is the case in, for example, online guest books or discussion groups, where people may have written a greeting or a message without signing it or by signing it with a pseudonym.

The Association of Internet Researchers (AoIR) was founded at the end of the 1990s to be an international "resource and support network promoting critical and scholarly internet research independent from traditional disciplines and existing across academic borders" (http://www.aoir.org). In 2000, AoIR launched a working group, whose aim was to discuss and work out ethical guidelines for internet research.[1] The publishing of these guidelines (Ess & Jones, 2003; http://www.aoir.org/reports/ethics.pdf) was one important step toward guiding internet researchers in their ethical decisions (also see earlier publications, such as Allen, 1996; Frankel & Siang, 1999; and King, 1996). However, there are still (and will probably always be) unanswered questions. This is partly due to the rapid development of the internet. The technology and the online environments have shifted so quickly that what is written one day is sometimes outdated and obsolete the next. But the rapid development is not the only reason for the uncertainty. Even if the internet had not changed at all, it would still be extremely difficult to foresee all possible situations a researcher might encounter online. This is due to the multi-faceted character of the internet, which makes it virtually impossible to create guidelines that will adequately cover all aspects of internet research. When asking ourselves whether our research is ethically sound, as in so many other cases in social science research, the answer will often inevitably have to be, "Well, it depends."

Because qualitative internet researchers come from different backgrounds, disciplines, and cultures, their perspectives on research ethics naturally vary. The AoIR ethics working group had some animated discussions on this subject. Some of the researchers were extremely careful to propose and follow ethical guidelines similar to the current or traditional ones (see, for example, Bruckman, 1997). Others (see, for example, Danet, 2001b; Sveningsson, 2001) had a more utilitarian approach and argued that existing guidelines had to be measured against the purpose of research.

The diversity of disciplines also meant that the group's researchers sometimes had different ontological and epistemological assumptions about what kind of knowledge was to be sought and how this knowledge could be attained (i.e., with what research methods). For some research questions, it might be reasoned, an experimental research design would do the job and yield the information sought; this strategy would solve all problems with getting informed consent and conducting research that is ethically sound. The problem is, however, that some other disciplines and research fields would not consider experimental situations to be satisfactory in providing the sought-for knowledge. This is the case, for example, for ethnologists, ethnographers, or anthropologists conducting naturalistic inquiry. In these approaches, researchers study people's actions and interactions in their natural online contexts to explore meanings, describe culture, and so forth. Does the problem of getting informed consent then mean that naturalistic researchers would have to abstain from doing such research, despite the knowledge it would give us? This was the vital point in many discussions of the ethics working group, and no absolute consensus was ever reached.

Finally, the committee did agree on a recommendation that collecting research data without informed consent could sometimes be acceptable if (a) the environment was public and (b) the material was not sensitive (see also the ethics working group's final report in Ess & Jones [2003] or at http://www.aoir.org/reports/ethics.pdf). However, the variables of public/private and sensitive/not sensitive are not as unambiguous as they may seem at first glance. They both require problematizing and further discussion, which is the focus of the rest of this chapter.

❖ DEFINING PUBLIC AND PRIVATE

When discussing issues of privacy and publicity, our first task is to define what we mean by the concepts. What is to be considered private and what is to be considered public? According to Thompson (1994), in Western societies since the medieval period we can distinguish two senses of the public/private dichotomy. The first one has to do with the relation between the domain of institutionalized political power and the domains of economic activity and personal relations that fell outside of direct political control. Thus, writes Thompson (1994, p. 38), "From the mid-sixteenth century on, 'public' came increasingly to mean activity or authority that was related to or derived from the state, while 'private' referred to those activities or spheres of life that were excluded or separated from it."

It is the second sense of the public-private dichotomy, as defined by Thompson, that has relevance in this discussion. According to this sense, "public" means "open" or "available" to the public:

> What is visible or observable, what is performed in front of spectators, what is open for all or many to see or hear or hear about. What is private, then, by contrast, is what is hidden from view, what is said or done in privacy or secrecy or among a restricted circle of people. (Thompson, 1994, p. 38)

How does this conception apply to online environments? What is to be considered open and what is to be considered hidden, when, for whom, and under what circumstances? Let us start with a look at the places where online interactions take place.

Public and Private as a Continuum, Not a Dichotomy

The first question we have to ask is which online environments are private and which should be considered public. A first step in answering this question is to ask additional questions that enable a deeper understanding of the contextual environment in which one is researching. Possible questions include the following: How exclusive is the environment? Is it possible for anyone to access the content, or is any form of membership required? If so, is membership available for anyone, or are there any formal requirements or restrictions as to who and how many are allowed to become members? Is it not even possible to become a member, and is the content restricted to those with an invitation and/or a personal relationship with the creator of the content? These questions can give some information as to how public (i.e., how open) the environment is, thus providing us with guidelines for how to act.

If we start to compare environments, we will probably discover that we are not faced with a dichotomy between public and private, but rather with a continuum in which several different positions are possible between the variables, private and public. A first conclusion is then that there are different *degrees* of private and public. A more nuanced way of categorizing environments might therefore be as public, semi-public, semi-private, and private environments. Here, we can use the same kind of variables as was suggested by Patton (1990) when describing the degree of openness in participant observations. There, an open observer is known by everyone, a partly open observer is known by some but not everyone, and a hidden observer is not known by anyone at all. Applied to specific internet environments, we then get the following structure:

1. A public environment is one that is open and available for everyone, that anyone with an internet connection can access, and that does not require any form of membership or registration. Public online environments can for example be represented by open chat rooms or web pages.

2. A semi-public environment is one that is available for most people. It is in principle accessible to anyone, but it first requires membership and registration. In this category we find most web communities or social network sites such as for example www.lunarstorm.se or www.myspace.com.

3. A semi-private environment is one that is available only to some people. It requires membership and registration, and it is even further restricted by formal requirements preceding membership, such as belonging to the organization that created the online environment. Examples in this category are companies' and organizations' intranets.

4. Finally, a private online environment is one that is hidden or unavailable to most people and where access is restricted to the creator of the content and his or her invited guests. In this category we find for example private rooms within chat rooms, online photo albums, or the areas within web communities where the sender specifies who is allowed to access the content; for example, only those who are classified as "close friends."

There are also some web sites that allow users to adjust the settings of their accessibility. For example, in livejournal or MySpace, a person can make certain information available to everyone or can adjust the settings so that only "friends" can access it. In this way, some sites are in some sense individual-controlled, and not just site-controlled.

Looking at public/private as a continuum may help clarify what kind of place we are dealing with, but it also makes ethical decisions and delimitations even more difficult. It illustrates a complication in implementing the recommendation of the ethics working group that researchers should be guided by examining whether an environment is either public or private. This decision may be more difficult than it would seem at first sight, because online environments may not fit so neatly into just one of the polarities. In practice or by design, the online environment in question may not be only public or private but something in between.

Researchers may instead focus on a slightly different question about their ethical path: Is the environment *public enough* for us to study it without getting informed consent? Of the four different positions listed above, the first one is clearly public enough to study without informed consent. Hence, we can study individuals' and organizations' web sites, online newspapers, and web shops without informing the users (although it may of course still be considered good manners to do so).[2] Studying environments in the fourth, entirely private position without informed consent is clearly unsuitable, or even illegal, and is also further complicated by the fact that we would probably not even get access to the site in question. If we want to study people's private e-mails, online photo albums, and private chat rooms, informed consent is an absolute necessity.

However, the second and third positions listed above are more complicated, and we may encounter problems in deciding whether semi-public and semi-private environments are public enough for us to study. This is partly due to their character of being on the one hand open and accessible for anyone or to some, but on the other hand first requiring membership and/or registration. But it is also partly due to the complex structure of many of these internet environments, which are often multi-faceted and where several different communication modes and arenas aimed at interaction coexist at the same site.

More than a decade ago, Allen (1996) noted that our conceptions of public and private can be blurred because both types of spaces can exist within the same internet arena. This is the case in web communities, in which users can choose among several different arenas in which to interact. There may, for example, be bulletin boards, discussion groups, and chat rooms that are closer to the public end of the continuum, and personal profiles, guest books and diaries, which may be thought of as closer to the private end of the continuum. Other internet environments may be constructed in similar ways. This mixture of different arenas under the same "umbrella" makes it difficult, as well as possibly unwise, to decide whether the environment in its entirety is public, semi-public, semi-private, or private.

Public and Private as a Perception, Not a Fact

The multi-faceted character of internet environments is of course a problem for the researcher, but may also be a problem to the users. In some cases, the fuzzy boundaries between private and public parts of online environments may make it difficult for users to grasp the gradual transition between private and public spaces. According to this view, people may perhaps not be aware of the fact that their actions and interactions may be observed by other people, even perfect strangers. Or even if they are aware of the publicness of the arena, they may forget about it when involved in interactions. It can sometimes be that even if a certain internet medium admittedly *is* public, it doesn't *feel* public to its users. For many users, the anonymity in terms of lack of social and biological cues that computer-mediated communication (CMC) provides may encourage a less restricted, more intimate communication than would be the case in offline contexts (Lövheim, 1999). As we found in previous research (Sveningsson, Lövheim, & Bergquist, 2003), writing an e-mail or a message to a newsgroup or chat room *feels* like a more private act than sending the same message to other kinds of public forums, and it is easy to forget that the message may sometimes be stored and be retrievable for a long time afterward. Furthermore, what is not easily available now may become easily available in the future, as happened when Google bought the Usenet archives and made them searchable and easily accessible years after posts were submitted.

Another important issue to bring up is that, even if users are aware of being observed by others, they do not consider the possibility that their actions and interactions may be documented and analyzed in detail at a later occasion by a researcher. If the content was created for one certain audience and context, the transmission of this content to other contexts may upset the creator (Walker, 2002). This raises two crucial questions, which are discussed later in the chapter; namely, for whom is the content created, and to which audience is the content intended or directed?

The above examples demonstrate clearly that social researchers are forced to grapple with at least two different views of privacy: One view is based on how easy it is to access the site, and the other view is based on how public or private do users *understand* their contributions to be. Early ethical discussions of qualitative internet research mostly implicitly dealt with the first of these views: If the medium is accessible to the public, we might assume that it is also perceived as a public place (Sudweeks & Rafaeli, 1995). This assumption is highly problematic, however, and we thus see a shift toward acknowledging the importance of and further exploring the second view (e.g., Sveningsson et al., 2003).

❖ USING OFFLINE GUIDELINES FOR ONLINE RESEARCH

For researchers, one way to decide whether obtaining informed consent is required is to look at the characteristics of the parts of the environment we wish to study. In some cases, we may conclude that only some parts of a specific web site are public enough to study, whereas we have to exclude others. When we are struggling to decide whether informed consent is necessary, we can get guidance by comparing online environments with their offline equivalents and looking at what existing ethical guidelines have to say about studying those latter settings. In some occasions, these ethical guidelines can be transferred to their corresponding online environments.

Starting with the first public position above, the offline equivalent comprises streets, squares, and shopping malls in city environments. Here, at least Swedish ethical guidelines state that one is allowed to collect data without informed consent, under the condition that no individuals are identifiable (HSFR, 1990/1999). The Norwegian equivalent to the Swedish Research Council expresses similar views: it is allowable to collect data in public places without informed consent, but only without making any audiovisual recordings of the material; for example, videotaping people's interactions on a street (NESH, 1999). The recommendations of the AoIR ethics working group coincide with those of existing guidelines. Again, it is important to note that ethical perspectives and guidelines vary widely by country.

The offline equivalent of the second type of environment above, the semi-public environment, might include libraries, schools, and hospitals. Here, it is more difficult to draw lines between what is acceptable and not acceptable to study, because different parts of the environments often have different characteristics. To do participant observations in a school cafeteria, for example, no informed consent is required. However, if one is to study classroom interaction, permission is required at least from the administrators and teachers of the school. The same goes for studies performed in health care institutions, wherein most activities are considered, if not private, at least strongly sensitive. To conduct social observation research in health care institutions in Sweden, one has to apply for permission from a specific ethical committee. However, the suitability of doing research also depends on what is the object of the study and, more important, who is under study. During the 1960s and 1970s, quite a few studies were done where the researchers gained entrance to mental hospitals and other institutions in order to study aspects of them (see, for example, Goffman, 1961). These studies were seldom if ever preceded by any applications for permission either from administrators, staff, or inmates. Instead the researchers gained entrance under false pretences and did participant observations that managed to capture the essence of the everyday life of these institutions. Had they informed the staff and patients about their research, it is not likely that the studies would have yielded the same results. In this and similar cases, the procedure can be defended by the object of disclosing bad conditions in society and emancipating people whose agency was otherwise restricted. Since then, however, research guidelines have changed, and the legal limitations of Institutional Review Boards (in the United States) and their equivalents elsewhere can hamper this sort of research.

The third position above, semi-private environments, has offline equivalents in the form of clubs and companies. As with the semi-public environments, some elements may be accessible and allow for observations without informed consent, whereas others may require it. Within many semi-public and semi-private environments, both on- and offline, there are spheres that count as, if not private, at least as something that resembles private areas and that therefore require more consideration from researchers and observers. One example of this kind of research was conducted by Svensson (2002), who studied gay communities and gay men's presentations of self. Svensson was known as a researcher to some of the people within these communities (i.e., her informants, whom she interviewed), but not to all them (i.e., all the other visitors at clubs and parties). We can thus conclude that the parts of the study that concerned informants' private spheres required informed consent, whereas the spheres that were more general and concerned publicly observed gatherings did not. As we can see, research in semi-private environments often falls into Patton's (1990) middle position, whereby observers are partly open. This multi-faceted and complex character is by no means restricted to online environments, but is also found in various offline environments.

Finally, the offline equivalents for the fourth position of private environments might be represented by the private home. It may be unnecessary to state that studying any such private environment requires informed consent.

Looking at geographically/physically oriented rules and regulations and applying them to internet research, we thus see that data collection without informed consent can be acceptable in certain environments that can be considered public. However, as has already been noted, researchers of internet environments must make additional considerations for the perceptions of the people who are under study—that is, whether they feel the arena is public or private. We may also have to consider the nature of the content, which is discussed more thoroughly in the next section.

❖ CONSIDERING BOTH CONTENT AND CONTEXT

Having stated what kind of places may be public enough to study, the next step is to look at the content. We have to consider not only whether the places we wish to study are public or private but also if the content of the communication is public or private. This consideration begins with a seemingly simple question: What kind of content can be considered public enough to be studied without informed consent?

One way to go about answering this question is to take our point of departure from Thompson's (1994) first definition of the concepts public/private, mentioned earlier. According to this definition, "public" is a matter of activity or authority that is related to or derived from the state, whereas "private" refers to those activities or spheres of life that are excluded or separated from it. Public content would then be content that concerns societal matters, whereas private content concerns individuals' private lives as separated from societal matters. Using this definition may keep us from making unethical decisions, but it also excludes all studies of people's online interactions unless they concern societal matters, such as for example discussions on politics and economics at a strictly general level. It would become impossible to study people's everyday lives and everyday interactions as expressed online.

A second way of examining this issue is to conceptualize it along a continuum of degrees of public/private. At a first level, we have what is public in Thompson's sense: content that concerns societal matters.[3] We then proceed across levels of increasingly private matters, moving from a macro to a micro level that concerns fewer and fewer people and moving into what we typically call private spheres.

Still a third option for considering this question is to bring in the AoIR ethics working group's concepts of sensitive/not sensitive. One would assume that people in general would not speak about sensitive matters of their lives in public, whereas they would share with the whole world those matters that they consider not sensitive (to the extent the world is interested in knowing about these matters, of course). However, using the concepts sensitive/not sensitive may be problematic too, because people do not necessarily think of sensitive matters as more private than nonsensitive ones. During the last decade, we have come to see what was once private made increasingly public. What started as talk show confessions, reality TV, and docudramas, in which ordinary people's private lives became the subject of TV entertainment, broadcast in prime-time national TV shows, developed into a formidable universe of confessions and exposures of private (in the sense of sensitive) matters in public. In personal web pages, personal profiles at web communities and social network web sites, and blogs, we see a good deal of personal information being exposed in public. People write and publish their online diaries, accessible for anyone with internet access; they provide personal information, including full name and real-life address; and they even share pornographic pictures of themselves with people they meet online (Daneback, in press). In his book, *Liquid Modernity*, sociologist Zygmunt Bauman (2000) suggests that, while theorists such as Jürgen Habermas feared the public would colonize the private sphere, what we see in today's society is in effect an inverse process where it is rather the private that is colonizing the public sphere:

> The "public" is colonized by the "private"; "public interest" is reduced to curiosity about the private lives of public figures, and the art of public life is narrowed to the public display of private affairs and public confessions of private sentiments (the more intimate the better). "Public issues" which resist such reduction become all but incomprehensible. (Bauman, 2000, p. 37)

The colonization of the public, says Bauman, is due to a process by which individuals to an increasing extent are made responsible for their lives—in short, individuals have no one else but themselves to count on to make decisions and choices to make their lives more successful and satisfactory. And should anything in their lives turn out to fail, they have no one else but themselves to blame. This responsibility concerns all aspects of life, from matters of career and wealth to fitness and health. Media and other public surfaces are filled with individuals speaking as private persons about their private matters. These individuals, says Bauman, offer themselves as examples, if not as counselors who can advise others. By watching or reading these examples, the audience can both get some guidance on how to deal (or sometimes not to deal) with their own life situations and get a sense of not being alone with their private problems after all.

This exposure of private matters in public space has made people think differently about the way public space is to be used. Bauman (2000, p. 40) puts it this way:

> For the individual, public space is not much more than a giant screen on which private worries are projected without ceasing to be private or acquiring new collective qualities in the course of magnification: public space is where public confession of private secrets and intimacies is made.

Therefore, what may seem private/sensitive to an observer is not necessarily apprehended so by the individual who exposed the content. Many scholars have found this to be the case. For example, in my study of a Swedish web community (Sveningsson, 2005), the users' practices suggest that they do not consider their personal pages, including personal profile, diary, and photo album, as specifically private. For example, they often put out "ads" in the more publicly visited spots of the web community, where they urge people to come visit their personal pages, to watch and comment on their photos and diaries, and to sign their guest books. Not only do the users seem to be aware of the risk of having their material observed by others but also the attention from others is often what they seek. There are strong indications that users tend to see the web community as an opportunity for public exposure, something that is further supported by social caseworkers who have been doing fieldwork among young people at the web community in question (Englund, personal communication). According to these social caseworkers, some users seem to see online environments as their chance of getting their 15 minutes of fame, and furthermore, these users are often influenced by the content of reality TV and docu-soaps, where extremely intimate matters are displayed frequently and prominently. Yet, this discussion could also very well be turned the other way around: What is seen as public and not sensitive by the researcher may in some cases be seen as private and sensitive by the people who use the online environment.

In this virtual jumble of potentially private and sensitive material, what *is* then acceptable to collect? Who is to decide whether a specific communicative act is to be seen as public/not sensitive or private/sensitive? This question is reminiscent of literary theorists' discussion of where the meaning of a text is to be found. Is it in the text itself? Or does it lie with the text's creator? Or, is the meaning, as more postmodernist thinkers claim, to be found within the eyes of the beholder; that is, is meaning created first when interpreted by a recipient?

How we reason in these questions may also have some influence on what decisions we think of as ethical. But in the end, unless we ask, we cannot know how the creator of online content apprehends it; we can only judge whether she or he *seems* to be seeing it as public. For those who believe the meaning resides in the text per se, the preferential right of interpretation will always be with the observer/interpreter. This may be suitable for those who believe that meaning resides within the recipient as well, unless they go ask members of an audience about how *they* classify the content (and even there, different audience members may hold differing opinions).[4]

Another consideration is that some content may not have been intended to be public in the first place, but was published online anyway, either by the user him- or herself by mistake or by someone else as a prank or as part of bullying or harassment. This was the case in a previous study of a chat room, in which content was published by mistake (Sveningsson, 2001). In that study I made observations of statements intended to be "whispered" (i.e., sent as private messages to a chosen recipient) that were transmitted by mistake to the whole public chat room. This inadvertent transmission often amused the other users, and some friendly teasing and mocking were likely to follow, which undoubtedly were part of the local color of the place (see also Cherny, 1999). Nevertheless, this kind of material was excluded from the analyses because it was seen as (too) private.

There are other, similar examples, such as photos or videos published as pranks or harassment, a practice made simple with the built-in cameras on many mobile telephones. At the same time, this and similar practices seem to have increased people's media literacy and general awareness of being observed. In general, informants say that nowadays young people tend not to do anything at all in public that could be experienced as embarrassing, in case someone is carrying a mobile phone with a camera (and in contemporary Sweden, virtually everybody under the age of 30 is doing so).

We thus see how the concept of social control takes one step further as the technology advances. Maybe we, as Bauman says, are no longer afraid of Big Brother, but we instead have come to fear an infinite number of little brothers, who spy on us and make their findings known to others, such as parents and teachers, but perhaps more annoyingly, to our friends and lovers and people we would like to impress. During the last few years, we have seen an increasing number of signs in, for example, the dressing rooms of public swimming pools prohibiting the use of cameras, something that was not even thought of before the advent of mobile phones with built-in cameras. Practices surrounding mobile phones with built-in cameras have also had consequences for people engaging in affairs. In one example, a cheating young woman traveling abroad had no idea she was being observed and photographed by friends of her boyfriend, who then sent him the pictures they had taken with their mobile phones. The boyfriend received instantaneous proof of the infidelity, whereupon he called his girlfriend on *her* mobile phone, asking her what the heck she thought she was doing.

Media-literate people in contemporary Sweden are well aware that what they do may be instantaneously known by others, not only with a simple mouse click, but even more easily, with the send button of a mobile phone. Of course, this affects our conceptions of private and public. Interestingly, we may have just resigned ourselves to think of everything and anything as potentially public. We may have become so accustomed to being exposed and seeing others exposing themselves that we may not even expect or care for any privacy online anymore.

To return to the question at hand, in the end, it is important to realize that our efforts to simplify the notions of privacy may be misguided. The discussion on public/not sensitive versus private/ sensitive content further complicates the matter. The conclusion has to be that matters of public and private content *are* extremely complicated. No content is ever either private or public, but potentially both, depending on who you are asking.

Further, in attempting to make sense of the notions of privacy, social researchers must consider the intended audience for an individual's online expression: Even those who are comfortable making all their contributions public may still resent their use as a topic of research. One first recommendation may therefore be for researchers to be reflexive about the object and process of research in an attempt to assess who is judging the publicness of the content in the specific study: Is it the researcher, the creator, or the audience? Second, who is the intended audience? The answers to these questions may very well affect our views of whether the research is ethically sound or not.

Another alternative could be to start to think differently about the whole issue, perhaps even deconstructing the entire notion of private/ public. Brin (1998) for example offers a different way of thinking about the notion; instead of privacy, he argues, the focus should be shifted to "accountability." Instead of struggling with problems of who is defining the publicness of certain content, we can instead look at our role as researchers to assess whether or not we are doing any harm by using a certain material.

This recommendation is neatly included by the Swedish Research Council in their basic principle, "the claim for individual protection." This claim summarizes their ethical guidelines as follows: People who participate in research must not be harmed, either physically or mentally, and they must not be humiliated or offended. Taking this claim to heart is a way, as suggested in the introduction of this chapter, to look beyond ethical guidelines to see what values we are seeking to protect. When we ensure that our research subjects are not harmed, humiliated, or offended, it may not always be necessary to follow single rules and regulations exactly.

❖ CONCLUSION

The issue discussed in this chapter is how to make sense of the variables, private and public, so we can better judge the appropriateness and ethical soundness of our studies. Our point of departure was the recommendations of the AoIR ethics working group. According to these guidelines, it can sometimes be acceptable to collect and use research data without getting informed consent, under the condition that the environment under study is public and that the content is not sensitive. However, as we can see, it is vital to problematize these concepts.

Our first conclusion is that the concepts of public/private cannot be seen as a dichotomy but must be conceived of as a continuum. In other words, there are several different degrees of privacy and publicity. The chapter therefore suggests the use of at least four different degrees: public, semi-public, semi-private, and private. The recommendations of the ethics working group could then be further specified that places to be studied without informed consent must be either public or semi-public.

A second conclusion concerns the fact that internet environments are multi-faceted and are often made up of several different types of communication modes that permit different degrees of privacy. Here, one recommendation is to examine the characteristics of the specific parts that we wish to study and look at what degree of privacy they permit before we decide whether it is suitable or not to collect data.

To determine the degree of publicness or privateness requires more difficult questions of classification and delimitation, which are complicated by the fact that many recent media genres focus on exposing people's everyday private lives in public. We seem to have become accustomed to seeing more and more such content in public media, possibly resulting in an immunity toward it. It appears to be increasingly acceptable to expose oneself and one's private matters in public; at least it is done considerably more often now than ten years ago when confession TV and reality soaps were relatively new phenomena.

When it comes to issues of whether certain content is to be seen as public or private, I admit that even after more than ten years of research, I find I am unable to take a clear stance—I am just as irres-olute now as when I started to think about the issue, if not more. In many ways, my indecision as a social researcher makes sense; we all probably have different notions of whether specific content is public or private, and what is seen as sensitive and not sensitive is a clearly indi-vidual question. This conclusion does not make it easier to make deci-sions, but it makes it necessary to rethink our implicit views of who is to judge whether a certain content is to be seen as sensitive or not.

Other questions relate to what we have discussed in this chapter. We could for example discuss whether the appropriateness of collecting and using online data differs depending on who the sender is and in what capacity she or he is communicating. Such questions may very well have implications for decisions we make in our research. A publicly known person may not be able to expect the same consideration of privacy as an average ordinary person. But who is to be considered a public or private person and under what conditions (i.e., when)? And how does one pro-ceed if one does not know who the sender is? This question concerns var-ious issues of identity: the role a sender adopts when communicating, the category or authority that is called on in the context in which she or he speaks, and the problems we may encounter when we do not know the age or the mental condition of the people we study.

We could also further discuss questions of audience—both the intended and actual one. As mentioned earlier, some material published online was never intended to be exposed in public, with or without the depicted person's knowledge. There are also situations in which mater-ial intended for a specific context and audience is transferred to other contexts. This transfer may sometimes change the way the material is interpreted; as Månsson and Söderlind (2003) acknowledge, a photo that could in some contexts appear sexually explicit could in another context appear quite innocent, and the other way around.

No matter how much we think about and discuss issues of research ethics, we may never be fully able to draw any definite lines or make any definite recommendations. Research ethics, on- as well as offline, seems to remain a dynamic and unsteady field that defies all attempts at drawing up any definite and overall sets of rules and regulations.

❖   RECOMMENDED READING

To learn more about the cultural variations in ethical approaches to social research, examine the governing documents, country by country. In the United States, the Belmont Report is considered a foundational document, whereas in

Norway and Sweden, the foundational reports are the NESH report (1999) and the HSFR report (1999), respectively.

For multi-disciplinary and international discussions and methodological advice about ethics and privacy, the 2003 AoIR report, *Ethical Decision-Making and Internet Research. Recommendations from the AoIR Ethics Working Committee,* is highly recommended as a starting point.

For more specific case studies and method-specific approaches and guidelines, I recommend Elizabeth Buchanan's edited collection (2004), *Virtual Research Ethics,* as well as her edited special issue of the *Journal of Information Ethics* (Vol. 15, no. 2), which outline key perspectives. Additionally, all of the members of the AoIR working committee on ethics have produced empirical and/or theoretical works dealing with specific ethical issues and guidelines.

To review the Scandinavian approaches to ethics and internet research, see May Thorseth's 2003 collection, *Applied Ethics in Internet Research,* as well as further research by the contributors to this volume.

Finally, David Brin's *Transparent Society* (1998), written for the mainstream press, provides a keen analysis and reconsideration of the concept of privacy, which can be useful in thinking about how we conceptualize this term traditionally, how our users might conceptualize this term, and how we might develop more productive notions in the future.

❖ NOTES

1. The members of the ethical guidelines committee that worked out the ethical guidelines were as follows: Poline Bala–Malaysia; Amy Bruckman–USA; Sarina Chen–USA; Brenda Danet–Israel; Dag Elgesem–Norway; Andrew Fernberg–USA; Stine Gotved–Denmark; Christine M. Hine–UK; Soraj Hongladarom–Thailand; Jeremy Hunsinger–USA; Klaus Bruhn Jensen–Denmark; Storm King–USA; Chris Mann–UK; Helen Nissenbaum–USA; Kate O'Riordan–UK; Paula Roberts–Australia; Wendy Robinson–USA; Leslie Shade–Canada; Malin Sveningsson–Sweden; Leslie Tkach–Japan; and John Weckert–Australia. The committee was chaired by Charles Ess–USA.

2. However, as is discussed further later, even though the site is public, it may still be too sensitive to use without seeking consent.

3. Although in repressive regimes this could be private; for instance, certain kinds of political discussion in some nations can result in prison sentences.

4. At first thought, using an independent audience as a method of deciding the meaning of the content of web pages might sound odd, but it has in fact been done, for example by Karlsson (2002) when classifying various genres of web pages.

A Response to Malin Sveningsson

Elizabeth A. Buchanan

❖   ❖   ❖

I entered the dialogue among scholars around internet research ethics (IRE) rather circuitously. My doctoral work was multidisciplinary, housed in a school of education, with a specialization in information studies. My dissertation research examined engagement and discourse in online education and how individuals experienced web-based communication and dialogue. The population I studied was in an online Bioethics program, studying such issues as informed consent, privacy, justice, and other foundational research ethics principles. Thus, the content with which my participants were engaging revolved around research ethics, while simultaneously, I was grappling with the *application* of these principles in an online environment. As a qualitative researcher, my methods included virtual ethnography, online interviewing, and log content analysis. While watching others debate research ethics in theory, I had to articulate my research into the institutional review board (IRB) model of human subjects protections.[1] I did this first out of necessity—in 1998, no one on my university's IRB knew quite what to do with my protocol that asked to use virtual observations, chat transcripts, click box consent forms, and e-mail correspondence. But, more than necessity, I was fascinated with the complexities of internet research ethics and wanted to learn more.

In 1998, there was not much in the scholarly literature. I found disparate pieces, some from communication, some from nursing, and the Frankel and Siang report in 1999. All seemed to be concerned about such issues as online privacy, ensuring consent, and data security, but how researchers adhered to traditional human subjects protections while conducting research online was less clear. Internet research was emerging—that was certain—but cross-disciplinary, cross-cultural guidelines were a few years off. Meanwhile, I was invited to sit on the IRB at my university as an "online data expert." Over the years, I watched and read as more researchers used various forms of the internet as both a research locale and as a research tool. Virtual worlds were studied, and online survey generators became most desirable, perhaps out of convenience alone. Online research protocols, reviewed by IRBs, increased dramatically, and yet, we still had few standards or guidelines by which to judge these protocols. Most of the research ethics concerns revolved around informed consent and privacy.

In 2002, I proposed a book that would be a compilation of disciplinary, theoretical, and practical approaches to IRE. The response to the call for submissions was amazing: Vast disciplinary and cultural differences were represented, which illuminated the complexities that IRE embodied. By this time, also, the AoIR Ethics Group had issued its guidelines, and two other fascinating compilations had been published (Johns, Chen, & Hall, 2004; Thorseth, 2003). The IRE field was truly established, and, one of the core issues in IRE was delineated in the literature: privacy.

❖ PRIVACY AND METHODS

Privacy is defined, in the research realm, as "control over the extent, timing, and circumstances of sharing oneself (physically, behaviorally, or intellectually) with others" (*IRB Guidebook,* n.d.). One may argue that online, an individual has more control, as she chooses what to present, when, and how in an online environment. Conversely, individuals may have less control online, given that disparate pieces of data exist on individuals and when taken together, in ways originally unintended, may comprise a false or distorted, image of an individual—the data persona. Furthermore, researchers may harvest data from an online environment out of context or without consent at all, thereby violating the control over the extent, timing, and circumstances of sharing oneself.

I would argue that online qualitative research in particular raises the level of responsibility that both researchers and researched share where privacy is concerned. Is it "easier" to violate one's privacy online? Does it seem less harmful, as it is "just" an online persona? We would not think of walking into a classroom, for instance, without justification or consent, whereas online, we may walk into a newsgroup or online world without such consent, as our presence, our observation, and our research are less obvious. This calls for greater reflexivity in online research. Researchers must address their roles, must account for themselves, in the research process. And, with online research, we can be something we aren't. Cases of deception and fake identities abound online—both researchers and researched can create false realities. What does privacy mean then?

Sveningsson's discussion of privacy articulates the complexities of research in general and of internet research in particular. Clearly, a paradox exists around the concept of privacy. On the one hand, there is growing concern about the loss of privacy to government and to the corporate world, both of which want access to personal information for different reasons. In the United States, for instance, great controversy has surrounded the Bush administration's surveillance programs and the link with such telephony giants as AT&T, Verizon, and BellSouth. Conversely, social networking sites, such as MySpace and Facebook, have grown exponentially and comprise places where individuals willingly present great amounts of personal information. There are distinct generational differences in expectations of privacy, as well as cultural differences. And, of course there is a major difference between having our information harvested without our knowledge, indeed our consent, and controlling what we present and how and under what conditions and to whom.

James Moor (1997) calls these conditions a "control/restricted access theory." For Moor, the nature of computerized information leads to loss of individual control over our own information—it becomes "greased," sliding easily and quickly from one place or person or entity to another. To maintain some control, we must establish zones of privacy, "zones [that] will contain private situations with different kinds and levels of access for different individuals . . . this conception encourages informed consent as much as possible and fosters the development of practical, fine grained, and sensitive policies for protecting privacy" (p. 32).

Brin's (1998) notions of the "transparent society" and "reciprocal transparency" offer another way of conceptualizing privacy that focuses less on protecting privacy and more on building accountability. In his vision, information would not be private, but this would apply to *everyone*. Open channels of information would flow even wider, thereby equalizing privacy: "If some company wishes to collect data on consumers across America, let it do so only on condition that the top one hundred officers in the firm must post exactly the same information about themselves and all their family members on an accessible Web site" (p. 81). Of course, Brin tempers reciprocal transparency by noting,

"There will surely be times when the only viable solution to some problem is to forbid the collection, distribution, and/or storing of certain kinds of knowledge, at least for a limited time" (pp. 82–83). Researchers in particular must address such limited transparency, as information may exist online for purposes other than research per se.

Thus, for Sveningsson, the idea of Moor's zones is applicable in the research sphere. As she notes, informed consent as an aspect of privacy is a foundational principle, or requirement, of research ethics. Both informed consent and privacy must be considered as process, not static. Yet, traditional models of human subjects work tend to present these concepts as static entities that are often conceptualized in a binary framework; Sveningsson's presentation of the public-private demonstrates this inherent dualism extremely well. For instance, a researcher conceptualizes her research; she presents it to her Ethics Board or IRB. It is approved, after which the participants or subjects are informed about the research. They either consent or not. They either participate or not. There is little negotiation among the researchers, the board, or the participants. In theory, this is often a linear process that denies reflexivity, whereas in practice, research is messy, gray, and processual—even more so online as boundaries of public and private are diluted.

Furthermore, a strong general criticism of IRBs or ethics committees has been that their perspectives are often too strongly biomedical or behavioral and do not necessarily articulate, or allow for, different models or conceptions of privacy, informed consent, or ethic as method, as Markham has described (2006). IRBs are forced to walk a tight line, balancing numerous interests: those of the researcher, the researched, and the institutions themselves (universities, colleges, granting agencies, and so on) that foster and promote research endeavors. IRBs therefore mediate legal, philosophical, and social definitions and contradictions of such constructs as privacy, consent, and justice. IRBs must, by practicality, impose order on the often very messy realm of research. To make this manageable, research models have been, and continue to be, conceptualized in binary thinking. As Maximilian Forte (2004) has noted in a critical fashion, there are "scientific takers and native givers," subjects and objects, agree to participate or do not agree to participate—the binaries go on and on. Rarely do we as the takers ask, as do Bakardjieva, Feenberg, and Goldi (2004), "What do the subjects get out of it all?" Are we afraid the answer may just be "nothing at all"? If that is so, what does our research mean? Do our participants have to get something out of their participation in research? These significant questions warrant more pursuit.

Recently, I conducted a survey of 600 undergraduate students on research in general. I asked why they participated in research studies on campus, what did they learn, and how did they think they were contributing to a knowledge base. The responses, overall, were disconcerting: 70% of the respondents said they participated in faculty's research projects either for the extra credit or, second, because they thought they were required to participate as part of their coursework. Another 16% simply didn't know why they participated. When asked meta-reflexive questions meant to see how they read and engaged with the informed consent document they received, it was clear very few had actually read the document at all.

Discussions of these dilemmas occur in many fields of social research; perhaps internet research can contribute to different ways of thinking about privacy, informed consent, and research in general.

Sveningsson's chapter continually calls into question the dialogic relationship between researcher and researched within the framework of privacy and informed consent. She accurately shows the possible—and probable—misalignments that occur when researchers enter a space *only* for research purposes. The perspectives, objectives, and expectations are inherently different, which is not to say incompatible. As such constructs as privacy are redefined in the face of technology-mediated spaces, and as research participants conceive of their roles in online research differently, alternative models of protections will evolve. When we walk away from Malin Sveningsson's chapter, we should take away a greater understanding of our roles as researchers. What do we give back? We take great pains to "protect" and to ensure our participants have consented to research, but we rarely look back to see what we've accomplished for our participants and how; she shows us what privacy means and how important it is. And, she shows us the great responsibilities researchers really have—online and off.

❖ RECOMMENDED READING

For foundational research ethics and for cross-disciplinary, foundational guidelines on ethical research in online environments, see the AoIR guidelines (2002) and the *IRB Guidebook* published by the Office for Human Research Protections (both available online).

Several edited collections specifically cover research ethics in internet research, including Buchanan (2004); Johns, Chen, and Hall (2004); and Thorseth (2003).

For philosophical perspectives on privacy and the information society, see work by Brin (1998), Moor (1997), and Spinello and Tavani (2004).

❖ NOTE

1. In the United States, human subjects protections were codified in 1974: "In July of 1974, the passage of the National Research Act established the National Commission for the Protection of Human Subjects of Biomedical and Behavioral Research. The Commission met from 1974 to 1978. In keeping with its charge, the Commission issued reports and recommendations identifying the basic ethical principles that should underlie the conduct of biomedical and behavioral research involving human subjects and recommending guidelines to ensure that research is conducted in accordance with those principles. The Commission also recommended DHEW administrative action to require that the guidelines apply to research conducted or supported by DHEW. The Commission's report setting forth the basic ethical principles that should underlie the conduct of biomedical and behavioral research involving human subjects is titled The Belmont Report" (*IRB Guidebook,* n.d.).

A Response to Malin Sveningsson

Susannah R. Stern

❖   ❖   ❖

Determining how notions of privacy influence decision making for qualitative internet researchers is a tricky business, not least of all because the concept of privacy itself is amorphous, evolving, and rooted in individual perceptions. How one defines privacy and/or private information, as Malin Sveningsson clearly articulates in her essay, has consequences for the types of procedures researchers will follow. In particular, she notes, that researchers must determine if it is necessary to gain research participants' informed consent for a study to be executed ethically. Sveningsson's chapter is valuable because it comprehensively identifies the diverse factors that affect conceptions of privacy. Moreover, it wisely repositions the relationship between "public" and "private" as continuous rather than dichotomous.

As a researcher who has studied teenagers' internet use for the past decade, I have spent a great deal of time considering issues of privacy and how they bear on the research process. My experiences lead me to agree wholeheartedly with Sveningsson's conclusion that for researchers seeking to know how privacy issues should guide their decision making about informed consent agreements, the best response is "it all depends." Nevertheless, there are some important considerations, beyond how one defines privacy, that provide useful guidelines as one endeavors to do qualitative internet research. These include keeping track of the big picture, allowing those we study to define their own privacy expectations, and considering how shifting notions of privacy affect the types of messages and interactions that researchers themselves will encounter in their online inquiries.

❖ KEEPING TRACK OF THE BIG PICTURE

I agree with Sveningsson that the principal way in which privacy issues are implicated in qualitative internet research decision making is via the informed consent process. However, it is important to remember that respect for privacy is about much *more* than this process. While this seems an obvious point, it is, I believe, well worth making. In the daily effort of designing and implementing a research project, we often concern ourselves with the notion of privacy only insofar as it will "tell" us whether or not we need to go to the trouble of getting consent from those we wish to study. However, when we focus only on the procedure ("do I need to get consent or not?"), we often fail to reflect on the broader issue that the procedure itself was centrally designed to raise: namely, how to treat individuals as autonomous agents who should decide for themselves if they wish their personal information and interactions to be studied.

I noticed my own tendency to focus on procedure early in my career, when I was studying teen girls' self-expression practices on personal home pages. As a graduate student in the United States, I was keenly aware that, to proceed with my study (and thus, earn my degree), the IRB at my university needed to sanction my research. Recognizing that the study of "private" data online would require me to seek informed consent (often a time-consuming and expensive undertaking in online contexts), I worked diligently to build a case for why personal home pages should be considered public documents. For the reasons Sveningsson articulates in this chapter, there was good reason to conceive of these publicly accessible and publicly directed home pages as public rather than private. The IRB agreed, signed off on my project, and helped me put the issue to rest so I could move forward with my project.

In retrospect, I began to lament my relative inattention to the very real reasons to be concerned with privacy issues. That is to say, I wish I had spent more time reflecting on how to show respect for the people I wanted to study, and less time coveting the stamp of ethical approval an IRB might bestow on my project. I might have pondered a bit further such questions as the following: How did the young female authors I wanted to study regard their own disclosures? How comfortable would they be with the knowledge that a researcher was analyzing their intimate confessions? How might this knowledge harm them? What might be the consequences of seeking consent? For them? For scholarship?

Questions like these are worth asking because they are meaningful in and of themselves, regardless of their utility in directing decisions about informed consent. Of course, IRBs hope and intend that researchers do consider such questions as they draft their proposals. But the temptation to attend exclusively to the very real, everyday tasks of executing a project sometimes works against this type of contemplation. Fortunately, researchers need not dwell aimlessly in a period of solitary speculation about questions like these, since they can be informed by some relatively painless pilot work, as suggested below.

❖ ALLOWING THOSE WE STUDY
   TO VOICE THEIR OWN PRIVACY EXPECTATIONS

Researchers who endeavor to study people online have a responsibility to investigate the privacy expectations of their research subjects/participants. One practical way to do this is by asking them, or people like them, directly. The participants' perspective need not replace researchers' good judgment or professional standards, but rather should inform their general understanding of the rights and duties involved in their research decision making. Admittedly, it will often be impossible or unwise to directly interact with people whose online communication we wish to study. However, it is nearly always possible to find people *like* those we wish to study to give us some additional perspective. For example, if a researcher intends to study a particular online community devoted to cancer patients, her pilot work might focus on members of a different online community for people with another type of terminal illness. It will also, admittedly, be impossible to learn about every single person's individual perspective on the privacy of his or her own information and interactions. Yet this impossibility should not foreclose the opportunity to at least solicit a deeper and broader understanding of privacy expectations than a researcher might otherwise acquire.

   After all, there is good reason to assume that those we study may adhere to an entirely different set of criteria in their conceptions of privacy than researchers. For instance, after I began to question my lack of reflection in the project described earlier, I devised a new project, aimed expressly at understanding how youth internet authors regarded the public/private nature of their online expression (Stern, 2004). My conversations with youth authors suggested that they considered their online communications to be private when they were kept hidden from the people they knew in their everyday lives, regardless of who else encountered them. This perspective helped account for some of their seemingly contradictory behaviors, such as posting comments like "no one knows how upset I am" to a (potentially) global audience online.

Sveningsson usefully identifies factors, such as accessibility and sensitivity, that can help guide our decision making about how to respect privacy in our online internet research pursuits. But my study suggested other criteria, such as reach and proximity, that might also be considered. Ultimately, this leads me to wonder, Why should we, as researchers, get to decide what the parameters of consideration are? Given that people have such varying understandings of privacy, why should the researcher's perspective be privileged? In an age in which notions of privacy shift ceaselessly, it is important that our decisions about our research be guided increasingly by those we wish to study, as our own conceptions may be expanded or even challenged in this process.

❖ CONSIDERING HOW RESEARCHERS' DUTIES MAY EXPAND OR SHIFT AS DO NOTIONS OF PRIVACY

One final issue that qualitative internet researchers might usefully consider is how varying notions of public and private translate into new experiences for researchers. Take, for example, the case of researchers' encounters with distressing disclosure online. By "distressing," I refer to disclosure indicating that an online communicant is considering harming him- or herself or others. Such disclosures are certainly not limited to the internet, nor are researchers exclusively likely to encounter them in an online situation. However, because the internet allows for anonymity, private authorship, and public reach, many internet users feel encouraged to self-disclose what we historically might have considered to be "private" information, including distressing information. For example, a teen boy who harbors suicidal thoughts might not share them publicly in his offline life, but he may feel comfortable elucidating them online. What is a researcher's responsibility when encountering this information? What is the most ethical way to respond? In another article (Stern, 2003), I identify why researchers might carefully consider these questions and provide suggestions for how they might handle such information should they encounter it.

I suspect there are many other types of new situations that researchers may encounter as notions of privacy shift in online and offline spaces. We would all wisely begin to pay attention to these experiences and contemplate what they mean, not only for research participants but also for researchers.

❖ RECOMMENDED READING

For some interesting reflections on the informed consent procedure and how it is complicated in online contexts, I recommend Reid's (1996) discussion of informed consent in the study of online communities and Frankel's and Siang's (1999) report on ethics and legal aspects of human subjects research.

To read more about the experiences and contemplations of researchers who concern themselves with various ethical issues involved in online research, consider reading the work by Binik, Mah, and Kiesler (1999); Christians (2000); King (1996); Mann and Stewart (2000); and Waskul and Douglass (1996).

QUESTION FOUR

How Do Issues of
Gender and Sexuality Influence
the Structures and Processes
of Qualitative Internet Research?

Lori Kendall

❖ ❖ ❖

I t's three in the morning. I'm extremely sick to my stomach and unable to sleep. I'm wondering if you're supposed to eat the orange peel segments in the Orange Beef I shared with others earlier this evening. Or perhaps the cause of my malaise is just the combination of fatigue, rich food, and nervousness. Worse, I'm lying in the guest room of a condominium belonging to someone I know fairly well online but am not completely comfortable with in person. How nice of him to give me a place to stay while interviewing him and others from his group. How awful to be here sick in the middle of the night and not at home.

Finally, I get up and reluctantly look through the medicine cabinet in the bathroom for something to calm my stomach. This feels wrong to me, as if I'm snooping, and I hope my host is asleep and can't hear me. But no, as soon as I return to my room, I hear him get up. I feel immensely lonely, embarrassed, and exposed, and about as uncomfortable emotionally and physically as I've ever been.

Responding essays by Jenny Sundén (pp. 119–123) and John Edward Campbell (pp. 124–130).

This discomfort is made all the more intense by the fact that earlier this evening I felt powerfully attracted to my host. During my interview of him, I struggled with feelings of sexual arousal. It was distracting, but I worried that if I completely suppressed my feelings I might seem cold or awkward. I managed finally to enjoy the glow but give no sign of it. (Or so I think.) It's not so much that I feel it inappropriate to flirt with someone I'm interviewing for a research study. It's more that I know with a fair degree of certainty that my feelings are not reciprocated. So ego as much as ethics guides my behavior.

Now here I am, sick in the dark, while out there in the hall I can hear the movements of someone on whom I have a powerful crush. If this were a romantic comedy, or perhaps if I were younger, more daring, more attractive, the end of this scene would be racy. Instead, I finally manage to get a little sleep (sitting upright against the wall). Neither my host nor I ever mention the incident.

In her groundbreaking article on sexuality in the field, anthropologist Esther Newton notes, "Rarely is the erotic subjectivity or experience of the anthropologist discussed in public venues or written about for publication" (Newton, 1993b, p. 4). She points out that many fieldworkers are young and unattached and that, in the long months of fieldwork (often, for anthropologists, in places far from home), "fieldworkers and informants do and must get involved emotionally" (p. 5). In "My Best Informant's Dress" (1993b) and in her ethnography of a gay resort community, *Cherry Grove, Fire Island* (1993a), Newton discusses her erotic (although not physically sexual) relationship with her primary informant, Kay. Preliminary reviewers of her book warned that "[t]his manner of working poses the danger of 'uncritically adopting [the informant's] point of view'" (1993b, p. 15). However, Newton argues that ethnographers need to be more forthcoming about their sexual feelings and actions during the course of their research:

> Until we are more honest about how we feel about informants we can't try to compensate for, incorporate, or acknowledge desire and repulsion in our analysis of subjects or in our discourse about text construction. We are also refusing to reproduce one of the mightiest vocabularies in the human language. (1993b, p. 16)

While Newton discusses her own flirtation with an informant in her Cherry Grove research, her article does not really provide a clear example of what difference the attention to sexuality makes in the analysis of fieldwork and writing of ethnography.

I want to push her analysis a step further. Taking to heart the insights of those few who have written on the topic of sexuality in the conduct of qualitative research, I explore what difference attention to sexuality might make specifically to those of us studying online interactions and doing fieldwork about people's use of computers and the internet in both online and offline settings. In the following, I revisit previous work I've done, with greater attention to the erotic aspects of my experience. I make the case for doing qualitative work with the whole body, and not cutting off certain types of experiences as irrelevant or inappropriate, even in situations, such as wholly online social interactions, in which the body might seem relatively unimportant.

❖ OTHER ACCOUNTS OF THE EROTIC IN FIELDWORK

Before the publication of Newton's 1993 article, accounts of sexuality in the field were few and rarely were integrated into the primary analytical work resulting from fieldwork. The famous anthropologist Malinowski's sexual feelings and exploits were relegated to private diaries, published posthumously (1967). Other works were published pseudonymously (Cesara, 1982), or they analyzed other fieldworkers' experiences, often in ways that were dismissive of both the fieldworker and his or her subjects (Wengle, 1988, as discussed in Kulick, 1995).

The discussion of sexuality in qualitative research still only occurs rarely. Perhaps the best work on the topic is the 1995 edited volume *Taboo: Sex, Identity, and Erotic Subjectivity in Anthropological Fieldwork* (Kulick & Willson, 1995). In his introduction to this work, Kulick provides a hint of where sex in the field might lead us:

> For many anthropologists, desire experienced in the field seems often to provoke questions that otherwise easily remain unasked. . . . The questions are basic, quite uncomfortable ones. They are questions about the validity and meaning of the self-other dichotomy, and about the hierarchies on which anthropological work often seems to depend. (p. 5)

This discussion positions the acknowledgment of sexual desire as a methodological issue: Suppression of the erotic in the experience of fieldwork potentially cuts off an important source of knowledge. That suppression can occur not only in the field but also in the resulting text, further limiting the knowledge gained and transmitted through qualitative work. As Altork (1995) says, "By funneling data gathered in this way through the senses, fueled by access to the full range of human emotions, it is possible to create texts which I contend will better enhance our understanding of other cultures (or groups within them) and of ourselves" (p. 109).

Suppression of the erotic is also, then, an epistemological issue. How do we know what we know? What do we tell people about how we learned what we learned in the field? These issues relate to questions of objectivity and the status of qualitative research as science. As Goode (1999, p. 320) writes in his article, "Sex with Informants as Deviant Behavior," "What better means of maintaining the traditional social science fiction of objectivity than to pretend that all ethnographers remain completely celibate when they conduct their research?" Despite the (now not so recent) turn to reflexivity in qualitative research, the ideal of the disinterested, "objective" observer lingers. All emotions, not just sexual feelings, can be suspect in ethnographies. As Kleinman and Copp (1993) note, "Fieldwork analyses reflect our identities, ideologies, and political views. Yet we often omit them from our published accounts because we want to present ourselves as social *scientists:* objective and neutral observers" (p. 13). Writing conventions in academic venues discourage the reporting of strong feelings about informants. In the post-Freudian Western world, sexual feelings are taken as a given to be "strong," seen as inspiring everything from artistic creation to murderous rage.

Providing information about our own erotic lives exposes us as researchers to risks. Even those of us who eschew the possibility of complete objectivity and neutrality in social research may worry that others will see our accounts as overly biased. The exposure of personal information may also feel uncomfortable and may affect other relationships, both personal and professional. These risks need to be balanced by significant analytical and ethical gains. By discussing several specific examples from my own research, I suggest some of these potential gains.

❖ WHAT DIFFERENCE DOES IT MAKE?

My book, *Hanging Out in the Virtual Pub* (Kendall, 2002), an ethnography of an online group, certainly includes reports of my own experiences and, to some extent, my feelings. Some of these made it into the main text, rather than being omitted altogether, as is most common, or at best relegated to the methodological appendix (Kleinman & Copp, 1993, pp. 16–17). However, even my methodological appendix contains very little specific information about my relationships with the other BlueSky participants. For instance, as excerpted below, I wrote that henri's early support of my project was probably instrumental to the success of my research.

> Highly respected on BlueSky for his wit and intelligence, henri contributes more to the mud environment than most other BlueSky participants.... His high status in the group and the early interest he took in me and my research were instrumental both to my being accepted as a newcomer on BlueSky and to the acceptance of my research project.... henri's introspective disposition, his long history of very active mudding with the BlueSky group, and his place at the emotional center of the social group made him particularly useful in this regard. (Kendall, 2002, p. 237)

What in retrospect is notably absent from this description is that henri was one of a handful of BlueSky participants on whom I had a crush. I can't recall whether I consciously considered whether or not to include such information, but I'm sure that not doing so was influenced by the same factors that Newton and others have identified. I (probably rightfully) feared that people might assume that everything I wrote in my ethnography reflected an uncritical acceptance of henri's (and other participants') points of view. This fear demonstrates the importance people give to sexual feelings. Although other emotions are also suspect, types of relationships with "informants" other than sexual ones do not result in as strong a suspicion of bias. Yet, importantly, nothing inherent in sexual feelings makes the researcher less likely to be critical.

Perhaps, including information about my very personal emotional and erotic feelings would not have added greatly to the analytic points I made in my write-up. However, as I review my interview notes and reflect on the sexual attractions and repulsions I experienced, I believe that consideration of these feelings does illuminate some aspects of online and offline relationships and connections between them. I think I was a bit too quick to think of these feelings as a "side issue" in the conduct of fieldwork. Including more information about my own relationships with my online informants might well have made for a better ethnography.

For instance, as I've noted previously, the culture of BlueSky included a significant amount of sexism and was often uncomfortable for me. Yet, I mostly enjoyed my many years of participation there. Reading sexist remarks and jokes that were written online disturbed me much less than hearing those same statements. As I put it, "I find it **much** easier [online] to ignore the sexism and other things that are obnoxious" (Kendall, 2002, p. 166; emphasis in original). So, on the one hand, as I have already reported, the text-based online conversation muted reactions to disagreeable aspects of people's personalities and of the group culture.

What did not get highlighted in my research, although I briefly mentioned it, is that positive elements can also be enhanced through solely text-based discourse online. This point is demonstrated by the duration of my crushes. The people on whom I had crushes on BlueSky had many attractive qualities. Yet, in every case, we were also incompatible in many ways. Realistically, I was not likely to become romantically involved with them, and I think that more face-to-face time spent with any one of them would have significantly decreased my erotic interest. But the fact that these were primarily online relationships extended that phase of a romantic relationship sometimes called "limerance." In this intense early phase, one imagines and enhances the good qualities of the romantic partner. In limerance, one does not see the person for who he or she really is, but sees only those aspects that meet one's criteria for an idealized potential mate. The limerance phase is even easier to maintain in an online relationship. The limited cues of the online environment allowed my crushes to be perpetuated and probably enhanced my relationships to these people online by increasing my good feelings toward them and my pleasure in participating.

Erotic interest in others in online fieldwork situations may also be paradoxically enhanced by the *lack* of sensual information. Altork (1995) connects the erotic imagination of the fieldworker to the sensual experience in general of the field site: "It has been my experience that any new locale sends all of my sensory modes into overdrive in the initial days and weeks of my stay" (p. 110). Since physically my field site was the familiar environs of my apartment, it did not engage my senses in this way. Further, the physical experience involved in online interaction ranges primarily from the banal to the uncomfortable. There is nothing pleasurably sensual about fingers tapping computer keys. The physical boredom and discomfort resulting from hours and hours spent online provide an incentive for creating situations that provide more pleasurable physical sensations. Feeling sexual attraction to the online participants sometimes made the time spent online more interesting, emotionally and physically, which enabled me to remain engaged intellectually.

Here then is an insight about how online interaction facilitates relationships, especially romantic ones—an insight that is lost without paying serious attention to the erotic dimension of fieldwork. My erotic reactions point to a specific effect of online interactions on relationships: Erotic attachments to others online may make text-based online communication more interesting and long periods at the keyboard more tolerable. This is a point that warrants further research and one that could potentially yield important insights into online participation and activities. For instance, it might provide a clue to the success of pornographic and other sexual industries online, beyond the more obvious advantages of allowing people access to sexual materials in the privacy of their own homes.

That my full participation on BlueSky included my erotic imagination points to the richness of that experience, and perhaps more of that belonged in my reports. My subsequent research projects have not yielded as deep a level of involvement. Possibly I have resisted getting that involved again. But aside from my personal wishes, the difference between my BlueSky experience and subsequent projects also reflects the particularities and importance of context.

For instance, I noticed that, in my interviews with LiveJournal participants for a later research project, many of my interviewees noted with relief and approval that I did not ask them too many "personal" questions. Yet many of them included quite personal information in their LiveJournal posts. Information received online did not necessarily translate into the offline relationship; online personal revelations did not lead to a greater feeling of closeness in person. In contrast, although interviews with BlueSky people I was meeting for the first time in person sometimes started out with some awkwardness, as the interviews progressed, we easily referred to online experiences and often ventured into the expression of personal feelings.

BlueSky's group identity and cohesion contributed to a more across-the-board acceptance of me as a group member and allowed each interview to start from that position of safety (which is not to say that some of the interviews of BlueSky participants weren't still quite uncomfortable.) With LiveJournal participants, by contrast, while some interviewees were interconnected, each such interconnected group from my set of connections had to be negotiated separately, and each interview started almost as a new relationship, despite the exposure to each other online.[1] Notably, I did not have crushes on any of my LiveJournal informants and found none of them particularly attractive (let alone distractingly so) during the interviews. I believe this lack of response highlights a difference between the kinds of relationships and group identity (or lack thereof) formed in different online situations. BlueSky constituted an online community, with a distinct group identity. LiveJournal, in contrast, follows a pattern of what Barry Wellman (2002) has termed "networked individualism," with much less group cohesion. This too I've discussed elsewhere (Kendall, 2005), but again, not including the full range of feelings and experiences that might help illustrate that difference.

❖ GENDER, POWER, AND EMBODIMENT

Most of my crushes began after meeting people in person. In short, they were physical attractions. For instance, I was attracted to one participant's androgynous good looks. I found him very cute and more personable offline than online. Another participant had graceful hands with long expressive fingers. These physical features came to mind during my online interactions with those participants. This is another area of online experience that is difficult to explore. I asked BlueSky participants, many of whom have met each other, about how they pictured others online, but didn't get much information from them about the importance of people's physical presence to later online interactions. These are difficult experiences to articulate, and many people are reluctant to acknowledge the importance of physical attractiveness, especially for nonsexual relationships. Thus my own reactions provide important information missing from other sources.

But perhaps physical attraction was only part of the equation. It is worth noting that all of my crushes were on high-status, high-profile participants. There were certainly high-status people I found physically and emotionally repellent, but I can't discount the possibility that I tend to be attracted to people I perceive as more powerful than me. That perhaps tells us more about me than about BlueSky (and perhaps more about me than you wanted to know). It also exposes one of the dangers inherent in self-reflexive strategies of qualitative research—that the researcher's expressions of his or her own feelings and experiences can be interpreted as somewhat narcissistic or unnecessary.

Yet when taken in context of the different social locations involved, these revelations also illuminate aspects of power and gender relations, and the intersection of those issues with both fieldwork and sexuality. Despite my own openness to such feelings, I did not, for instance, develop crushes on any of the women participants on BlueSky. In fact, my impression during most of my interviews with them is that they didn't like me very much, and I wasn't sure I liked them very much either. Here's an example from field notes taken after one such interview:

> Don't like Susan much. Looks kind of sullen and seems a bit suspicious of me. This contrasts with how she was earlier (online and in the group meeting last night). Her answers are short and she says "I don't know" a lot. We're crowded on a little loveseat. I'm trying to eat snacks. She almost can't move without her feet touching me. It bothers both of us. (handwritten field notes, 9/10/1995)

This is quite a different kind of physical discomfort from that provoked by the arousal experienced in the interview that I described at the beginning of this chapter.

Susan was not a very frequent participant, nor particularly high in status on BlueSky. She was also one of the few women participants. Each of these women described a history of involvement in groups and activities in which they were the only or one of the few women participants. They were all quite used to being the exception. Often, for women in circumstances in which they are in the minority (as in nontraditional occupations), the experience of exceptionalism leads to a distancing from other women. As Kanter (1977) explains, "some women . . . bend over backwards not to exhibit any characteristics that would reinforce stereotypes" (p. 237). When there were only a few women in a male-dominated occupational group, Kanter found that they resisted the group's tendency to pair them together "by trying to create difference and distance between them and becoming extremely competitive" (p. 238). Bagilhole (2002) similarly found that "many women [in non-traditional occupations] . . . do not want, or do not feel able to associate with other women or to be seen to be concerned about 'women's issues'" (p. 161).

While not an occupational setting, BlueSky was similarly male dominated, both in numbers and in culture. Like the women studied by Kanter and Bagilhole, many of the women I interviewed made a point of differentiating themselves from women they perceived as more "traditional" or feminine, as in the following conversations:

HalfLife: It seems like there are a lot of women on DeepSeas who play really stupid characters. Airheaded, bubbly, and they're not treated very well except by people who support them and want them to be bubbly. . . .

Lori: Give me an example of a bubble-headed one.

Halflife: Sparkle. A lot of them I don't pay attention to . . . Trillian is sort of one of them.

*****

Beryl: Have you talked with Sparkle?

Lori: No. Well, I've talked to her some online.

Beryl: I consider her very much a traditional female. And Tina—Tina's her real name, what's her mud name—Melissa. She really was traditional. She acted like there wasn't a brain in her head. She went around chasing guys.

Lori: Is this Susan?

Beryl: Not Susan. Susan, even though she chases guys a lot, you know, she's an engineer, she enjoys computers, she enjoys science fiction. She's one of us. [laughs] But Sparkle, and Tina, and there've been a few other women who have been what I've considered traditional. Tina even said that, if you asked her what she'd like to do, she really wanted to be a housewife. You don't hear that much. . . . And now she's not online anymore, because she found a nice rich guy and she's a housewife.

These women reject anything that seems at all stereotypically feminine, such as a bubbly demeanor or the desire to be a housewife. Beryl specifically identifies interest in computers and engineering as not traditionally feminine, demonstrating that even women with such interests perpetuate the idea that these are masculine pursuits.

There was not, in short, a lot of female bonding around our identity as women or in reaction to sexist behavior by the men. Each woman's position in the group, her acceptance as smart, funny, and witty (all qualities especially valued on BlueSky), in short as "one of the guys," depended somewhat on her ability to show that she was *not* like other women. While this did not preclude friendships among the women, having to play by the boys' rules (or perhaps, what we perceived as the boys' rules) left us with a somewhat impoverished basis for connection.

This discussion points to the complexities of gender identities, especially as expressed in relationships, as well as to the importance of considering sexuality in conjunction with gender. My relationships to the participants on BlueSky, and their relationships to each other, varied not just according to a simple notion of gender (male or female), but also with consideration of different ways to be male or female. For instance, Beryl distinguishes between "traditional" women and women who are "one of us." HalfLife explains that the poor treatment of some women on BlueSky stems from their portrayal of themselves as "stupid" or "bubbly." To cultivate positive relationships with both men and women on BlueSky, it was important that I was also perceived as nontraditional.

Thus, like many gender theorists, women on BlueSky portray gender as a spectrum rather than as a duality. Sexuality and sexual identity also create variation in the gender spectrum. People have different understandings of each other's gender, and different relationships to others' gender identities, based in part on their sexuality and sexual preferences. Sexuality also can best be viewed on a spectrum, or perhaps on several axes of variance. Dating back to Kinsey's famous sexuality studies, scholars have often viewed homosexuality and heterosexuality on a continuum, with few people being exclusively one or the other. But people also vary greatly in levels of interest in sexual activity, as well as in other aspects of their sexuality. (For instance, there is considerable difference in sexual identity between a heterosexual person interested in "mainstream" or "vanilla" sexual activities and a heterosexual person very actively involved in the sadomasochistic subculture.)

Even in nonsexual situations and nonsexual relationships, sexual aspects of identity influence interactions at the most basic and minute level. This is one of the reasons online participants so often attempt to ascertain each others' gender. As one participant who was flirting with me online put it after asking if I was "really" female, "I don't like being switched genders on . . . so I don't inadvertently use the wrong social mores with anyone" (Kendall, 2002, p. 124). How we behave toward people, even people we never expect to see again, varies according to our own and their gender identity, which includes attention to sexual identity as well.

Scholars have long considered the effect of the researcher's gender on the information obtained. Denzin (1989) suggests that interviewers need to share aspects of identity and background with their interviewees as much as possible (p. 115). I find this an almost unrealizable goal and too limiting for most research projects. But researchers should be aware of differences and similarities between their own identity and that of the people they research, with attention to how those similarities and differences might affect interactions and responses to questions. I believe most researchers are aware of such differences with regard to gender and suggest that they must also take sexuality into consideration.

❖ SEX AND POWER

The advantage, once one is accepted as a member of a predominantly male group, is the increase in status this acceptance entails. In theory, at least some of the usual intergender tensions decrease as well. As I've noted elsewhere, the women on BlueSky said they appreciated the lack of sexual innuendo on BlueSky, contrasting it favorably with other online spaces. My own erotic feelings and my own enjoyment of the sexual humor on BlueSky should have caused me to question this perception more. Looking back at logs of BlueSky interaction and at my interviews with the women participants, I find that in fact my depiction of BlueSky as a haven from the sexual harassment prevalent elsewhere online is not completely accurate.

On the one hand, BlueSky norms precluded most overt sexual activity or flirtation, especially if affectionate or romantic. As Peg reported, concerning her relationship with another BlueSky mudder, evariste, "if evariste and I are demonstrative, it's like 'Get a Room!' They don't want to see that." Yet other types of sexual attention and innuendo occurred frequently on BlueSky.

Peg: I think actually because I'm not available it gives them license. The guys can feel like they have more license to do lustful things.

Lori: They can tease you.

Peg: Say "Woo Woo!" . . . It's known that I'm attractive. . . . People talk about that because it's always been talked about. It's okay. . . . Usually I ignore those things, because if I respond to them it reinforces it. . . . So now it's to the point where I'll come home sometimes from work and [evariste] tell[s] me that he's been online and people will ask him questions about our sex life or something like that and they'll say like "Peg, Woo Woo!" or something like that. And instead of saying "yeah well" or something like that he'll go the other way—I'm trying to think of [what he does] . . .

Lori: He says "don't you wish?!"

Peg: Yeah and they'll be like "sigh" and he'll be like "yeah I'm going to go have sex with Peg RIGHT NOW!" And he's like "you guys asked for it" and they're like "you're a cruel man" or something. But that happens mostly when I'm not there. But I don't know if it's because . . . they don't want to offend me?

Thus not only did many of the men on BlueSky openly avow their attraction to Peg, but her husband, evariste, blatantly tormented them for it. He often made comments online that highlighted his sexual relationship with Peg and taunted the other BlueSky men with the knowledge that he had sex with her and they could not.

Another interviewee, BlueJean, reported an incident in which a BlueSky participant began calling her at home. I happened to mention the name of this other participant during our interview, and reacted to a face she made at its mention.

Lori:	[laughs] Did you have an experience with Rockefeller? What was that?
BlueJean:	There was a point where we were talking online once and he was getting kicked out of his computer lab and he convinced me to give him my phone number.
Lori:	Huh. And he called you up?
BlueJean:	[annoyed tone] Several times.
Lori:	That doesn't sound like it was a good experience.
BlueJean:	[there's a pause; she seems reluctant to talk about it] It . . . was . . . an interesting experience. And then as soon as I mentioned that online, everyone was "oh god no! why'd you do that? Why'd you give him your phone number" and I was "oh no!"
Lori:	Yeah, he has kind of a reputation.
BlueJean:	Yeah, he has a definite reputation. But I figured it was my dorm number and I'd be out of there in less than a few weeks anyway, so it couldn't hurt. Interesting guy. I mean, I can't say, I haven't met him in person, but I guess talking on the phone.
Lori:	Is he still calling you?
BlueJean:	No. He doesn't have my current phone number.
Lori:	Well that's good.
BlueJean:	Yeah. I mean, he would—crazy hours. My roommate would be like "that guy from Missouri called again." . . . Usually when I was [on BlueSky] . . . there weren't usually a whole lot of females. So I get a lot of attention.

In looking at the contrast between the perceptions of women like Beryl and Susan, who both reported feeling very comfortable on BlueSky, and the experiences of Peg and BlueJean, I note that my own interpretation sided more with Beryl and Susan. I too perhaps was seeking to distance myself from the experience of being female. Possibly also, my attraction to men whom I knew to have no reciprocal interest led me to empathize less with those women who attracted sexual attention on BlueSky.

Within the unequal power structures of a patriarchal culture, sexual attention both regulates and delineates status positions. Unwanted sexual attention that women receive positions them as sexual objects, limiting their role and status. However, sexual attention also illuminates finer distinctions, positioning some women to benefit more from the existing hierarchy than others. Hegemonic masculinity represents an ideal for men that positions all men to benefit to the degree that they fit that ideal. Emphasized femininity similarly represents the hegemonic ideal for women. However, while women benefit from the degree to which they meet that standard, it is always seen as inferior to masculinity, and thus for women there is an additional cost to conformity (Connell, 1995). Women like Beryl and HalfLife criticize women who meet the standard of emphasized femininity, siding with masculinity, despite never fully benefiting from it.

Women on BlueSky and other similar male-dominated forums must carefully negotiate their own status with regard to their gender and sexual identity within these hierarchical constraints. While an understanding of this dynamic informs my earlier writing on BlueSky, the more carefully I consider my own reactions and feelings in that situation, the better I am able to articulate the particular maneuvers and power plays that occur in day-to-day interactions.

Conforming to emphasized femininity carries both costs and benefits. Some women manage to lean more toward masculine identity (as in avowing interest in activities deemed masculine). These women accrue some benefits from masculinity's higher status. But some women neither conform to emphasized femininity nor successfully perform a masculine identity. These women are likely to be the most denigrated group in a male-dominated culture.

At the other end of the spectrum of sex talk about BlueSky participants from the acknowledged longings for Peg were repeated allusions to an image called "tawny.gif."[2] Tawny was a past BlueSky participant who was still friends with some current participants, but was not at all active on BlueSky. She was known to have slept with one of the other participants, but as he was at that time affianced to another BlueSky participant (later his wife), the topic of that liaison was one of the few out-and-out taboos on BlueSky. Tawny was also a very large woman, and tawny.gif was an artistic nude photo of her that circulated online during my research on BlueSky. BlueSky participants often made negative references to tawny.gif, calling it nausea-inducing and jokingly threatening others with it. In the following conversation, one of the women on BlueSky (Alisa) reacts negatively to a typical discussion of Tawny by several BlueSky men:

BJ says "alisa doesn't wear clothes."

Dave says "neither does tawny."

Steve EEEEE [Steve's representation of a scream]

Alisa makes a note never to put a n00d jpeg of
    herself on the net so bozos on muds can scream
    with horror at how fat she is.

BJ for one, is thankful.

Alisa says "Since net.guys seem to like them
    starving thin with silicone balloons in their
    tits."

BJ is not too picky, but hell. There's LIMITS

Such discussions outlined the hierarchy of female attractiveness on
BlueSky. Petite, friendly (and relatively demure) Peg, whose looks some
compared to the actress Gillian Anderson (of *X-Files* fame), inspired
fawning and crushes, while fat (and absent) Tawny became a joke
punch line and the very standard of repulsion. In addition to not fitting
the norm of feminine attractiveness, fat women's bodies highlight the
association of women with the body and bodily functions. Thus, a fat
women—especially a fat woman who dares to see herself as attractive
and to publicly exhibit her body—is seen as one of the furthest identities from masculinity, and thus becomes one of the most denigrated.

Within this hierarchical spectrum, I could only see myself as being
on the Tawny end. Not only am I also relatively fat but I was also quite
a bit older than most BlueSky participants. These factors, at least as
much as my professionalism, kept me silent about my own sexual feelings for group members. Whatever discomfort this silence caused me
might matter little, except as a methodological issue. However, issues
of sexuality, of perceived attractiveness, and especially of expressed
standards for women's attractiveness were very much part of what I
analyzed. For instance, in *Hanging Out in the Virtual Pub*, I recount discussions in which BlueSky participants depict "nerdettes" as fat and
unattractive. My own feelings as the potential butt of these jokes
therefore became part of my analysis, but that is nowhere represented
in the text. Making that linkage clear could only have strengthened the
analysis.

In general, I spent much more time analyzing the sexuality of the
men on BlueSky than that of the women. Had I more fully accepted
my own erotic feelings as data, this might have been different. My
analysis of several men on BlueSky portrays them as "heterosexual
dropouts" (Kendall, 2002, pp. 90–94). I analyze heterosexuality as contradictory within patriarchal society, causing tension for men who
must view women both as denigrated and desirable. Where does my

own desire for these often openly sexist men position me within these contradictions? Not surprisingly, my crushes were on some of the least sexist men on BlueSky, men who sometimes supported my feminist analyses of BlueSky in online discussions. This tells us more than just my own particular tastes in men. It also points to some of the contradictions for *women* within heterosexuality, something I did not previously analyze.

Most of the female BlueSky participants I interviewed were married to, or later married, other BlueSky participants. Taking my own sexual feelings for BlueSky participants more seriously as data might have led me to consider this fact a bit further. I analyze the women on BlueSky as having to fit into a male-dominated social context and depict them as being "one of the guys." Their marriages show that, like many heterosexual women in mostly male groups, the BlueSky women managed a complicated presentation of self as "like the guys" and simultaneously "not guys."

Had I been more conscious of these aspects, and in particular, had I taken more seriously my own feelings and concerns, there are several different directions I might have taken in my study. Most particularly, I probably would have asked different questions of the women I interviewed. While they downplayed sexual aspects of their interactions online, they clearly encountered sexual talk and also had sexual feelings for at least some other participants. This would have been worth pursuing more than I did.

❖ SEXUALITY AND RESEARCH ETHICS

Issues of power, gender, and sexuality are also important to researchers in regard to the ethics of social research. Ethical standards for social research stress the degree of care that researchers must take not to abuse the power they have over research participants. Some of this power may come from their status in society, as people who are well educated (and usually economically privileged). Power also accrues from their activities as the ones controlling information about the people they study.

The depiction of the researcher as having power over the researched is sometimes at odds with how qualitative research *feels* while in process. For instance, Goode (1999) writes as follows:

To me, in interactions with my marijuana informants in 1967, the relationship seemed completely nonhierarchical. In my interviews, it was I who was invading the users' turf, begging them for their time and words. If anything, I reasoned, I was the subordinate party in this transaction, not the other way around. (p. 316)

Goode indicates that he gave no thought to ethical issues during his research project and would not, at the time, have considered his sexual activities with informants unethical. His 1999 reflections seem to indicate he still does not consider those actions unethical but understands that others might.

Like Goode, I did not feel more powerful than my informants, whose social location in many cases gave them more social status than I had. But feelings of powerlessness are not the same as actually being powerless. Such feelings ought instead to signal a particular need for caution. *We are most likely to abuse our power when we least feel we have it.* This is especially crucial during the writing phase of qualitative research. It is when writing up the research that the ethnographer particularly exercises power: the power of representation. As Fine (1993) writes, "A spurned ethnographer can be a dangerous foe. . . . Those of us with access to 'the media' have power that others cannot match" (pp. 273–274). I believe I did take care to describe the BlueSky participants carefully and honestly, and to protect their identities from exposure. Yet it is interesting that although I to some extent describe *their* sex lives (or at least their talk about their sex lives), I don't at all discuss my own, even as it intersected the field site. As Markham (2005c) points out, researchers have the privilege of choosing whether or not their own embodiment is an issue in the research, even while critically observing the embodiment of participants (p. 809).

Does this mean that researchers who look at sexual behavior online necessarily need expose their own? The vulnerability of the researcher in doing so might somewhat balance the power hierarchy. On the other hand, that can be a tricky balance to maintain. As Fine (1993, p. 285) points out,

Sexual contact stigmatizes the writer, particularly female writers. . . . Participant observation is a methodology in which the personal equation is crucial, and yet too many variables remain hidden. The question is whether we can preserve our privacy while we reveal the impact and relevance of our behavior, both private and public. Where is the balance?

My own sexual feelings are doubly stigmatizing because of my identities as a woman and as a professional ethnographer. Acknowledging sexual feelings in the field is antithetical to traditional notions of professionalism. Professionalism is associated with masculinity, and academic research is a male-dominated field. Sexuality, as connected to the body, is also associated with femininity. By talking about sexuality, I emphasize my stigmatized female identity in a context in which power accrues to conformity to masculinity. Writing about such feelings also exposes me more than similar statements expose my informants. I have at least taken pains to protect the identities of my informants. The reports of my own sexual feelings have no such protection.

Beyond the issue of my own exposure, the ethics of balancing the exposure of informants' feelings and behaviors by reporting on our own is by no means clear. Famous anthropologists who revealed sexual feelings (and/or actions) regarding informants in other cultures—as in Malinowski's (1967) private diaries, and Rabinow's (1977) discussion of a sexual experience in the field—could rest assured that most of their subjects would not read these tales. Modern field researchers, especially those who study people online, have no such assurance. Since my respondents might find my revelations as uncomfortable as I do, the ethical choice might be silence.

❖ CONCLUSION

Unless you count online jokes and sexual innuendo, I never engaged in any sexual contact with BlueSky participants. Had I done so, I'm not sure I could have written this chapter. I tip my hat to several of the authors I've cited herein for their bravery in discussing transgressions I only fantasized about. Even so, this is one of the hardest pieces I've ever written, illustrating the depth of the taboo I'm breaking. Despite increasing openness about sexuality in general in Western culture, and despite decades of self-reflexivity in qualitative research, talking about sex in fieldwork still crosses a line.

Researchers are generally quicker to acknowledge the importance of gender to qualitative (and other) research. Yet sexuality too needs to be recognized as an important part of our experience. Both gender and sexuality affect and are affected by our sense of self and our experience of fieldwork. These aspects of identity also interact and jointly affect people's relationships with each other, including relationships between researchers and the people they study.

Sexuality may seem irrelevant to research projects that focus on people's use of information technologies, especially when that research is conducted online. Yet it forms an important part of our identity and enters into day-to-day interactions far more than we usually credit. Further, as Markham (2005c) points out, "perception always involves embodiment, and this cannot be set aside in the context of studying life online" (p. 809). In the context of ethnographic research, we make of our bodies measurement instruments, and should be careful before considering some perceptions (such as erotic feelings) merely noise or error while privileging other perceptions (sight, sound) as more relevant. In most in-depth ethnographic studies, attention to the erotic dimension in both analysis and ethnographic reports can yield important insights.

❖ RECOMMENDED READING

Fine, Gary Alan. 1993. "Ten Lies of Ethnography: Moral Dilemmas of Field Research," *Journal of Contemporary Ethnography,* 22(3), 267–294.

   Fine, a sociologist who has published many oft-cited ethnographies, outlines the virtues expected of ethnographers and the problems that arise when moral expectations meet the realities of fieldwork. His article illuminates ethical and methodological dilemmas, many of which defy simple solutions but instead require continual struggle and consideration. This essay is particularly useful for considering issues of power between researchers and participants.

Goode, Erich. 1999. "Sex with Informants as Deviant Behavior." *Deviant Behavior,* 20, 301–324.

   This at times troubling essay goes against the dominant position among researchers that sex with informants should be avoided. Goode argues that this position may be true in some cases but not in all. The journal issue also includes two commentaries on Goode's article by Clifton Bryant and Columbus Hopper.

Kleinman, Sherryl and Martha A. Copp. 1993. *Emotions and Fieldwork.* Newbury Park, CA: Sage.

   Both authors are well-known experts in the sociology of emotions, and this book is an invaluable guide to an important aspect of fieldwork. Kleinman's earlier article "Field-Workers' Feelings: What We Feel, Who We Are, How We Analyze," in *Experiencing Fieldwork: An Inside View of Qualitative Research,* edited by W. Shaffer and R. Stebbins (Newbury Park, CA: Sage, 1991, pp. 184–195), provides a briefer exploration of many of the same issues.

Kulick, Don and Margaret Willson, Eds. 1995. *Taboo: Sex, Identity and Erotic Subjectivity in Anthropological Fieldwork.* London: Routledge.

This excellent volume includes many thoughtful essays regarding sex and eroticism in fieldwork. These anthropological tales mostly depict U.S. scholars in encounters with other cultures.

Newton, Esther. 1993. "My Best Informant's Dress." *Cultural Anthropology,* vol. 8 (February 1993): 1–23. Also available in Newton, Esther. 2000. *Margaret Mead Made Me Gay.* Durham, NC: Duke University Press.

Newton's essay provides a good introduction to the issues discussed in this chapter, including an overview of some of the earlier anthropological writing on the subject of sex in the field.

❖ NOTES

1. The exception is the few BlueSky participants who were also part of my LiveJournal study.

2. Just as I have changed the names of participants herein, I have changed the name of this file.

Response to Lori Kendall

Jenny Sundén

❖ ❖ ❖

❖ DOUBLE LIFE ON THE SCREEN

In the spirit of confessional ethnographic reflexivity, I too have a story to tell. While conducting my two-year online ethnography in a text-based virtual world called WaterMOO (Sundén, 2003), I did, occasionally, visit another online world—a parallel universe if you like—to explore the potentials and promises of cybersex.

My researcher character in WaterMOO carried the highly inventive name "Jenny," sporting sensible boots and a rather loose-fitting woolen sweater, tapping away consistently in her virtual office or hanging out with WaterMOOers to better understand their notions of online embodiment, gender, and sexuality. As opposed to Lori Kendall's study of BlueSky, my ethnography never took me offline to face-to-face encounters and interview sessions. The reason for this choice was primarily that most WaterMOOers didn't meet offline either, and I wanted to understand this particular online culture "on its own terms." This is not to say that people, myself included, are not curious about who the person is behind a certain character. But I insisted on the realness of imagined worlds for those involved, and I wanted to bring into the picture a fundamental online condition: the state of not knowing who you're meeting. The inhabitants of WaterMOO sometimes struggled with this uncertainty, particularly in terms of what they experienced as troubling gender incoherence, and I wanted to perform my ethnographic work in the midst of the very same insecurity.

If Jenny was the "serious" researcher, her doppelganger was very different. Sometimes, after having put Jenny to sleep in her office (which is what happens when you log out from the system), I would dress up virtually as one of the fairly anonymous guest characters at a different site, seeking out a late-night adventure. Sometimes in a very femme dress, sometimes butching it up with a tie and slacks, and sometimes, pretty straightforwardly, putting a single word in the description field: "Naked." Oh dear. I don't think of these textual escapades as having sex in the field, since they neither involved my field site nor the inhabitants of WaterMOO. Some would probably add that it wasn't even sex, since no physical bodies were involved in any "immediate" sense. Here, I would have to disagree. But no matter which way these steamy, sensuous, online encounters are labeled, they did have important consequences for my understanding of online embodiment and sexuality. These were experiences that I certainly brought with me to the field, and that were helpful in advancing my understanding of the connections among sex, text, and the virtual body, to paraphrase Shannon McRae (1996).

As opposed to the kind of fieldwork where being, living, and staying in the field is the only option, online ethnography brings with it the possibility of "cycling through" (Turkle, 1995, pp. 12–14) different layers of windows and locations, to the point where the borders between them may start to blur. What consequences does this cycling through have for the kind of knowledge we can form in online field sites? Is it relevant to make visible experiences that border the field, but that are not *of* the field? Or, as Kendall puts it in her chapter, "How do we know what we know? What do we tell people about how we learned what we learned in the field?" (p. 102).

Kendall's chapter is an act of bravery. I sympathize deeply with her ambition of "doing fieldwork with the whole body, and not cutting off certain types of experience as irrelevant or inappropriate" (p. 101), and I find the ways in which she revisits her fieldwork with heightened attention to its erotic aspects to be potentially important sources of knowledge both productive and daring. In particular, I am intrigued by her discussion of gender, sexuality, and power. She brings in the question raised by Markham (2005c) of researchers' privilege to chose "whether or not their own embodiment is an issue in the research, even while critically observing the embodiment of participants" (p. 809), but simultaneously argues that putting oneself out there—in particular as a female researcher—is risky business. We risk our credibility as researchers, no matter whether we ourselves regard the ideal of neutral detachment in social science as neither obtainable nor desirable.

Kendall pushes her case even further and argues, "Despite increasing openness about sexuality in general in Western culture, and despite decades of self-reflexivity in qualitative research, talking about sex in fieldwork still crosses a line" (p. 116). I could not agree more.

However, Kendall and I differ in our understandings of what characterizes online embodiment and sexuality. In her chapter, I sense a certain ambivalence in relation to the role of "the body" in online interactions in general and in online fieldwork in particular. She makes a fairly clear distinction between the offline world as the world of bodies, sensuous experiences, crushes, and physical attraction, and an online world in relation to which embodiment and sexuality are, if not irrelevant, then not quite present. Bodily experiences in her writing enter online fieldwork primarily through aching backs, stiff shoulders, and sore eyes from spending too much quality time with your computer. Although a certain amount of physical attraction plays into the online sessions, making long sittings at the keyboard more interesting and tolerable, most of Kendall's crushes on her informants "began after meeting people in person. In short, they were physical attractions" (p. 106).

My take on embodiment and sexuality online is different. Leaning on the experiences, stories, and secrets that WaterMOOers shared with me about the many intimate connections between textuality and desire—as well as my own experiences in a parallel, text-based universe—I make the case that online attractions, indeed, can be highly physical affairs. On a methodological note, this characterization gives a different meaning to the notion of "doing fieldwork with the whole body." If the virtual can be erotically charged, then this quality highlights the fragility of the limit between body and text in online encounters. It renders unstable the borders of online ethnography, raising an issue discussed elsewhere in this volume about whether the notions of online and offline are as self-evident as they might be portrayed in the writing of internet methodology. To say that the boundaries between bodies and texts are fuzzy in online ethnographies (of the WaterMOO variety) is more than a rhetorical trick. It demands a reformulation of what it means to do fieldwork with the whole body in a field that relies on intense mediations of bodies.

Then again, even if the border between physical and virtual locations is continuously crossed in online experiences—including online ethnographies—there is also a distance separating the two. Actively having to type oneself into being creates a certain gap in this construction. This distance between "the typist" (the person typing) and the textual character can help provide some breathing space—a reflexive understanding of research procedures and of the ways in which oneself as a researcher is always intertwined with these processes. The possible distance between fingers typing and on-screen performances coming to life at your fingertips can be used to create room for reflection on how I, as a researcher, am not only a producer of texts (such as this one) but also always a co-producer of the reality that is being written.

Kendall never moves her discussion of sexuality online into the domain of cybersex, but if she did, her argument might have engaged more clearly with the sensuous, erotic potentials of online textuality itself. In a text-based virtual world, cybersex takes on the character of a rhythmically co-typed narrative of seduction in which typists engage their characters in sexual acts and enactments (see, for example, Branwyn, 1994; Döring, 2000; Hamman, 1996; Marshall, 2003; Waskul, 2003). In fact, the passionate textual acts of cybersex might be the ultimate case study of embodiment online, since in few other moments is the line between the textual and the corporeal so obviously fragile. I agree with Sadie Plant (1998, p. 30) in stating that cybersex is "a merging which throws the one-time individual into a pulsing network of switches which is neither climactic, clean, nor secure."

In the WaterMOO study, I attempted to turn this sense of not being safe into a methodological strategy. Donna Haraway (1997a, p. 190) uses the term "ethnography" in an extended sense, which "is not so much a specific procedure in anthropology as it is a method of *being at risk* in the face of the practices and discourses into which one inquires." Following Haraway, I used the concept of ethnography to allude to a particular mindset in relation to which her notion of being "at risk" seems crucial: "The WaterMOO project was never primarily about 'taking sides.' It was rather about exposing others, as well as myself, to critical inquiry—to engage in the making of online texts in ways that braved initial beliefs and passions" (Sundén, 2003, p. 19). This is a path well worth exploring. The question I need to ask myself at this point is how much I really exposed myself. Looking back, it does not seem like I was at risk quite as much as this quote implies, at least not in the sense of self-exposure.

I did align my project with the reflexive ethnographic tradition of sharing reflections on the research process (such as how I handled the early phase of entering the field, building trust, etc.), as well as of making visible the dynamics around my own presence in the field as a researcher. For example, WaterMOOers tended, initially, to quite self-consciously "put on a show" when I entered a room, well aware of my recording devices and special interest in them. With time, they became more relaxed. I also did bring into the picture the creation and impact of my own online embodiment, from the initial act of creating an online persona, to the embodied motions within and between rooms and locations together with other WaterMOOers. But the WaterMOOers put themselves at risk in a different way by sharing with me their most intimate thoughts and texts. Compared to them, I was playing it safe. We were close, but never intimate. It was a closeness that cannot quite be described as happening on equal terms.

The possibility of getting sexually intimate in the field—as a way of exploring online embodiment and sexuality differently—barely crossed my mind. It must have appeared incompatible with the kind of research ethics that asks questions of the researcher's (mis)use of power over the people he or she studies. The question then is rather, Are there ways of developing ethically responsible risk-taking?

If the conclusion is that making visible our own embodied experiences would be valuable for analyses of (online) embodiment, we should realize that such efforts might backfire in an academic context of departmental hierarchies and traditional gender politics. At the time of the WaterMOO study, I was a relatively young doctoral student in a department with primarily middle-aged male professors. It became clear to me that bringing sexually explicit material to the table (in general, without explicitly including myself) certainly got their attention, but not always in productive ways. "I haven't had time to read it all, but I have, indeed, read *certain* parts of your text," one of them told me with a smile and a wink. Such episodes should not stop us from examining the critical role that sexuality and desire might play in ethnographic work. We need to keep taking risks to continue the expansion of the field of possible and legitimate knowledge production.

❖ RECOMMENDED READING

For discussion and research on cybersex, see, for example, Branwyn (1994), Döring (2000), Hamman (1996), Marshall (2003), McRae (1996), Plant (1998), and Waskul (2003).

For discussions of gender and feminist ethnography, see, for example, Balsamo (1990), Callaway (1992), Enslin (1994), Lengel (1998), Skeggs (1994, 2001), and Warren and Hackney (2000). In addition to Lori Kendall's references on intimate methods, sexuality in the field, and research ethics, see Irwin (2006).

To better understand the kind of "ethnographic attitude" of being "at risk" that Donna Haraway argues for, see Haraway (1997a, 1997b, 2000). See also Lather (2001). For this type of ethnographic approach in cybercultural studies, see Escobar (1994).

Response to Lori Kendall

John Edward Campbell

❖ ❖ ❖

❖ LET'S (NOT) TALK ABOUT SEX:
  CONSIDERATIONS OF SEXUALITY IN ONLINE RESEARCH

In 1994, Pat Califia wrote that there is "something unsatisfying and dishonest about the way sex is talked about (or hidden) in daily life" (p. 11). I would extend Califia's observation by suggesting that there remains something unsatisfying about the way sexuality is talked about (or ignored) in much academic scholarship. This discourse proves both curious and troubling when one considers the inescapability of sexuality—along with race, gender, class, age, and even body type—in the constitution of our social identities. Indeed, Foucault (1978) argues that sexuality is the primary means by which the body is discursively subjugated; it is the mechanism by which social hierarchies are extended over physical sensations and life processes.

The absence of candid discussions of sexuality in online qualitative research is particularly problematic in light of the abundance of sexual representation in cyberspace. Whether examining chat rooms on IRC or AOL, profiles on social networking sites such as MySpace.com or AmIHotOrNot.com, videos uploaded to YouTube.com, or video chat on ICUII, we find individuals expressing their sexual fantasies, fetishes, and pleasurable practices with great alacrity. The very fecundity of this online erotic universe begs the question of how qualitative researchers could *avoid* discussing expressions of sexuality in cyberspace. With such a question in mind, I build on Lori Kendall's discussion of gender and sexuality in online fieldwork by focusing on some of the theoretical and methodological considerations confronting the researcher when studying sexual communities in cyberspace. Guiding this discussion is the understanding that the erotic is present in every social situation, regardless of the site studied or the sexual identities of either the subject or the fieldworker.

Kendall rightly observes that sexual desire is at once a methodological and an epistemological issue. I would further Kendall's observation by noting that sexuality, as an integral dimension of our subjectivity, is an ontological issue to which the fieldworker needs to give careful consideration. Bette Kauffman (1992) insightfully points out that "the particularities of the ethnographer shape the very selection of what constitutes a 'problem' worthy of study, whose reality or social knowledge will be construed as 'answer,' and what techniques will be privileged for the selection of 'facts' from the flow of things" (p. 192). In practical terms, the fieldworker needs to remain aware that he or she will be sensitive to certain expressions of eroticism while oblivious to or even dismayed by others.

For instance, my sexual identity (which situates me as a gay man) and my particular sexual desires (which draws me to the gay male "bear" subculture) infuse every decision I make (and may not be fully aware of) about what communities I will study and how I will approach those social aggregations. A restricted view of the sexual universe is a challenge confronting every qualitative researcher both online and off. However, the limitations of a singular perspective are compounded by a hegemonic model of sexuality that denies or censures sexual practices that are societally deemed "non-normative." Such epistemological myopia is apparent in the general absence of sexual-minority communities from the existing literature on social relations in cyberspace despite the substantial number of sexuality-minority members who have been early adopters of computer-mediated communication technologies. This omission of sexual-minority experiences from the cyberculture literature has the danger of enacting what Gross (1991) identifies as the "symbolic annihilation" of people who do not conform to the dominant sexual paradigm.

I wrote my monograph—*Getting It On Online: Cyberspace and Gay Male Sexuality* (2004)—to address some of these troubling oversights. At the time I started the study in 1997, most generalizations made about social interaction in cyberspace were based on observations of online straight (and predominantly white) communities, resulting in an incomplete understanding of online social relations. I set out to investigate the presence of sexual tension when conducting fieldwork in a sexually charged space, even if that space was virtual. Problematizing conventional understandings of sexuality, I interviewed men (some identifying as gay, some identifying otherwise) whose erotic desires and sexual practices utterly diverged from the societal norm and often from each other as well. Of particular fascination was how often these men would speak of their own sexual practices as perfectly "normal" or "healthy"—whether those practices involved gaining, muscle worship, bondage, water sports, or vanilla top-and-bottom anal sex—while discounting the erotic practices of others. To avoid privileging or naturalizing my own sexual desires, I continuously reminded myself of the idiosyncratic nature of my own sense of the erotic.

Although, as Weston points out, recent "work in cultural anthropology has stressed the importance of recognizing the researcher as a positioned subject" (1991, p. 13), studying sexual communities necessitates pushing self-reflexivity beyond conventional levels of comfort. Such research involves confronting invasive questions regarding one's own sexual identity and sexual desires. In addition to acknowledging that the researcher's particular "turn-ons" are as culturally constructed as those of subjects, such study also requires an awareness that sexual identity involves more than a binary claim to being "straight" or "gay." Sexual identity equally encompasses the researcher's particular sexual desires, how these desires intersect with other axes of identity, and, most importantly, how these desires inform the very sense of self. As such, sexual identity is thoroughly enmeshed with issues of hierarchy and power.

Bell and Valentine (1995) discuss the power dynamics inherent in the researcher-researched relationship in regard to the study of sexuality. Specifically, they warn of collapsing a shared marginalized sexual identity with a shared power position in conducting research, noting that "our research relationships and the way we report them cannot (indeed must not) be kept impersonal and clinical"; instead we must "be reflexive about how we feel about our respondents—owning up if we feel sexually attracted to them rather than struggling to maintain a false front of objectivity" (p. 26). Bell and Valentine attempt to open a space for more critical and positioned ethnographic work in which the researcher reflexively interrogates his or her own role as researcher *and* as positioned subject, acknowledging that although reflexivity makes the potential audience more aware of power inequities, it *does not* erase them. Thus it is vital for the researcher to acknowledge if there is a sexual interest on either the researcher's or the subject's part even when the researcher makes a concerted effort to *bracket* his or her desires in the field.

By "bracketing," I refer to the methodical monitoring of the researcher's own online discourse, communicating clearly to participants whether he or she is speaking to them as a researcher or as a community member. In my own research, when conducting formal interviews, I avoided initiating any discussions I suspected would be construed as libidinous or even as inappropriately personal. If I wanted to engage in a personal (sexual) discussion with an individual, it would have to wait until another occasion when we were not interacting under the auspice of research. This is not to suggest that my personal experiences and desires do not shade my interpretations. Indeed, it would be dishonest to suggest that one can "bracket out" all of one's expectations and sentiments regarding a group with which one has significant personal investment. Rather, my methodological strategy in approaching these sexually charged relations between myself as researcher and my subjects is simply to be honest with the reader—to include these very social dynamics as objects of analysis and critique. As Hammersley and Atkinson (1995) remind us, the researcher's interpretations "need to be made explicit and full advantage should be taken of any opportunities to test their limits and to assess alternatives" (p. 19).

Of course, there are analytical dangers to studying any subject to which one has such a close identification. In her work on gay kinship, Weston (1991) discusses the unique challenge of conducting research within a community with which one has "a common frame of reference and shared identity," noting that the greatest difficulty confronting such a researcher is in the "process of making the familiar strange" (p. 14). In this regard, my strategy in online interviewing has been to keep conversations open-ended and to ask participants to explain to me the significance of online social practices to which I was already accustomed. In this process of making the implicit explicit, I hoped to be surprised by the connotations of things I thought I already understood. In the written account, I allow as much as possible the "voices" of those participating in this study to "speak" directly to the reader, endeavoring to have members of these online communities explain their practices in their own words while never losing sight of the constructedness of any written account.[1]

It is vital then for the researcher as "the research instrument *par excellence*" (Hammersley & Atkinson, 1995, p. 19) to open him- or herself up for inspection, allowing the seams of the research to show. One means toward this goal is incorporating what Grindstaff (2002), and earlier, Van Maanen (1988) identify as the "confessional tale" into the written account. Reflecting the influences of both feminist researchers and poststructuralist thinkers, the "entry of confessional tales into the fieldwork canon is part of a larger culture moment in which disciplinary canons of all sorts are being challenged and in which truth and knowledge are taken as historically situated, partial, and incomplete" (Grindstaff, 2002, p. 276). This "confessional tale" should not be mistaken for some self-indulgent narcissistic practice, but rather as a way of maintaining an open channel of communication with the reader. Put into practice, maintaining that open channel involves keeping a detailed journal of events in the field as well as incorporating the researcher's own online discourse into the written account so the reader can see how the researcher actually interacted with subjects.[2] The final account should include the oversights and limitations of the fieldwork in the understanding that all research enterprises are inherently incomplete.

With this in mind, researchers need to assiduously contemplate what ethical responsibilities they have in constructing representations of sexual communities in cyberspace. I felt a deep sense of privilege and responsibility that those participating in my study were willing to talk candidly about their online experiences even when recounting events that had proven emotionally painful. As those participating in the study were so forthright about their online experiences—including their online erotic experiences—I was intellectually and ethically obliged to be open about my own online (erotic) experiences with the reader, despite the fact that such candidness often left me feeling vulnerable and exposed. This openness involved discussing how my desires and those of my subjects were negotiated in the field, admitting that at times any distinction between my role as researcher and my role as friend or even sexual interest blurred.

In confronting these ethical considerations, the safest strategy for the online researcher is simply to be honest with the reader. One does not need view an ethnographic monograph as an instrument of confession (which Foucault suggests functions as a disciplinary means of surveilling and containing sexual behavior) to have a forthright discussion of erotic tension in the field. However, acknowledging the sexual identity of the researcher in relation to those studied enables the reader to more critically assess which social dynamics may have been neglected and which privileged in the field.

Kendall notes that gender seems a safer topic for academic discussion than that of sexuality, even though Foucault (1978) and Butler (1990) see the social construction of the gendered body as inextricably intertwined with the social construction and deployment of sexuality. Still, gender is often discussed in terms that avoid the sexual, for the sexual remains forbidden territory. As Kendall points out, "despite decades of self-reflexivity in qualitative research, talking about sex in fieldwork still crosses a line" (p. 116). I invite the online qualitative researcher to hold that line up to interrogation. Who draws the line and who is positioned on the other side? Such interrogation will reveal much about the hierarchies our culture has constructed around sex and sexuality.

❖ RECOMMENDED READING

For some of the earliest cyberculture work to look at online expressions of sexuality, including the experiences of sexual minorities in cyberspace, see articles and book chapters by Correll (1995), Hamman (1996), Shaw (1997), and Woodland (2000); two essays by Nina Wakeford (1996, 2000); and, more recently, a chapter by Poster (2002). Kate O'Riordan and David Phillips' recent collection, *Queer Online: Media, Technology, and Sexuality* (2007), reflects the continued evolution of this line of inquiry.

For insightful discussions of sexuality and space, see Bell and Valentine's (1995) edited collection, *Mapping Desire: Geographies of Sexualities,* and Bouthillette, Retter, and Ingram's (1997) collection, *Queers in Space: Communities, Public Places, Sites of Resistance.*

For theoretical discussions of the social construction of sexuality and gender, read Foucault's (1978), *The History of Sexuality: An Introduction, Volume I* ; Butler's *Gender Trouble: Feminism and the Subversion of Identity* (1990) and *Bodies That Matter: On the Discursive Limits of "Sex"* (1993); and Stone's (1996), *The War of Desire and Technology at the Close of the Mechanical Age.* Examples of the metholodogical application of some of these theoretical insights to the enactment of gender in cyberspace can be found in Mia Consalvo and Susanna Paasonen's diverse collection, *Women & Everday Uses of the Internet: Agency & Identity* (2002).

For theoretical discussions of the role of the body in cyberspace and online embodiment, see Braziel and LeBesco's (2001) collection, *Bodies out of Bounds: Fatness and Transgression;* McRae's (1997) "Flesh Made Word: Sex, Text and the Virtual Body," in David Porter's collection, *Internet Culture* (1977); and O'Brien's insightful article (1999), "Writing in the Body: Gender (Re)Production in Online Interaction," in Smith and Kollock's collection, *Communities in Cyberspace* (1999).

For readings on the gay male "bear" subculture, see Mosher's (2001) chapter, "Setting Free the Bears: Refiguring Fat Men on Television," in Braziel and LeBesco's collection, *Bodies out of Bounds: Fatness and Transgression* (2001), and Wright's (1997) collection, *The Bear Book: Readings in the History and Evolution of a Gay Male Subculture.*

For an experimental approach to the online ethnographic study of gender, see Schaap's (2002), *The Words That Took Us There: Ethnography in a Virtual Reality.*

For particularly insightful discussions of sexuality and reflexivity in ethnographic fieldwork, see Weston's *Families We Choose: Lesbians, Gays, Kinship* (1991) and *Long Slow Burn: Sexuality and Social Science* (1998).

For a method of discourse analysis incorporating the thought of poststructuralist thinkers such as Michel Foucault, see interpretive repertoire analysis introduced in Potter and Wetherell's (1987) *Discourse and Social Psychology* and employed with great success in Hermes' (1995) *Reading Women's Magazines.*

❖ NOTES

1. Methodological considerations do not end with the collection of data in the field. Historically, careful decisions had to be made about the best approach to transcribing the discourse of subjects. Concerning the transcription of oral narratives, Catherine Kohler Riessman (1993) indicates that transforming "spoken language into a written text" is a serious endeavor, involving theoretical and interpretive decisions "because thoughtful investigators no longer assume the transparency of language" (p. 12). Riessman continues: "Different transcription conventions lead to and support different interpretations and ideological positions, and they ultimately create different worlds" (p. 13). However, research in cyberspace presents different considerations as the very technologies underlying computer-mediated communication can also provide the researcher with analyzable data of online interaction. The fundamental difference, however, is that this transcribed text is static, whereas with synchronistic modes of online interaction, the text appears fleeting.

2. In analyzing the discourse of subjects, a useful approach originates in social psychology: Developed by Potter and Wetherell (1987), "interpretive repertoire analysis" involves identifying "recurrently used systems of terms used for characterizing and evaluating actions, events and other phenomena" (p. 149). Hermes uses this approach in her study of women's magazine consumption, noting that repertoire analysis, "though grounded in poststructuralist theory, differs from other forms of discourse analysis in that the social subject is theorized not just as an intersection of discursive structurings but as an active and creative language user" (1995, p. 26). This approach is helpful in discerning what interpretive strategies participants employ in making sense of community practices and the researcher-subject relationship.

QUESTION FIVE

How Can Qualitative Researchers Produce Work That Is Meaningful Across Time, Space, and Culture?

Annette N. Markham

❖ ❖ ❖

What we understand to be "global" is itself constituted within the local; it emanates from very specific agencies, institutions and organizations whose processes can be observed first-hand.

(Michael Burawoy, 2001, p. 151)

Mutual understanding [cannot] be accounted for in terms of either unequivocally shared knowledge of the world or linguistically mediated literal meaning. It becomes . . . actual and reciprocal assumed control of what is meant by what is said and, in some sense, a self-fulfilling faith in a shared world.

(Ragnar Rommetveit, 1980, p. 109, emphasis in original)

In 2004, I moved from Chicago to the U.S. Virgin Islands (USVI) to take a post at the university there. Before I moved, I had visions of swimming in the coral reef during lunch hour and contemplating new research topics while sitting in the shade of the palm trees lining the

Responding essays by Elaine Lally (pp. 156–164) and Ramesh Srinivasan (pp. 165–171).

beach on campus. I would be teaching and researching in paradise. Although I had traveled extensively before, I had never before worked in a Second World environment. I learned a lot in the first few weeks of being on the island, but perhaps the most surprising moment was when I realized I had completely forgotten about electricity.

I lived just above the sea cliffs on the remote northern side of the island, where the Atlantic meets the Caribbean. One day during hurricane season the power went out for several hours. A major storm was brewing; in the eerily dark afternoon, I had my cordless telephone, a mobile phone with no service signal, a laptop, and several e-mail addresses. None of these, including the URL addresses to streaming online radio, helped me figure out how bad the storm was or how long the power outage would last. All my tools required an external power source that was no longer available.

That afternoon, looking past the pile of useless gadgets toward the swiftly darkening storm clouds, I realized three important things about myself and my research: My everyday behaviors were developed in a cultural context of ready access to basic goods and services, my modes of communication were overly dependent on electronic technologies, and my working theories about new technologies for communication were embedded in invisible infrastructures of privilege. As a middle-class white mainlander American academic, I enjoyed the luxury of taking for granted the existence of such a mundane thing as electricity.

This was going to really mess up the tidy categories of my academic and social life.

I had to rethink everything. How could I have forgotten about electricity?

My only exposure to internet use in the Caribbean had been Miller and Slater's (2000) study of Trinidad. As an internet researcher in the Virgin Islands, I soon realized that I cared about and was attached to the internet far more than anyone else. On the islands, the internet is useful but not indispensable. Radio is much more ubiquitous and central to everyday life, because its transmission survives when the power—or the money—is gone. These islands have the highest cost of living as well as the lowest average income in the United States. Those with money can afford to pay the high monopoly prices for connectivity. For the vast majority of people, however, broadband (much less internet) is not even tenth on their list of needs.

When technologies fail economically or physically (and the question on the islands is when, not if, they will fail), the residents' very palpable struggle to survive continues. For many, life is lived close to the bone.

In 1995, when Hurricane Marilyn hit St. Thomas, USVI, it wasn't the biggest news on the mainland United States, but to the local population it was devastating. In addition to the immediate physical destruction of property, the infrastructure crumbled. Although some people had electricity and running water in a matter of weeks (not unexpectedly, those with money and connections), others waited more than nine months (read: Nine months?!) for those basics. Certainly, life without running water, refrigeration, or adequate communication systems might describe everyday life in many places around the world, but surely not here, in this U.S. Protectorate, proclaimed to be "Paradise" and acknowledged as the #1 cruise ship destination in the Caribbean.

The same year, but worlds away, I was living in an insulated college town in the Midwest, learning that all academic inquiry necessarily involves abstraction. Almost immediately upon turning our analytical gaze to examine a phenomenon, we extract it from its context. We study phenomena (and in qualitative inquiry, this is often in situ), we capture particular moments as snapshots, we package and present our findings in a mode suitable to our target audiences. The product of our research is several times removed from experience.

Scholars have long discussed the concept of being "situated," though feminist scholars brought this concept to the foreground of social inquiry in the 1980s and 1990s.[1] Laying out powerful critiques of the ethnocentric, patriarchal, and colonialist traditions in the practice of science and the production of knowledge, scholars across disciplines called for more direct attention to the identification and/or interrogation of the frames delimiting the processes of inquiry, as well as the social, economic, geographic, cultural, racial, and gendered position of the researcher.

What I didn't comprehend at the time I was first exploring these stances in qualitative inquiry was the extent to which each of us is situated in a particular locale as well as point of view. Our theories about how the world works are bounded by invisible frames, built not only from our disciplinary training but also from our position, as described above. I had *thought* that I was conducting interdisciplinary, multisited, even "global" qualitative research of the internet. I had been well trained in the methods of interpretive sociology, in negotiating my own voice within multiple perspectives and situating my work. Yet all of my premises, all my reactions to stimuli in the field, all my interpretations of discursive behaviors, and even all my frames for writing seemed still locked within some powerful and, more importantly, invisible structures for sense-making.

No matter how much I had strived to reveal the frames influencing my life and work over the years, I had still forgotten about electricity. There is often, if not always, a disconnect between the idyllic paradises of tourist brochures and the realities of Second or Third World living. Likewise, there are disconnects between our imagined lives as reflexive researchers and the extent to which we are one of the "Others" of our research projects.

I glibly entered into a new cultural context in 2004, dreaming of white sand beaches and snorkeling during my lunch hour. Each day brought a new definition to and sobering reality about where I had chosen to live. But I only truly identified the cultural presuppositions I had used to conduct internet research when I faced my useless technologies in a storm and bemoaned my inability to *do* much of anything except hope that my accidental supplies of peanut butter (which I had obtained without realizing this was a perfect food choice for emergencies) would allow me to ride it out.[2]

This experience may seem tangential to the topic of qualitative internet research, but it speaks to what, for me as an interpretive ethnographer, lies at the heart of the question of this chapter: Is it possible to make one's research more global and meaningful across time and cultural boundaries? Even if it is possible to do so, and I argue it is not, should this even be a primary goal? This dire-sounding response to the question of the chapter is not meant to deter us from our efforts, but is intended rather to emphasize that our research theories, methods, and interpretations are bounded by particular and situated rationalities. We live, conduct research, and find meaning from particular positions. As researchers, our understanding of others is limited by unnoticed frames of reference. Thus, when it comes to the global phenomenon of the internet, social researchers must remain cognizant that global scale does not inherently yield global understanding. The best we can hope for is a shared *faith* that our experiences have common ground or our research findings can be comparable. Featherstone and Venn note that because of digitalization and globalization, "we have to abandon many of the [Western] universalistic assumptions, for example about linear temporality and progress, and instead start from a perspective which emphasizes global *variability*, global *connectivity*, and global *intercommunication*" (2006, p. 2, emphasis in original). Even so, as Burawoy notes in the quote beginning this chapter, understanding, sensemaking, and cultural meaning are all constituted within the local, and as qualitative researchers, that is fundamentally where we are situated.

In this chapter, I focus on the concept "global" and discuss the ways in which building reflexivity into one's research design can help situate one's work, internally and externally. By "research" I mean both the process and product of inquiry. By "situated" I mean located in a particular historical, local, and political place. By "internally and externally," I mean to include those factors influencing the design, process, and write-up of the study, as well as those elements that link the specific study to larger contexts of meaning, whether physical, theoretical, or cultural. By "reflexive processes" I mean the method of looking recursively and critically at the self in relation to the object, context, and process of inquiry. In a crass sense, this is less like looking in a mirror and more like trying to look at yourself looking in the mirror (for more elegant treatments of this concept, see Ashmore, 1989; Lynch, 2000; or Woolgar, 1988).

❖ QUALITATIVE INTERNET RESEARCH: A LOCAL AND GLOBAL ACTIVITY

At least in the United States, new communication technologies—including the internet—are decidedly among the hottest areas of study in the social sciences and humanities disciplines. Even after a decade of exponential growth of these areas of research, there is still the alluring opportunity to study something that nobody has studied before, to develop new theories, and to access and use amazing technologies in one's research.

In this environment of swift, global transformations and marked shifts in disciplinary attention, it is vital to remain firmly rooted in and aware of the local—not just because all objects of inquiry are localized but also because it is only by examining one's local premises, situated in a physical locale and saturated with certain particularities, that one can hope to recognize how one's work is situated in larger contexts.

I take communication and information technologies to be subsumed within the concept of the global, because they are the means by which we are more able to conceptualize and concern ourselves with "the global." Arguably, all internet use is local, but unless it happens within the same room among members of the same kinship group, it occurs within and constitutes the global. It behooves us to consider, then, what the term might entail. I find myself asking three questions:

1. What does the term "global" mean, anyway?

2. How can qualitative methods be used to address global concerns?

3. How can qualitative researchers produce research that is meaningful and relevant to a global audience?

It may be risky to perpetuate a binary distinction between the terms "local" and "global," because lived experience in a media-saturated world seems to meld together into a hybrid, the "glocal" (see Kraidy, 1999, for a clear articulation of this term). However, it is useful to retain the distinction for purposes of focusing less on how people in general experience this hybrid existence and more on how qualitative researchers have approached social phenomena, using particular (situated) procedures to define the parameters of the field, collect information, apply theoretical and analytical lenses in the interpretive process, and write research reports.

For example, globalizing trends as well as media attention to the term "global" encourage researchers to conduct studies based on global datasets, use global frameworks, or speak to a global audience. Yet, social problems themselves, which help us identify topics for research, always occur at the local level. It is at the local level where qualitative research contributes a wealth of possibilities, because it is uniquely developed to grapple with in-depth study of the individual case.

Given this, one might ask, Can qualitative research be global? This question is interesting because it immediately raises the a priori questions of whether or not qualitative research can be conducted on a global *scale* or in a global *manner*, which lead us in decidedly different directions. Another way to get at the difference is to ask this question: Does the term "global" refer to the dataset collected, the author's mindset, the applicability or generalizability of findings, or the audience of the work? These are key questions to address, individually and in tandem.

A related but less explored way to approach this issue is to look at the other side of the same coin: What does it mean to be local? Does the term "local" refer to the physical location of the object of study or the proximity of the researcher to this object, the theoretical situation (standpoint and/or historicity) of the researcher, or the closeness of connection or fit between the researcher and the researched?

Exploring each of the multiple definitional delimiters mentioned in the previous two paragraphs is a useful exercise while recalling that, in practice, these elements are intertwined. This exploration in turn can remind us of the complexity of the process of conducting internet research in and of global contexts.

❖ OPERATIONALIZING THE TERM "GLOBAL"

Considerable caution should be used when tossing around the term "global." As has been remarked about general systems theory, this term encompasses everything and therefore explains nothing. "Global" and other related terms such as "globalizing" or "globalization" encompass so much that they have little definitional value alone, without significant qualification. In this section, I complicate the definition of the term to demonstrate the value of its exploration.

The internet is certainly globally distributed, which without clarification can seem to imply that it is a universal or monolithic technology available everywhere to everyone. Naïve application of this premise leads to oversimplification of technologies that are, in actuality, *differentially* distributed and have different meanings in different global contexts. Even as this premise is laid out, it assumes what it seeks to critique: the unproblematized use of the phrase "global contexts." What is a global context? The term is terribly vague, based on a presumed but unclarified understanding of "global." Is it a verb, noun, adverb, or adjective? An object, subject, or predicate? Process, product, or epoch? Or just a broader categorical code word for "Other," used mostly by Westerners? Of course it can be any of these things, but if it remains undefined in published accounts using the term, the term loses power, even as it enables, often usefully, the illusion of shared understanding through its ambiguity.[3]

Before one can consider how to be "more global" in one's research, one must determine what that term actually means in the specific context of one's research project. I present in this section some possible operational definitions, but the researcher should look beyond these definitions. A simple Google search for "define: global" yields a dizzying array of meanings, each of which is legitimate and, in practice, should be operationalized carefully, continuously problematized in the course of research, and spelled out for readers.[4]

Global can provide a shorthand way of describing anything beyond the local, anything other than the singular, anything beyond one's own scope of knowing.

Global can be a generalization of or to the whole (planet, typically), generalized to include not just all noted locations but those unnoted as well, in much the same way that sampling techniques are used to generalize to entire population groups.

Global can be a unit of measure, whether it seeks to encompass the entirety described earlier or not. In this way, researchers can discuss the global nature of their data.

Global, when used in relationship to "globalization" can be usefully conceptualized as an *effort* or, from another perspective, as an *effect*.[5] Certainly, there are many efforts toward large-scale (global) homogenization or unification on some front. One can note such entities as the WTO, such companies as McDonalds, or even the operation of such concepts as democracy when beginning to think about this notion (these topics have been well developed by a range of scholars too numerous to mention here). Shifting one's vantage point from production to consumption or from mainstream to margins, these same examples can be used to illustrate globalization as an effect.

Global can refer to the concept of capacity, when discussed in the context of the internet as an information network, one might focus on "global" as a capacity. From one angle in the prism (as Kendall discusses in Chapter 1), the internet provides people with access to the same information resources from many points on the planet, or multiple information resources from a single point. Shifting the prism slightly enables another operationalization of the concept: The seemingly limitless and, more important, all-encompassing capacity of the internet promotes the illusion that access to this *entirety* of information yields knowledge and sometimes even power; this illusion is founded on the faulty notions that access equals use and transmission equals understanding.

Global, when discussed in the context of the internet as a place, can mean, among other things, distributed (not physically centralized) cultural units, unified and homogeneous (as implied in the colloquial English usage of McLuhan's term "global village") or independent and isolated nodes of special interest.

The definitions of the term "global" are endless. Identifying one's predispositions and frames, whether in relation to this term or to others, is an essential methodological move that enables one to reflexively choose what is relevant and meaningful to the specific study, as well as what is equally plausible but not chosen as a frame or path.

If one is not explicitly studying global internet issues or conducting inquiry from a "global" perspective, why is it important to engage in reflexivity about the term? Arguably, it is increasingly necessary as one's network of study participants, colleagues, and readers become more widespread and diverse because of internet-based communication technologies, crossing occupational, disciplinary, national, and, clearly, cultural boundaries.

To inject a note of caution—it is important to remember that in the iterative, nonlinear process of qualitative research, questions about the global character of one's inquiry might be more satisfactorily addressed retrospectively, rather than a priori. This is not always the case, of course, but dwelling on the global can lead one too swiftly away from the concrete into the abstract. Qualitative inquiry enables us to focus on the detailed local level, shifting from the forest to the trees in an iterative fashion. Any study of communication and information technology will be simultaneously local and global, but the power of qualitative approaches is most aptly realized at the local level.

❖ GLOBAL AS THE MANNER VERSUS SCOPE OF RESEARCH

Let us return to a question posed earlier in this chapter: *When does one's work become global?* At the beginning of the project, when the research is being designed? In the conduct of the study, which is at a global scale? In the analysis, which may be using global rather than local frameworks? Or in the conclusions of the study, when the local and the global are compared or otherwise connected? Arguably, these are not the most useful questions. Although the term "global" might imply a planet-wide field site for research or the application of universal principles in the interpretation of social behavior, qualitative research methods are designed and best suited for close analysis of the local. The term "global" gains more usability when applied as a guide for one's sensibilities rather than for one's scope.

Whether one follows the people, the object, the metaphor, the conflict, or the story line, the use, influence, production, and effects of the internet are not homogeneous and ubiquitous, but instead specific and concrete. Local experience is always the object of analysis. How one makes sense of it, on the other hand, is a situated act that can enact more global sensibilities. For instance, Michael Burawoy's multi-authored collection *Global Ethnography* (2000) illustrates excellent comparative interpretations across population groups or shifting locales. In some cases, data were collected in more than one context, which means those studies were multi-sited, but they are not global in the sense of encompassing the entire globe. In other cases, researchers apply multiple perspectives from different cultural understandings to interpret data. I take this to mean (and I believe Dr. Burawoy and the other authors of chapters in his collection would agree) that the interpretation is multi- or poly-vocal, but not that there was some sort of universal, global perspective. Miller and Slater's *The Internet: An Ethnographic Approach* (2000), is often categorized as an illustration of global ethnography, when in fact, it is an intensively localized study of the use of globally accessible media (albeit in two primary locales, London and

Trinidad). Likewise, George Marcus's (1998) writings on "multi-sited ethnography" are often interpreted as discussions of global inquiry but, when read closely, are more reflective of the need, in an era of globalizing media, to connect the local to the global and to allow boundaries of the field to be emergent and fluid rather than predetermined and unnecessarily restricted, as was natural in traditional ethnographies.

I oversimplify these works not because they are simple but to point out that, on close inspection, key advocates of global ethnography are actually arguing for close, local work that incorporates global sensibilities, not work that is global in scale. This is not a simple task for most of us. The notion of "having global sensibilities" may be difficult to comprehend, much less enact. Our interpretive lenses generally focus at the close level of discourse. Although we may be trained to shift our lens from the empirical to the abstract or theoretical, our gaze to the extant edges of the forest stops at the limits of our own situated, local imaginations. So, although the local context is never disconnected from larger contexts, it is impossible to think at global scales. The interpretive frame of the researcher is trained to work inductively. This approach requires sensitivity not only to the context we're studying but also sensitivity to ourselves as objects foreign to the world around us, both in the context we're studying and outside it, in the rest of the world.

Being global, then, is not a matter of developing a larger range or scale; this goal is incommensurate with the general principle of qualitative inquiry that seeks depth within case, rather than generalization across cases. Given the primary strength of qualitative research as studying human social behavior using close, inductive interpretive methods, it is appropriate to strive to approach research in a more global manner.

❖ REFLEXIVITY: A METHOD OF FINDING THE
    LOCAL(E) SO AS TO PLACE IT WITHIN THE GLOBAL

How do we understand ourselves beyond our personal experience in order to understand our orientation to the world? How can we become, as Bauman (2005) describes, nomads making our homes at the crossroads of culture? Being saturated with global stimuli does not necessarily allow us to truly know some sort of "Otherness" outside our local context, nor will it grant us a global orientation. Even if it did, this saturation is not an equal transfer, as privilege, politics, and even media habits determine the extent to which one has access to multiple perspectives and can reflexively incorporate them into one's research practice.

To even begin to think "outside the box," it is necessary to grapple with the notion that, because we live and work within invisible frameworks, we are to a certain extent foreign to ourselves. For most researchers (indeed for most people), these frameworks are not easily identified, much less acknowledged. Yet, to adopt more global sensibilities, this inwardly directed reflexive inquiry is necessary. Such inquiry is partly a matter of recognizing that the self, the phenomenon, and the research project are all located in particular, small arenas, yet must be woven with or contextualized within other encompassing ecologies that themselves cannot be comprehended or encapsulated. It's a matter of "placing" oneself, which requires the practice of "othering" one's own premises, actions, and interpretive tendencies.

Logistically, reflexivity is a method of gaining greater sensitivity to the local and global contexts, of identifying one's own location, and of establishing a sense of rigor in one's research.[6] Reflexivity can be practiced in all stages of research.

❖ REFLEXIVITY AS AN ANALYTICAL AND RHETORICAL METHOD

Whether one strives to be global or not, one's research will be read globally by audiences who have varying experiences with and attitudes toward the technologies discussed or used in one's research. So while one should remain closely focused locally, one should be prepared to deal with a global, technologically—as well as otherwise—diverse audience for research reports.[7] I take this to be initially a *reflexive* and, later, a *rhetorical* challenge. How can I help guide my readers so that they understand my work?

My first challenge is to interrogate my cultural and conceptual frameworks to situate my object of analysis and method of inquiry in relation to other people, places, and things. Later, as I try to convey my interpretations to the world of readers, my challenge is to try to make my work sensible and meaningful to people situated elsewhere, while understanding that "shared understanding" is ultimately impossible in an intercultural or even interpersonal sense. At this impossible juncture, one can only interrogate one's own research premises to a certain degree. Then, one's challenge is to find rhetorically sensitive strategies to help locate these premises for readers. It may involve guiding the reader through one's reasoning process or providing links from context to theory as a way of mapping the path of one's unique, situated interpretations. Stepping back to the basics, one might begin by considering how one's basic terms might be understood—or not—by someone with a vastly different set of experiences.

Consider these different opportunities for situated reflexivity throughout the research project:

Situate the research question into larger frameworks.

Situate the local context into larger contexts.

Situate the research approach within other approaches and research "camps."

Situate specific procedures within larger sets of assumptions and practices.

Situate decisions among other, alternate choices and paths.

Situate the gendered, racial, classed, affiliated, disciplined self.

Situate the study, as a whole and in its component parts, among larger conversations.

Even if this list is collapsed into a seemingly simpler guideline, such as "Situate the Self and Other" (Other as an all-encompassing term involving everything outside the self), it still constitutes a fairly massive requirement that, if tackled fully, would be laughable in its impossibility.

Attention to this list, at various critical junctures over the course of the study, lends strength to the global quality of one's interpretation. Reflexivity allows one to maintain focus not only on the details of the study but also on the puzzle of how one is making decisions that influence the evolving design of the study. This sort of reflexivity also enables the researcher to situate the lens, the context, and the findings so the work remains relevant even as the technologies change. In this way, research can sustain meaning over time to more global audiences far beyond the local.

Engaging in reflexive self-analysis won't yield some all-encompassing, global, capital "T" truth, but it is extremely productive along with other strategies in building rigor into one's research. Reflexive self-analysis is a part of every phase of the study, from the design to the data collection to the editing and sorting of information, the interpretation process, and the writing.

❖ REFLEXIVITY IN ACTION: FOCUS ON THE OBJECT OF RESEARCH

Situating the object or context within the larger picture is again a matter of understanding how the locale of the researcher and the researched is placed inside larger and larger systems of meaning as well as geographies. Here, reflexivity can be thought of as a method of meta-analysis, whereby a researcher can analyze his or her working hypotheses (stated or, more important, unconscious), analytical processes, and ongoing conclusions. This process shifts both naturally and deliberately from the empirical to the theoretical and back again in such a way as to include room for an analytical gaze on the self doing the analysis.

A practical method of beginning this process is through writing, using research journals, making sure to date all entries or modifications. Rather than erasing one's previous thoughts, one simply notes new additions or modifications. Noting the dates of each entry can help illustrate how the researcher is changing through the course of the study. During this process, it is useful to ask questions of oneself such as the following:

How do I know that?

So what?

Why did I conclude that?

What led me to that perception?

In the process of attempting to answer these questions, a researcher is constituting the self as an subject of study along with the other objects. These "data" are interrogated through a critical reflexive lens. This process can help one determine how one's research questions are shifting, how one's perceptions are changing, how these changes influence concordant shifts in research questions, etc. One can see that this focus on method is less about "application of procedure" and more about the "rigor of interpretation." Both fall under the category of "method," but are often thought to occur at different stages of research. Rigor of interpretation is far less discussed in methods texts, partly because interpretation is often considered a subjective, individual act of discussing implications or drawing conclusions. Such conceptions can be misleading; the interpretive process begins even before the first research question is formulated. Because the interpretive process rarely appears in the final research report, its procedural elements remain elusive.[8]

Here, I do not address this issue fully, but provide an example of iterative reflexivity in process. During a collaborative study of Dominican newsgroups with a student, several moments of self-analysis enabled us to refine our analytical lens and identify some of our own foreignness to each other and to the context.

Lesson 1: Even the simplest descriptive details are filtered through the researchers' localized understandings.

In a very early written description of a Dominican newsgroup, the student described the various topics available for conversation. Rather than list all the topics separately, she elected to create categories. She did not consider this an interpretive move but a practical way of reducing a long list of hundreds of topics to a manageable number and presenting specific material in the written report that otherwise would be a too-vague mention of "various topics."

This choice was sensible in that it served to organize her thoughts. But in the process, she was formulating categories and themes before having any systematic intent to guide this selection. In this early description, for example, she listed "gay marriage" under the category of "social discussion," and "politics" under "entertainment discussion."

I asked her, "Do you think it makes a difference how you're grouping these topics into these categories?" After reflection, she realized that it made a significant difference, particularly to people outside the Dominican culture who might not understand the specific context that guided her categorization.

I then asked her, "Why did you select these categories for these two topics?" She began to talk about political discussion in Dominica in general, speaking as a Dominican familiar with this environment. She remarked that political discussions in Dominica or among Dominicans were very different from her experience of political discussions in the United States. She noted that her categories for the online discussion boards were based on her opinion of how people in Dominica discuss things in general, when they're not online.

I asked her, "How are you defining entertainment?" She provided a definition that was much different from what I, as an American, expected to hear. Among other things, she said, "Because Dominicans talk about politics more frequently, as part of social encounters, we consider it a form of entertainment."

"Well, then, how is that different from social discussion?" I asked, and at this point the conversation became too convoluted to retrace here. Suffice it to conclude that we were both struck by the extent to which our definitions differed.

The dialogue helped us recognize the ways that a seemingly practical action of simplifying data into categories was in fact an interpretive act, revealing but also constructing a complex schema of social interaction. Reflexive dialogue helped her identify some invisible aspects of her own perceptions that were influencing the way she characterized others' interactions in her study.

Lesson 2: Our cultural assumptions will influence our interpretation.

At a different juncture in the research project, the student began using gender-specific labels for participants, a move that didn't seem to make sense to me. I asked her how she could identify the gender (biological) of the user. She replied that it was "very straightforward," because "a voice emerged" such that the reader/listener could discern if the user was male or female. Her reasoning, upon questioning, was that the gender roles in Dominican culture are stabilized and people adhere to traditional gender roles. I mentioned an opposing viewpoint: that this internet forum might actually provide one of the few anonymous venues to reject or interrogate pre-assigned gender roles. As she reflected further on her gender assignments, she realized that she was perhaps making hasty decisions based on her own comfort zones and cultural assumptions of uniformity.

Lesson 3: Culturally specific understandings of power and authority influence the interpretive lens.

As we continued to converse over the next two days, the student began to shift her understanding of the environment. Without reading any previous literature about gender in online environments, she modified her interpretation, switching from her original perspective to a new perspective I had mentioned in passing as an alternate explanation.

When we discussed this sudden switch in interpretive lens, she acknowledged that she had allowed my own comment to override her initial, instinctive interpretation. I then asked, "Why did you give up your initial interpretation so readily?"

She replied, "I feel like I need to follow your advice and that I'm not in a position to argue with you." She elaborated that the shift was almost automatic, because of my expertise in internet studies and my position of power.

"This may be indeed true," I said, "but what if I'm wrong?"

As she paused to consider this question, I added that in both her original interpretations and my counterpoint, we were merely making guesses about gender. We decided, eventually and with a great deal of self-directed irony, that it might be useful to ask the members themselves.

During this conversation, the student expressed discomfort with the idea that I might be wrong and continued to pursue my own line of analysis rather than following her own instincts, even though she was closer to the context and far more familiar with the data. Her reaction made sense to me only because I had been living in the Caribbean for a while. There, students are taught that to disagree with a teacher is to show great disrespect. The respect for authority and hierarchy made it very difficult for her to disregard a comment that I made in an off-hand manner.

Notably, the focus of the study narrowed solely because we were attending to this "gender role" detail of social life more than other, potentially equally interesting, viable, or relevant details. The research questions changed. A seemingly small point got bigger and more relevant while other plausible paths faded away. This point became an object for further data collection and analysis (which points to the issue of constructing boundaries developed by Hine in Chapter 1).

Although these lessons may seem tangential to the issue of making one's qualitative internet research more globally meaningful, they actually lie at the heart of the matter. Once we begin the process of interrogating our own premises and interpretations as foreign, we can begin to find ways of connecting them with other contexts for understanding.

This reflexive exercise was conducted in oral form with my student. I find that it is also productive if conducted (with or without help from a colleague) in writing, thereby producing a documented trail of perception and a chronological record of the related shifts in the shape of the study, which might involve shifts in the shape of the field site and focus of study.

Clearly, these shifts in research focus can and do happen naturally. One's perceptions change as one becomes more familiar with the field, one meets and talks with people, or one studies the data. These shifts are characteristic of qualitative research, and attempting to actually avoid this tendency marks a more positivist/modernist orientation to research, in which accuracy is predetermined by the method of measurement rather than inductively derived through introspection and modification of method. The power of qualitative methods can be actually limited if one uses criteria for quality and rigor that are intended for other approaches or if one sticks too rigidly to the study's design as initially planned.

To sustain internal consistency and a good fit between epistemology and method, it is vital to understand and embrace qualitative induction and flexibility; one must understand that research is an ambiguous, messy process that changes constantly until the researcher determines he or she has reached an endpoint. Far from diminishing the quality of the research, this reflexive and messy process lends rigor to the qualitative project. Iterative self-critical writing in research journals is one means of developing reflexive rigor.

❖ REFLEXIVITY IN ACTION: FOCUS ON THE SELF

To make one's work readable by a potentially global audience of people is an impossibility, but if one does not even attempt to connect the local to the global, one's work can remain isolated and foreign to readers. If readers have no signposts to orient themselves within your work, they won't know where you or they are. This is a concern for any writer, but it is particularly important in a global community of internet scholars, each of whom ostensibly studies in the same general arena but comes from a particular standpoint and limitation. As members of that academic community, it is part of our responsibility to provide contextualization for our work.

Locating myself is a process of trying to figure out these issues:

> . . . *where I stand*

> . . . *where I'm coming from*

> . . . *where I can move from, given where I am,*

which helps me understand more about

> . . . *where I'm not*

> . . . *and where others have been that I'm not going, but might be relevant to helping me understand where I am*

Qualitative approaches assist in this process because they are marked by iterative, reflexive processes. Much can be gained by attending closely to those moments when the analytical gaze shifts from the empirical details to the theoretical big picture. As inquiry cycles through observation, analysis, and interpretation, critical turning points provide opportunities to engage in reflexive analysis about the fit between the questions and the phenomenon and between method and question, the ways in which answers are emerging, and the context in which the interpretation is taking place. As this process of reflexive inquiry is sustained, arguably one's research becomes more accessible and comprehensible to audiences outside the self, the context of the study, and the discipline within which the study occurs. Hence, it becomes more global (using global here as a manner or attitude of research rather than a scale or unit of measure).

Extricating one's own history is a specific part of this process. In a sense, by doing so one is creating data for further analysis within the context of the study in progress. Far from being self-indulgent, it is a valuable means of identifying one's frames and boundaries and, through reflexive analysis, considering the connections and disconnections that first inform and, later, situate the study.

Self-reflexive writing exercises can be conducted in any number of ways. The activity of laying out one's premises, standpoints, and so forth should be a part of one's research process (and is a formal part of such methods as phenomenology or grounded theory). Having said that, I also maintain that there are varying degrees to which this stuff should show up in the final report. Even when advocated or supported by the general philosophical approach, weaving this information into the research may not be warranted or advisable.[9] If not understood and therefore handled properly as a method, it can be easily judged as solipsistic.

Still, one might pursue this question: How does this sort of reflexive exercise aid in the process of making research conducted in Finland relevant to people reading it in Japan? Or a study of Dutch community networking relevant to community networking research in any location?

As an exercise within the course of conducting a study, it is aimed at revealing some of the hidden intersections of the self, the local experience of the participants, local history and culture, and scientific inquiry. The outcome of such an exercise is not illustrated above because the example only reflects an initial, externally demonstrable phase of reflexive analysis. This level of detail is often missing in general qualitative method textbooks because it is arduous, messy, and lengthy. The best insights happen outside the texts one might produce in these exercises, so the benefits may not be transmitted in writing.

Another example of this sort of exercise illustrates one way I might begin the process of analyzing the connection (or lack thereof) between my methods of inquiry and possible readers. The exercise helps me identify several possible disconnection points, which through further analysis I can attempt to bridge by applying various persuasive strategies. I begin by addressing a series of questions:

Why might my work be incomprehensible to someone else?

My perspective is unique to me and not accepted by everyone—or possibly anyone—else. I have mashed together such a mess of methods, I'm not sure my work would be seen as "reliable" or "valid" to others. Further, though I may not like or believe in those terms, they're used all the time to assess my work.

What is my perspective?

I'm an ethnographer conducting research on how users feel about technologies. My activities in the field are informed by my use of and familiarity with interpretive qualitative methods, rhetorical criticism, feminism, and critical theory. I believe that interpretations must be derived from and be supported by discourse collected in situ.

What methods do I tend to use in collecting data?

Interview and participant observation, directly, but research journals, indirectly. I write constantly in my research journal, in which I record both my direct observations and my thoughts about my observations. My bad habits in research journal writing: I tend to spin in reflexive circles until I lose focus on the phenomenon. I can second-guess myself endlessly.

What methods do I use in analyzing data?

As someone who calls herself an ethnographer, I'm sometimes baffled by the fact that the one tool I don't use is ethnography. From my perspective, this term describes a mindset or epistemological approach more than a specific set of interpretive procedures. I find it lacks the procedural specificity required to systematically analyze actual field data.

So what do I use? Initially, I just dump my toolbox upside down and try different approaches. Everything that can be considered as data is at some level "text." Whether it's an interview or an observation, visual or verbal, it can be read and analyzed as text, sometimes more literally than other times.

I borrow heavily from rhetorical criticism methods, because the systematic procedures help organize the data early in the process. I might conduct a metaphor or narrative analysis. I find these methods particularly useful in breaking down the structure of text into thematic categories that can be then further studied, using still other sense-making lenses.

Later in the process I use deconstruction methods, mostly in the way they've been applied in organizational analyses. I pay attention to how stories, arguments, or web sites might be rewritten, how binaries are being displayed, how my own binaries are operating on my analysis.

I generally try to follow grounded theory procedures as these have evolved from original conception, looking for themes and categories, but end up being less systematic than I believe the method warrants.

Sometimes in the back of my mind, I think about conversational analysis, but I am not rigorous in my application of this method as it is practiced in the United States. Rather, I think about the premises of this approach as I pore through interview transcripts and conversations.

I use the idea of genealogy offered by Foucault, looking backward to find a difference that makes a difference. I find that Foucault's work enables a mindset much more than it provides specific procedures, so I tend to use this as a macro level of interpretation, rather than in early stages of close analysis of texts.

After I conduct rough analyses using a range of methods, I settle into a more refined analysis that utilizes a narrower set of tools.

What else might make my work incomprehensible to someone else?

I mix methods from interpretive, postmodern, and critical schools of research. I have potentially inconsistent theoretical grounding if I think there is such a thing as a logical "argument" but also believe in the postmodern premises that reject binary thinking or "one right answer."

I also differentiate between methods for framing the study, methods for collecting data, methods for analyzing data, methods for interpreting, and methods of writing. This can appear messy or incommensurate to others when it actually is not, because I borrow from multiple schools of thought.

Even my definitions of "Qualitative Internet Research" may be completely bizarre to someone else.

Obviously, as mentioned above, this information will not make my work immediately comprehensible to the audience. This is just an initial exercise to interrogate the self. The objective of reflexivity as a method is to attempt to understand one's own framework in relation to other choices one could make, so that one can make well-founded decisions and articulate these to others. Understanding the fit between one's subject, one's theoretical frameworks, one's methods, and other phenomena in other places is a continual, iterative process in the qualitative project, not a beginning or endpoint. Notably, reflexivity is often an unconscious process, especially if one is not trained to pay attention to this phase of research. In laying out some of the more visible procedures associated with reflexive writing, I seek not to simplify or standardize, but simply to exemplify one way this activity can occur.

❖ CONCLUSION

I have described one aspect of interpretive methodologies, reflexive situating, as a useful way to better understand where the self and research stand and, therefore, how process and product weave together into the larger pattern. Reflexive situating can help facilitate more globally sensitive research, but it is also a keen rhetorical strategy for producing and sharing knowledge. We don't have the opportunity to engage in one-on-one conversation with all the readers of our research, so we cannot anticipate the innumerable questions posed by a potentially global (unit of measure, here) audience. Yet, we can articulate findings more clearly by addressing some of the questions these unknown readers might ask.

When it comes to pragmatic thinking about how to address the question of this chapter, I advocate going back to the basics; the adroit management of contingencies in the ever-changing internet contexts relies on solid grounding in the practices and principles of social inquiry. As any seasoned qualitative researcher will attest, good qualitative research takes time, trial, and error, regardless of how easy and swift the technologies seem or how quickly research papers seem to flood the market after the release of some new technology for communication.

How well will our studies fit within the larger conversations? The interdisciplinary quality of the field of inquiry means that most researchers will fall short of someone else's expectations for adequacy in reviewing previous literatures (excellent criticisms of ahistorical or atheoretical trends are written by Sterne, 2005; Sterne & Leach, 2005; and Carey, 2005). The task of covering one's bases is monumental: Required reading can potentially include all previous studies of internet-related phenomena across multiple disciplines, studies of communication technologies in general (historical and contemporary), as well as attention to discipline-specific literatures. Additionally, to really use the right tool for the job, we ought to have comprehensive knowledge of those methods and practices housed under the increasingly unwieldy and perhaps inappropriate term "qualitative" (see, e.g., Hine, 2005a).

It requires no great leap to realize that one's research will more often than not fail to satisfactorily address even a fraction of those issues, theories, and previous studies relevant to individual readers. This situation therefore requires a keen sensibility to rhetorical strategies, whereby the researcher is able to situate the self and the study. Part of one's methods, then, must include the goal to convey meaning at the crossroads of culture, providing maps and guides for an audience who potentially knows nothing of the method or the criteria used to evaluate quality.

The question of this chapter is interesting because it challenges us to think about our research beyond the narrow confines that are often encouraged if not required by our disciplines. At the same time, because qualitative approaches are most applicable and appropriate to local, detailed study of human social behavior in specific contexts, the question must be critically interrogated. Early in this chapter, I stated that it is impossible to carry meaning across cultural boundaries. This statement is not intended to stymie cross-cultural, globally sensitive research. It is only to remind us that research will always be an abstraction from lived experience—at any level.

Situating one's research is a way of enacting global sensibilities. More specifically, reflexive analysis of one's own boundaries is an ethically powerful way of identifying for the self and for others those limitations and factors influencing one's research choices. Even such an invisible (for me) thing as electricity, for example, influences everyday conceptualizations and uses of the internet, not just for those people in locations where electricity is not guaranteed, but for researchers in privileged and insulated environments.

Thus, beyond the impossibility of operating at a truly global level of scale, there remains the problem that, no matter how global you think your work is, someone else will find a flaw in your thinking, or you might realize these flaws long after the research report is completed. Such is the nature of the larger academic conversation. It's something to accept and embrace, acknowledging as Clifford Geertz (1973) did, that understanding any social setting is like trying to translate a manuscript that is faded and torn. The outcome will always be partial and incomplete.[10] In this way, reflexivity becomes an essential component of inquiry—not to provide a bird's-eye map of the terrain within which knowledge production occurs, but to provide a glimpse of one local position for others, whose local positions inform our own.

❖ RECOMMENDED READING

For a good introduction to and overview of the interpretive turn in qualitative approaches, which grounds and promotes a situated, reflexive stance for researchers, I recommend the collection edited by James Clifford and George Marcus, *Writing Culture* (1986). To problematize the concepts further and to approach the issue from a feminist perspective, I recommend the collection, *Women Writing Culture*, edited by Ruth Behar and Deborah Gordon (1995). To further address this issue in ethnography, I recommend Robin Patric Clair's edited volume, *Expressions of Ethnography* (2003).

For specific methodological advice within this general interpretive framework, I often return to the several works by Harry Wolcott (1994, 1999, 2005) and the three (very different) editions of the *Handbook of Qualitative Research* edited by Norm Denzin and Yvonna Lincoln (1994, 2000, and 2005).

To understand some of the complexities associated with the concept of "global" in relation to qualitative internet research methods, I recommend Michael Burawoy (2000, 2001), George Marcus (1998, 2005), Marwan Kraidy (1999), and Zygmunt Bauman (2005).

Reflexivity is a huge topic. Michael Lynch (2000) lays out a very useful inventory of reflexive positions with reference to associated disciplines/authors/proponents. The specific connection of reflexivity with epistemological standpoint positioning is well developed by Sandra Harding (1991, 1992). Steve Woolgar (1988) offers another useful place to begin. To see reflexivity built into a discussion of reflexivity as a concept, I often return to Malcom Ashmore's *The Reflexive Thesis* (1989). To explore how reflexivity has been applied in contemporary ethnographic research, see various studies published in the *Ethnographic Alternatives* series, published by AltaMira Press and edited by Art Bochner and Carolyn Ellis.

❖ NOTES

1. Haraway's *Simians, Cyborgs and Women: The Reinvention of Nature* (1991a) provides excellent exemplars of this sort of thinking within feminist studies. Also see Sandra Harding's work (1991, 1992)

2. Two notes here: First, this moment calls to mind Goffman's (1974) useful notion of a "frame break," an anomaly that jars the normally transparent frame of reference into visibility. Second, to explain peanut butter to those of us who don't live in storm regions: Peanut butter is a good source of protein that does not need refrigeration and has a long shelf life, thus making it a popular food choice for "hurricane closets," those larders that should be stocked annually with food, water, batteries, radios, and so forth. Another lesson I learned.

3. See Eisenberg (1984) for an explanation of the concept of strategic ambiguity. As applied to emerging disciplinary practices in Internet Studies, see Markham (2005a).

4. Notably, I offer these definitions from the perspective of the researcher interrogating research design. These concepts would be framed differently if detailed from the perspective of lived experience.

5. See Burawoy (2001) for an excellent explanation of this distinction, as well as a more general discussion of the concept of globalization as it is linked to the practice of "global ethnography." For an intriguing take on globalization and rethinking the production of knowledge, see the special 2006 issue of *Theory, Culture & Society* titled "Problematizing Global Knowledge" (edited by Mike Featherstone and Couze Venn).

6. The notion of "rigor" brings up yet another conundrum in qualitative approaches. A useful distinction is made between rigor in application of methods and rigor in interpretation, the latter of which is crucial, but much less discussed in qualitative methods texts (Guba & Lincoln, 2005).

7. The term "glocal" may apply to this state, which, while a useful amalgam of terms, doesn't provide much in the way of practical advice as to how this can be accomplished in one's study.

8. For instance, even in Lori Kendall's explicitly reflexive reanalysis of her BlueSky study (Chapter 4, this volume), the outcome of her reflexivity is far more visible than the process. As she and other interpretive ethnographers have aptly noted, this is a tricky dilemma: How much of the interpretive process does one lay out in the finished report? How much can this process be taught versus simply enacted and refined through practice and time?

9. Such inclusions are more familiar in certain academic arenas, including but certainly not limited to autoethnography (as illustrated by AltaMira Press's *Ethnographic Alternatives* series by Bochner and Ellis), confessional tales (Van Maanen, 1988), feminist narratives (as illustrated by Wolf, 1992),

fragmented narrative (Markham, 2005b), layered accounts (Rambo-Ronai, 1995), and other forms found significantly in postmodern, feminist, postcolonial, and contemporary ethnography arenas.

10. Since this is actually a strong foundation of interpretive qualitative approaches, it may relieve some pressure, if one is taking this approach, to know one's work is neither all encompassing nor, for that matter, the final word.

Response to Annette Markham

Elaine Lally

As Annette Markham argues in her chapter, we all exist in places that shape our perspectives on the world. In particular, the modes of our situatedness that are relevant to our work as researchers include (at least) our disciplinarities and place-specificities. In this response I focus more closely on important issues from my own situated perspective as a technology researcher based in Australia:

- The location you do research from is as important to any consideration of the local and the global as the location you do research in.

- Definitions of "global" may be quite different for people who are differently positioned with respect to mainstream Western modes, and a focus on globalization, as a process with attendant political and economic structures of privilege, can be more useful than looking at the global in terms of unifying perspectives through comparative research.

- Our situatedness gives us a sense of feeling at home in particular places and times, but as researchers we have a responsibility to use research practices that are dialogical and creative and that stretch our comfort zones.

As Donna Haraway (1991b) points out in her influential essay, "Situated Knowledges," there is an ethical dimension to the situated nature of a research practice that is aware of its own situated and embodied nature. Arguing "against various forms of unlocatable, and so irresponsible, knowledge claims" (p. 191), Haraway suggests that the unlocatable fantasy of infinite vision "is an illusion, a god-trick" (p. 189). We need to have

> a critical practice for recognizing our own 'semiotic technologies' for making meanings, *and* a no-nonsense commitment to faithful accounts of a 'real' world, one that can be partially shared and friendly to earth-wide projects of finite freedom, adequate material abundance, modest meaning in suffering, and limited happiness. (p. 187)

For Haraway, such a research practice necessarily "privileges contestation, deconstruction, passionate construction, webbed connections, and hope for transformative systems of knowledge and ways of seeing" (p. 191).

As Markham points out, we inevitably privilege our own situated perspectives, since they are the center of our worldview, but by "examining one's local premises, situated in a physical locale and saturated with certain particularities," we may come to "recognize how one's work is situated in larger contexts" (p. 135). Doing so generally involves, in my own experience as a qualitative researcher, the ongoing development of a willingness and commitment to stretching the bounds of one's personal comfort zone. It's not always easy to do this, since it involves living with a sense of intellectual uncertainty and self-questioning, and there are certainly times when, not infrequently, one wonders whether the effort is worthwhile.

My own situatedness certainly has had a significant impact on the research I've conducted and published. My physical location, a university in the western suburbs of Sydney, Australia, is one dimension of this specificity. Here in Australia, the scholarly community is highly aware of the "tyranny of distance" manifested in the expense and time needed to travel outside the country to conferences and for face-to-face collaboration. While information and communications technologies have transformed the possibilities for feeling connected with our academic networks, it is still the case that time-zone differences, particularly between Australia and Europe and the United States, intervene in the flow of communication, slowing down the dynamic pace of communication that is possible with more synchrony.

The question posed by this book's chapter interrogates the notions of the "global" in relation to studies of new digital technologies. What does the "global" mean? How can we use qualitative methods to address global concerns? How can we produce research that is meaningful and relevant to a global audience?

From the point of view of the "antipodes" (literally the points diametrically opposite their points of reference on the globe), these questions seem much more ambitious and less readily achievable than concerns about processes of globalization or trans-national aspects of life in a relatively isolated locale. Such terms as "globalizing" or "globalization" seem more useful than the '"global" as a thing-in-itself, because they can be defined in terms of processes that have an impact across all ranges of geographic scale.

An important strand in the literature on information and communication technologies (ICTs) deals directly with the relationship between the local and the global; see, for example, Miller and Slater's (2000) ethnographic study based in Trinidad and the United Kingdom; Holloway and Valentine's (2003) study of the cybergeographies of children's online and offline worlds; or Hine's (2000) study of the way the internet is made meaningful in local contexts. But is it important to include the global as a dimension in our research? Perhaps not. From the geographic periphery of the globe, in English-speaking population terms, if not in terms of centrality to academic cultural networks, the urge to "be global" seems less urgent than the need to understand our neighbors. Following Bauman, Markham suggests that to understand our place in the global we must become "a nomad who makes a home at the crossroads of culture" (p. 140). For pragmatic as well as intellectual reasons, many Australian scholars are increasingly developing an orientation toward academic networks in Asia and the Pacific. Scholars from the global South continue to point out that much research written in English continues to be Western- or Euro-centric. Language is certainly a barrier, as English-speaking scholars generally don't have access to the writing of scholars in languages other than English.

Markham asks how one can be more global in one's research. Yet, one could question the desirability of a more global focus in the research we undertake. Even within what seem like very local contexts, say the western suburbs of Sydney with its population of less than 2 million, heterogeneities proliferate at all levels of scale. Diversities of social formation mean that, in practice, things seem to become more rich and interesting as one focuses closer into the local. Arguably, there is now no place in the world where trans-national (rather than global) connections are not fundamental to the processes that are producing local specificities. Perhaps by becoming "more local" in one's research we can dig down to gain greater insights about the specific connections between disparate dimensions of local contexts and gain greater understanding of their dynamics and processes.

What is needed is a better understanding of the local, lived experience of people who may be geographically near but culturally far.

Qualitative research, at its best, conveys not just factual observations but also generates empathy in its readers for the subjects of the research. In *Local Knowledge,* anthropologist Clifford Geertz elaborates the relationship between "experience-near" and "experience-far" concepts (2000, p. 57). The challenge in qualitative research is "to grasp concepts that, for other people, are experience-near, and to do so well enough to place them in illuminating connection with experience-distant concepts theorists have fashioned." This is a task "at least as delicate, if a bit less magical, as putting oneself into someone else's skin" (p. 58). The massive popularity of reality television over the past few years provides good indication of the receptivity of mass audiences to media forms that approach the ethnographic in their depictions of what they observe, no matter how constructed the representations may be to conform to traditional narrative forms and conventions (e.g., the genre of soap opera).

❖ RESEARCHING TECHNOLOGY

How well do our studies fit within the larger conversations? This is a key question. What value will our work have in 5 years, 15 years, 150 years? The findings of research must be useful to other scholars and to the wider society. Our research must provide insights that are generalizable, in the sense that other scholars will find them applicable to the (situated) fields that they study. The application of sound, tried, and tested methodologies for data collection and analysis—that is, those for which there is a widespread consensus about their utility—ensures a level of quality control in the process. When we speak of soundness or rigor in our research processes, we mean, because research is a social activity, that we are speaking within frameworks of discourse and action that are accepted by a community of scholars.

In my own work on home computers (Lally, 2002), my concern in relating the particular and local observations I was making of the people in my study, in combination with the disciplinary background outlined earlier, led me to discuss domestic ICTs from the point of view of several different contexts. I related home computers to other domestic appliances and consumer goods and drew connections to more general concerns expressed in academic literatures on consumption and mass production of material culture. I related home computers to trends in technological development via the history of computers as business and educational technologies and the changes entailed by incorporating them into homes, including transformations in their marketing. Finally, I considered computers from the point of view of how we make ourselves "at home" in our domestic environments (and elsewhere), to the point that an affective and practical relationship of *ownership* is enabled. From the point of view of this final context, although I was dealing with a technology that was outmoded (in terms of contemporary culture) by the time I had finished writing about it, this particular case study had contributed to my own developing understanding of how we construct and maintain our sense of being "at home" in the world.

Our sense of belonging to and feeling at home in the spaces and times we inhabit in our everyday lives is

> inextricably linked with practices and practical knowledges because it involves being able to marshal a set of narratives, . . . appropriate segments of the object world (almost inevitably including nowadays all manner of consumer goods), a repertoire of bodily stances, and so on. Together, these resources generate a "sense of belonging," a feeling that the agent does not have to qualify as a member of a network, being already competent in its spaces and times. (Glennie & Thrift, 1996, p. 41)

It is the everyday practices and practical knowledges of the participants that we are attempting to understand in our qualitative studies. But it is also the case that, as researchers, our sense of belonging to academic networks and fields of study is based on a sense of being competent in these particular spaces and times. We can think of this sense of at-homeness in the everyday social and cultural environments we inhabit as academics/researchers as a kind of "comfort zone."

There is a lot at stake in maintaining a comfort zone as a stable zone of everyday living. Giddens uses the term "ontological security" to refer to "the confidence that most human beings have in the continuity of their self-identity and in the constancy of the surrounding social and material environments of action" (1990, p. 92). Ontological security, as Markham found out in the U.S. Virgin Islands, is only ever a fragile illusion, maintained by our trust in the continuity of our material, social, and technological environments.

The sense of intellectual uncertainty I mentioned earlier in discussing the situatedness of our knowledge production as researchers is always, I believe, a reliable indicator of a comfort zone that is indeed being stretched as we attempt to come to terms with the complexities of research sites and materials, endeavor to achieve new insights into their structures and dynamics, and hope for a favorable reaction to the written results given to others to review.

❖ REFLEXIVITY AND CREATIVITY
AS PART OF THE RESEARCH PROCESS

To what extent is it possible to achieve reflexivity as a researcher? Markham describes it as "like trying to look at yourself looking in the mirror" (p. 135). Reflexivity necessitates a commitment to sticking with uncertainties and recognizing that one's own perspective might be skewed. Research participants[11] are themselves the experts in their own life-world. We need to find ways of challenging our preconceptions about what they may tell us, but importantly, reflexivity is only one part of this process. We need to find "tricks" to bring what we may be taking for granted to the fore, and often these tricks are part of our methods. Focus groups, for example, by putting participants in dialogue with each other, can tell us things that an in-depth interview might not reveal.

Indeed, Markham gives an illuminating example of her discussion with the student studying Dominican newsgroups. The mutual surprise stood out for me as a diagnostic indicator of the disjuncture between the frames of reference and the taken-for-granted "common sense" of both teacher and student. By trying to open up the student's thinking through questioning, Markham exemplifies a pedagogic style that has been referred to as *maieutic* inquiry (Dimitrov & Hodge, 2002, p. 15). Originally developed by Socrates, maieutic inquiry (from the Greek work for "midwifery") proceeds by asking questions in a way that brings about the birth of new ideas in the student (hence Socrates' use of this term). It draws out of students a knowledge that is already latent within them, in potential if not actual form. While this mode of interaction is common in research pedagogy, it is also a component critical to success in the field, as we use the qualitative methods of in-depth interviews and focus groups.

Maieutic inquiry takes the form of dialogue and is a process that reveals the limits of available knowledge and facilitates the emergence of new insights. "If such an emergence occurs, the inquirer and respondent move together beyond the limits of what was considered known by them before initiating the process of inquiry" (Dimitrov & Hodge, 2002, p. 15). It is important that the questioner admits the possibility that her knowledge is limited and that the student or interviewee has independent expertise.

Participants often surprise us in interviews, and one of the most fulfilling experiences in qualitative research is this sense of surprise and wonder. Participants are the experts in their own reality, and our qualitative research methods are often designed to facilitate their own reflexivity—sometimes to the point of them becoming co-researchers, as in the methodology of participatory or action research (see overviews of these methods in Denzin & Lincoln's *Handbook of Qualitative Research,* 2000, 2005). When participants say something surprising, it often feels like being given a precious gem or nugget of gold.

In my home computer study, for example, a retired schoolteacher referred to her PC and the skills it had allowed her to develop as giving her "a handle on the future." As she used this phrase, I knew immediately that it was not only a wonderful turn of phrase (which became a chapter heading in the report and part of a conference paper title) but also that it was like the tip of the iceberg, indicating the existence of a much larger truth (Lally, 2002, Chapter 4). As I told other older participants about this phrase, it emerged that they could all identify to some extent with this sense that computing could give them control over their lives and futures. I found that it resonated with many other study participants too, especially those who had encountered computing as adults and who had a sense that it was important to keep up with technological developments or risk being "left behind."

It's important, I feel, to follow your instincts as an interlocutor with study participants. Another indicator that something very interesting is going on, I have argued, is laughter in the interview context. Laughter can often be read as an indication that there are underlying contradictions or paradoxes that we tacitly agree not to try to resolve, such as a contradiction between what we say we believe and what we actually do. Examples from my own work include attitudes toward software piracy (Lally, 2002, p. 90), a child's exploitation of a parent's goodwill (p. 140) and game playing, and mothers' roles within the family (Lally, 2002, p. 160; Mitchell, 1985, p. 124).

What we take for granted is just that, and perhaps no amount of reflexivity is going to give us the "aha" moment that the storm gave Markham through the sudden loss of power. An undermining shock to ontological security, as she experienced it, is certainly something that can cause a total rethink, necessary to incorporate a new perspective into a worldview. But it's really the reflexive thinking and investigation that we engage in *after* such an "aha" moment that count and that can give us profound insights into our situation in the world.

Importantly, research is a creative process. As Negus and Pickering point out, creative activity is not just about designing and manufacturing artworks or commodities, but is about making collective meaning and communicating our shared experience: "Creativity is a process which brings experience into meaning and significance, and helps it attain communicative value" (2004, p. vii). Through creative activity we combine and recombine symbolic resources in novel ways, so that they tell us something we haven't heard before or had only dimly recognized. Further, partial and situated perspectives are no barrier to the creative process: "Creativity often builds on the shards and fragments of different understandings. . . . we don't just collaborate with people; we also collaborate with the patterns and symbols people create" (Schrage, 1990, p. 41). By actively engaging with new contexts of our social, cultural, and technological lives, as researchers we achieve new ways for creating and sharing our ideas, our views of the world, and our unique experiences.

❖ RECOMMENDED READING

For classics works of ethnographic writing, any of Clifford Geertz's work can be recommended: *Local Knowledge: Further Essays in Interpretive Anthropology* (2000) is a beautifully written and engaging collection of essays on how to study and write about local cultures in broader context. For ethnographic approaches to the internet see Hine's *Virtual Ethnography* (2000) and Miller and Slater's *The Internet: An Ethnographic Approach* (2000).

For empirically based studies of information technologies in family and domestic contexts, see Lally's *At Home with Computers* (2002) and Bakardjieva's *Internet Society: The Internet in Everyday Life* (2005). Livingstone's *Young People and New Media: Childhood and the Changing Media Environment* (2002) provides an excellent mapping of children and young people's use of a variety of media, both old and new. Holloway and Valentine's *Cyberkids: Children in the Information Age* (2003) draws on extensive empirical research to explore children's engagement with ICTs from a cultural geographic perspective.

Moores' *Media and Everyday Life in Modern Society* (2000) situates ICTs within the context of older media forms, including television, radio and telephones, and investigates the position these media play in everyday life and relationships. For recent Australian perspectives on this issue, see the collections edited by Cunningham and Turner (*The Media and Communications in Australia*, 2006) and Goggin (*Virtual Nation: The Internet in Australia*, 2004).

Situating academic debates around the impact of ICTs on society in long-term perspective, Robins and Webster's *Times of the Technoculture: From the Information Society to the Virtual Life* (1999) charts a shift in emphasis from political-economic to cultural. Diverse theoretical approaches to the internet are explored in the edited volume, *The World Wide Web and Contemporary Cultural Theory* (Herman & Swiss, 2000). Bringing together diverse interdisciplinary findings from a UK-based large-scale research program, Woolgar's edited collection, *Virtual Society? Technology, Cyberbole, Reality* (2002), focuses discussion around the question of the relationship between the virtual and the real.

❖ NOTE

1. I prefer the term "participants" to "informants" because the latter seems to imply a level of privilege on the part of the researcher.

Response to Annette Markham

Ramesh Srinivasan

❖ ❖ ❖

Global and local, often separated in scholarly research, are more intertwined today than ever. Annette Markham has problematized this issue persuasively. Opening with a personal anecdote regarding infrastructures that vary across different regions of the world, she has highlighted the importance for the researcher of questioning his or her assumptions when working globally. This type of reflexivity, an unpacking of the self relative to the environment to be studied, enables qualitative researchers to overcome their own biases.

Reflexivity is an important and honest paradigm in ethnographic research. It considers the intersections between the observer and observed and admits that the researcher affects the cultural environment he or she observes. Deconstructing our assumptions can help us all question our own power as researchers and can provide us with fresh perspectives. Internet research can integrate ethnographic methods with participatory approaches to engage the former subject of a study to evolve into the author, critic, and designer of new media.

To truly embody reflexivity, we as researchers must acknowledge the power inequities we carry with us into field environs, particularly in remote and rural regions of the world. These visible inequities structure the interaction researchers have with communities and nongovernmental organizations (NGOs). The ethnographer may be seen as a source of funding and publicity, Westernization, and modernity, and possibly as a vehicle for international or urban mobility. Reflexivity involves an understanding that the researcher can be framed as a symbol of that which the community is not and perhaps as what communities believe they aspire to be. Deep reflexivity involves an honest disclosure by the researcher and the conveyance of his or her life on a level that exposes its positives and negatives. In that regard, it helps the researcher escape objectification as a symbol of modernity and Westernization.

Ethnography can be used to understand and acknowledge local realities and then stimulate participatory forms of research. This approach motivates my own research. I supervise a number of field-based projects that follow reflexive methods and also involve assembling teams of community members to design their own digital media systems. For example, the Tribal Peace project, conducted in collaboration with members of 19 Native American reservations spread across San Diego County in California, engages community members in creating and sharing digital content (video, audio, and image) within a system based around their own local ontologies (e.g., cultural categories). Engaging local communities to create and design their own internet systems involves the specifics of situated ethnomethodological practices, the "grounds" that connect the social group to its particular environment (Garfinkel, 1967; Suchman, 1987). Systems can therefore acknowledge context and transcend simplistic user studies.

Providing power to communities to create and design their own internet systems increases the potential for engaging in more culturally sustainable and meaningful initiatives (Srinivasan, 2006, 2007; Srinivasan & Huang, 2005). In this regard, integrating reflexive and participatory approaches empowers researchers to answer questions of how a digital system fosters culturally and indigenously sustainable activities. As the internet has become a global technology it has also become a cultural technology, a technology that raises the classic question of homogeneity (erosion of cultural difference) vs. heterogeneity (information spaces where diverse discourses are presented and shared with an ethic of equity and social justice).

Emerging from this conception is the dilemma of making such research global in impact. One important issue to consider is that internet research must directly consider trans-national networks of communication, authorship, and movement. Given this, are reflexive, locally isolated ethnographies satisfactory? While approaches toward cultural and phenomenological description are important, the internet must be grasped for what it has become—multi-sited, multi-authored, and multiply received and acted on. Therefore, global internet research must consider its trans-national elements without sacrificing local reflexivity.

Moreover, it has become clear, as with its "older media" analogues, that internet policy and movements are framed by the scalability of the research finding. The recent World Summit on the Information Society proceedings state as much—that standardized, transformative policies toward the internet must be broadly applied across the global South. The mantra of scale implies that locally derived observations hold global applicability only if they can interact and communicate seamlessly with other social and technical systems. As Castells (2000) and others have argued, the diffusion of one's idea, and its ability to survive and master the complexity of networks, ultimately is a statement of the power of the research. Researchers can no longer afford to overly privilege the local without considering networks, scale, and socioeconomic agendas that emerge from commercial and political institutions.

One can accomplish this aim by considering the globe itself as a potential field site, conducting multi-sited ethnographies, and examining the nature of how technologies and information flow between different geographical locations. In this context, I invoke the writings of Arjun Appadurai (1996), who argues that globalization can be understood in terms of the uneven movements of persons, finances, images, technologies, and so on. Globalization is a product of these motions, what Appadurai describes as -scapes. This manifestation is more relevant than ever, argues Appadurai, as physical place is best understood in terms of its placement within a network, in relation to a set of other places. Globalization is therefore best understood by looking at the movements within the network.

For example, Appadurai points to the nationalism movement in the 1980s that advocated for an independent Sikh homeland, Khalistan, within India. A local analysis would imply that ethnographic work should simply be situated within India and focus on particular points of local resistance, such as where protests took place, etc. However, doing so would ignore the fact that this movement itself obtained financing, imagination, and membership from trans-national sources. Without the trans-national focus, researchers would misunderstand the reality of this social movement.

I believe this argument applies when considering the internet as the basis for qualitative research. The internet is the ultimate constellation of networks, integrating actors that are human and nonhuman (Bowker & Star, 1999; Callon, 1999). Therefore, locally focused ethnographic research is of utmost importance, yet must be balanced by research that considers the following:

1. *Trans-national "third spaces,"* which acknowledge the reality of an immigrant group by its "cultural positionality, its reference to a present time and a specific space" (Bhabha, 1994, p. 36): This model challenges

an understanding of a culture or a community as a homogenized entity that can be directly correlated to a single social factor, such as ethnicity (e.g., the experiences and realities for all those of Indian descent are the same).

2. *Social networks:* These are methods to generate structural mappings of how the internet affects the diffusion of social connections and flows of resources in ways that exceed the bounds of physical and local place. Wellman (n.d.) has argued that we should discard both the small-box model of merely considering local place and the networked individualism model of considering the internet as connecting spatially distributed individuals. Instead, researchers must consider the "glocal" qualities of the internet, its dual local and global manifestations.

3. *Virtual worlds:* These are digital spaces that represent a different type of locality that is not physical but still plays a significant role in forming identity. Research has uncovered how identities can be formed and social movements can be imagined via these spaces that would otherwise be impossible given physical realities. For example, Second Life has become an important system/environment to consider for ethnographers.

How can these approaches be reconciled in a field-based effort? Ajit Pyati and I have argued that internet ethnographies must maintain this duality of considering local and global, and in the context of our e-diaspora research we proposed a Diasporic Information Environment Model (Srinivasan & Pyati, 2007). Understanding immigrant information behavior through the lens of diaspora expands the terrain for analyzing immigrant information behavior and raises a new set of research questions. For example, much of the work on immigrants and information is based on the proposition that immigrants have certain needs that are not met. While this approach provides a useful lens for information behavior research and information service delivery, the focus on "lacking" negates discussion about the agency of immigrant groups in contributing to the work of building information environments that remain invisible to researchers who only consider local, place-defined domains. The topic of e-diaspora is one relevant internet research theme, and it shows the potential of research that triangulates multiple methods. More generally, the questions and answers together gathered by a variety of research methods should be closely scrutinized, and researchers and communities alike must engage in sense-making exercises (Dervin, 1998) to recognize patterns and inconsistencies in the data they gather. Given this example, how would one conduct internet-related qualitative research?

We have begun collaborations with the South Asian network, a local grassroots organization dedicated to serving the South Asian diasporic community in Los Angeles. To understand the potential role of a cultural information system for this community, we have engaged in the following five strategies so as to conduct global internet research:

1. Using ethnographic methods to identify the diverse realities and experiences faced by community members: Using field notes from participant observation efforts, we can recognize that community is not a homogeneous entity and, indeed, that certain subcultural groups must be worked with to develop a meaningful information resource.

2. From the ethnographic work, identifying focus groups of participants who reflect the diversity of these subcultures of South Asians: For example, in our initial outreach, we identified that class, gender, age group, and language spoken are important social variables within the community.

3. Working with these focus groups to identify existing public spaces, informational behaviors, and connections with information sources, including web sites that may be of relevance.

4. Engaging these focus groups in techniques of participatory design to assist with modeling a social network system. Using these techniques, community members will sketch out the topics, categories, and interfaces that would be appropriate for such a system.

5. As the system is created, interviewing and engaging in ethnographic observations with users vs. nonusers while also running social network surveys of users vs. nonusers. This will allow researchers to identify the global scope of a community member's social network connections, yet also understand how these social networks may be changing over time and differentially between system users vs. nonusers.

This approach combines globally derived social network surveys with multi-sited local ethnographies. Through the local immigrant community, the study extends out to access global factors and attempts to create and study the impact of a digital system in this context.

One mechanism by which local cultures can share knowledge globally may involve the use of "folksonomies" (Vanderwal, n.d.). These spaces not only allow users to create and share information but also to add their own local "tags" to digital objects being shared. Perhaps a key to understanding an internet that collaboratively shares diverse and multiplied local knowledge would involve considering how databases and systems can enable incommensurable categories and ontologies to be presented along with the contributed information object. David Turnbull has argued that such an approach would be key to rethinking diversity and locality in the global net:

> How can differing knowledge traditions, differing ways of mapping be enabled to work together without subsumption into one common or universal ontology? . . . It is argued that one way in which differing knowledge traditions can interact and be interrogated is by creating a database structured as distributed knowledge emulating a complex adaptive system. Through focusing on the encounters, tensions, and cooperations between traditions utilizing the concept of cognitive trails—the creation of knowledge by movement through the natural and intellectual environment, the socially distributed performative dimensions of differing modes of spatially organized knowledge can then be held in a dialogical tension that enables emergent mapping. (Turnbull, 2007)

The global internet can connect multiple, local, and diverse cultures. Without this perspective, technologies could homogenize and disable the sharing of diverse knowledges. For example, a collapsing of all global health systems into a single database organized by the hierarchies of Western science would erode the power of Ayurveda or Chinese medicine, both of which are uniquely tied to the semantic means by which they reconsider categories (e.g., plants as medicine, etc.). Such an initiative is underway in a collaboration with Cambridge University (United Kingdom) and the Zuni Nation of New Mexico (United States), focused on developing a digital museum around the ontologies contributed by diverse stakeholders, including indigenous groups, archaeologists, and museum curators (Boast, Bravo, & Srinivasan, 2007). As we open up the semantic terms by which objects in this digital museum are described, so too may emerge further projects focused around the possibility of developing information societies and systems that are not just global in user demographics but in voice and authorship. And we must continue to consider and build on foundational studies in structural and cognitive anthropology (Atran, Medin, & Ross, 2005; Lévi-Strauss, 1966, for example) that reveal the power of categories in cultural cognition and difference.

Global internet research enables the tension between different knowledges to be present, yet also to mutually interact. The significant shifts enabled by the Web 2.0 allow us to renegotiate what "global" means in an internet that has replaced personal web sites with blogging, the online encyclopedia with Wikipedia, and taxonomical directories with folksonomies (O'Reilly, 2006). The pattern here is a movement from closed, homogenizing internet systems to a "social" web that enables sharing, collaboration, and global membership. Qualitative researchers must critique, design, and evaluate these spaces reflexively.

Therefore, in summary, I applaud Markham as she urges researchers to consider their reflexivity in conducting cultural research, and I argue for a focus on the following strategies:

1. Using trans-national methods that allow focus on the movements, flows, and socially distinct uses of information, multi-sited ethnographies, and textual analyses of virtual worlds

2. Considering scalability of results through multi-method triangulation and sense-making

3. Focusing on the networks: glocal (Wellman, n.d.) social network studies

4. Building collaborative digital spaces for knowledge: focusing on Web 2.0 technologies that integrate diverse knowledge traditions and systems

Let me close by revisiting the reference at the end of Markham's chapter. While Clifford Geertz has suggested that comprehension of any social setting will always be incomplete, perhaps researchers can better understand a social setting by triangulating their focuses—balancing the depth-based focus of a particular case by looking at the contextual, trans-national, and network-oriented factors that shape today's internet and society.

❖ RECOMMENDED READING

For a further focus on the nature of how sociological research can engage with situated, embodied practices, see Harold Garfinkel's foundational (1967) book, *Studies in Ethnomethodology*.

Appadurai's (1996) *Modernity at Large* and Bhabha's (1994) *The Location of Culture* are foundational texts that trace uneven and often immaterial characteristics that tie local and global cultural studies together.

For insightful descriptions of the nature of how objects maintain social lives, yet are often constrained by their immutability according to scientific standardizations, see Bruno Latour's (1990), "Drawing Things Together," in Lynch and Woolgar's edited volume, *Representation in Scientific Practice*. Another highly relevant text in this vein is Geoff Bowker and S. L. Star's (1999), *Sorting Things Out: Classification and Its Consequences*.

QUESTION SIX

What Constitutes Quality in Qualitative Internet Research?

Nancy K. Baym

❖   ❖   ❖

M ost of us would find it easier to conduct research if there were a clear set of rules to follow, if we could be assured that the paths of least resistance would be the most fruitful, or if were we guaranteed at least one "aha" moment in which it all fell into place and the right route was revealed. Qualitative research is never going to offer those things. As the writers in this collection show, doing qualitative research well is a matter of finding practical and defensible balancing points between opposing tensions. We always make trade-offs in our research choices. The trick is to understand the trade-offs we are making well enough to defend them to others.

The introduction and subsequent chapters and responses show that the internet presents novel challenges to qualitative researchers. In responding to these challenges, many of the scholars included here problematize issues germane to all qualitative research. None of our authors was asked to directly address the question of what made qualitative internet research good, but taken together, their writings offer a number of guidelines. In this concluding chapter, I offer some guidelines for conducting "good" qualitative internet research. To do this I draw on the chapters and responses in this book, my experience conducting and supervising qualitative projects about the internet, and a selection of writers who have been particularly helpful to me as I've learned about and taught the issue of quality in qualitative research.

❖ QUALITATIVE RESEARCHERS MUST CONTINUOUSLY BALANCE TENSIONS

The writers in this collection all discuss their research as a continuous process of decision making in which they must assess and balance what is to be gained and lost with each choice that lies before them. Drawing on the dialogic approach of Mikhael Bakhtin (e.g., 1981, 1986), researchers have described a dialectic approach to relationships that views relational maintenance as a continuous dynamic process of attending to multiple simultaneous contradictory needs (e.g., Baxter, 2007; Baxter & Montgomery, 2007; Montgomery & Baxter, 1998). The goal of relational research from this perspective "is not to catalog the definitive set of contractions in personal relationships, but to contribute to the understanding of the processes by which couples create, realize, and deal with dialectical tensions" (Montgomery & Baxter, 1998, p. 158).

Qualitative research is also a dynamic process in which, on an ongoing basis, researchers must find balance between opposing pulls. This dialectical perspective offers guidance for thinking about research goals and processes. As Montgomery and Baxter suggest, while one could develop typologies of dialectic tensions in qualitative research, each might have merit, yet all would be incomplete. What's important is understanding processes for dealing with these tensions. Nonetheless, identifying particular dialectics at play in particular contexts is extremely informative. Reflecting on what a dialogic approach to methodology might mean, Montgomery and Baxter (1998, p. 172) posit several methodological dialectics, including "rigor and imagination, fact and value, precision and richness, elegance and applicability, and vivication and verification." In this collection, the dialectics that receive the most attention are tidiness vs. messiness, depth and breadth, local and global, and risk (which brings intellectual benefit) and comfort.

One of the most basic tensions to be managed, as Hine draws on Law to discuss in Chapter 1, is the extent to which one develops an approach and interpretation that form a tidy whole in the face of research contexts that always reveal complexity rather than simplicity when examined closely. In a review of my book, *Tune In, Log On*, Wendy Robinson (2001) criticized it for being too much like the neat trim worlds of Jane Austen novels and not dealing adequately with the issues that could have been raised regarding gender, consumerism, and other important matters. I can't disagree (nor can I find comparison to Austen a bad thing). Though I do not think I oversimplified,

I certainly did err on the side of neatness over messiness by excluding many relevant potential analyses. This exclusion was also, as I discuss later, an issue of focus. However, by identifying processes through which diverse voices in the group continually constructed their social contexts, I did offer an analysis that opened doors to those complexities rather than rendering them irrelevant.

Related to this tension is the one between breadth and depth (e.g., Hammersley, 1998). There are always tempting ways to expand projects—after all, the more vantage points, the more perspectives on what you're studying. In a time of globalized networked convergence, a study involving the internet can go almost anywhere and still stay on topic. Yet, indefinite expansion is rarely practical and—even if it were more "accurate"—almost always invites more complexity than a researcher can manage. Moreover, the close examination of small things that under-pins so many of qualitative research's greatest contributions means that other important things must be left unexplored. As Hine puts it, some questions are always "left dangling." As a practical matter, one has no choice but to bound the project and offer a reasonably tidy interpreta-tion of a modest slice of a research field, sacrificing other interesting and integral routes of study along the way.

When one balances a project to keep it manageable and focused on the kinds of close examination that qualitative research offers, one also faces the inevitable tension between explaining a specific phenomenon under study and offering something to those involved in other contexts in which that phenomenon may be meaningful. How can we bring out the great strengths of qualitative research with close study of the local while offering something of meaning in the countless global contexts of internet use? This issue has often been seen as a problem of "general-izability." For instance, I think my students ask *how many* subjects they need to interview or *how many* observations they must make of *how many* messages in hopes that I will give them an answer (23?) that ensures generalizability. However, from a qualitative perspective, par-ticularly a dialogic one, generalizability is neither relevant nor possi-ble. The goal instead is comparability and the ability to offer analyses that can be coordinated with others (Montgomery & Baxter, 1998). The writers in this collection do not argue that findings should offer gener-alization to other contexts; quite the contrary, they argue that local specificity is essential to making sense of the internet in contemporary life. Yet their work offers insights that are of value outside of the spe-cific context of their study. As Srinivasan puts it in Chapter 5, "Global internet research must consider its trans-national elements without sacrificing local reflexivity" (p. 166).

Another tension the authors in this collection frequently note is between sticking to what is comfortable, easy, and predictable and taking risks that can lead to greater insight. The research paths that offer the most novel insight are those that challenge researchers' ingrained ways of seeing things and the interpretations they build throughout the research process. Intellectual benefits are often accrued through taking practical, intellectual, logistical, and emotional risks, pitting novelty against predictability. In this book, Lally in Chapter 5 advocates for risk, as does boyd, who writes in Chapter 1 about spending time looking at the uncomfortable hate-based areas of Friendster to force herself to see things she could otherwise easily ignore. Kendall writes in Chapter 4 about the ways her interpretations might have been richer had she attended to her own emotional interpretations rather than seeking a more scientific distance from those she studied. To bring one's own emotions and sexuality into the analysis as Kendall and others in this collection advocate is to put one's self at risk in regard not only to one's research subjects but also to an academy that may be increasingly comfortable with the concept of self-reflexivity in research, but whose norms often interpret this degree of personal disclosure as inappropriate irrationality or self-focus, rather than a thoughtful analytic strategy.

Dialectic tensions cannot be made to go away; they can only be managed. The challenge, as Silverman (1989, p. 222) reminds us, is to "avoid choosing between all polar oppositions." "Good dialogic inquiry," write Montgomery and Baxter (1998, p. 173), "should have a both-and rather than an either-or orientation." We need to accept that we will inevitably lose some things regardless of the choices we make and, given that fact, must make considered choices we can articulate to others that guide us toward what we are there to understand.

The remainder of this conclusion turns to what "making considered choices" might mean. I begin with an abstract discussion of whether there can be standards for quality from a dialogic perspective that takes the multiplicity of social meaning as a basic premise. I then move into a more concrete discussion of recommendations. Although the book's focus is ostensibly on internet research, none of the guidelines that emerge regarding quality are specific to that domain. Instead all of us in this volume have found that our internet research quandaries are best solved not by assuming we are facing brand-new situations that call for entirely new approaches, but by assuming we are facing people behaving in styles that call for many of the same ways of thinking that were called for before there was an internet.

❖ CAN THERE BE QUALITY STANDARDS?

Qualitative researchers agree that making wise research choices has never been about distinguishing right from wrong but about finding the most appropriate path given the specific point in the specific project. As Stern puts it in Chapter 3, the best answer is always "it depends." "There are no right or wrong methods," writes Silverman (2005, p. 112); "there are only methods that are appropriate to your research topic and the model with which you are working." Some might take the notion of "no wrong methods" to mean that all methodological choices are equally good. This fresh thinking may facilitate innovative new approaches to qualitative research (some of which work out better than others), but it also provides a wide opening for critics of qualitative methods to challenge the rigor and therefore the value of research claims.

One incentive for putting this book together was Annette's and my sense that too much of the qualitative internet research we read could use a healthy dose of rigor. Silverman, along with Hammersley and Atkinson (1995), are among the qualitative methodologists who argue for the necessity of standards, even as they (and we) run into phenomenological trouble specifying the exact nature or justification for standards. Silverman (2005, p. 15), for instance, argues that "qualitative research should offer no protection from the rigorous, critical standards that should be applied to any enterprise concerned to sort 'fact' from 'fancy.'"

This book's introduction raised several issues that problematize the question of what standards might be applied. We live in a time marked by convergence, mutability, and overlap, which greatly complicates our research objects. When our subjects can be viewed from so many valuable perspectives, all of which are deeply interconnected to one another and each of which is itself ever changing, on what bedrock can our analyses be evaluated? Disciplinary traditions have often provided that foundation, but academic norms and institutions are not immune to the cultural pressures that push us toward multiplicity and relativity. The role of disciplines in setting standards for the evaluation of research in interdisciplinary domains such as internet research is increasingly problematic as our work must be grounded in and speak to multiple traditions.

We argue that the problems of qualitative internet research are fundamentally questions of qualitative methodology, yet as the introduction noted, qualitative methodologists and theorists disagree about the possibility, let alone specifics, of standards. While Silverman urges us to sort "fact" from "fancy," others reject the premise that there are "facts" that can be discovered or found through inquiry. This disagreement is particularly apparent in a line of interrelated qualitative methodology texts, beginning with the first edition of Denzin and Lincoln's *Handbook of Qualitative Research* (1994), which offered critical and postmodern articulations of qualitative practice that celebrated diverse ways of knowing and questioned any research claims to "truth." Hammersley and Atkinson (1995) and Silverman (2005) cite that text and, in response, stand by a more postpositivist line that believes in and values notions of reliability and validity. In the second edition of the *Handbook of Qualitative Research* (Denzin & Lincoln, 2000), Smith and Deemer (2000, pp. 428–429) critique Hammersley and Atkinson, admonishing readers that "the epistemological project is over and relativism must be accepted. We must change our imageries and metaphors from those of discovery and finding to those of constructing and making." Smith and Deemer do not deny that we make judgments, nor do they argue that we should suspend judgment; rather, they argue that there cannot be predetermined standards for those judgments. In their view, judgment criteria "must be seen as always open-ended, in part unarticulated, and, even when a characteristic is more or less articulated, . . . always and ever subject to constant reinterpretation" (Smith & Deemer, 2000, p. 445).

From a perspective that takes the multiplicity of modern life seriously enough to do away with appeals to a unitary truth as the arbiter of quality, a perspective with which I am sympathetic, the question becomes how can we "make and defend judgments when there can be no appeal to foundations or to something outside of the social processes of knowledge construction" (Smith & Deemer, 2000, p. 438). How can we "honor pluralism and multiplicity while avoiding its excesses?" (p. 452).

If there is no truth, isn't doubt always justified? Can "accurate" be a measure when reality is socially constructed and multiple? Aren't quality standards ultimately decided not by what is closest to truth, but by the norms of the scientific research community? These are excellent questions, but the practical issue remains that even a cursory stroll through the halls of an academic conference-in-progress will convince almost anyone that not all work is equally good. That there is no direct access to truth does not mean that all studies are equally compelling. All of us make judgments based on standards, even if our standards are tacit and open to reformulation.

One path to resolving this philosophical dilemma is to take the phenomenological problem as irresolvable and then to shift the focus from whether we have really found the true state of things to whether we have built interpretations of affairs that meet our audience's standards for what they will accept as a basis for action. On the one hand this path is circular: Trustworthy research is research that people think is true. On the other hand, operating without knowing for certain that one's standards get to "The Truth" is the basic state of human affairs. We can take heart in Jackson's (1986) claim that every method—even those (experimental and statistical) methods that seem to have truth-claims built into their procedures—is a form of argument. Whether there is a single truth out there to be discovered or multiple truths waiting to be constructed, to be persuasive, researchers must convince readers that "their 'findings' are genuinely based on critical investigation of all their data" (Silverman, 2005, p. 211).

In sum, then, I take a practical approach to thinking about quality in qualitative internet research. Though there are thorny ontological problems one can wrestle with, there are also many moments in qualitative research that call for pragmatic judgments about what to do. We need standards to guide us as we resolve the inherent dialectics in qualitative research; at the same time we should recognize that standards must be flexible and situated and that others may hold other standards (and truths) yet function just as well. Elsewhere (Baym, 2006), I have offered a list of criteria that I believe make for "quality" in qualitative internet research. In an analysis of exemplary qualitative internet studies, I argued that their quality was due to at least six inter-related strengths: (1) they are grounded in theory and data, (2) they demonstrate rigor in data collection and analysis, (3) they use multiple strategies to obtain data, (4) each takes into account the perspective of participants, (5) each demonstrates awareness of and self-reflexivity regarding the research process, and (6) each takes into consideration interconnections between the internet and the life-world within which it is situated.

In what follows, I turn from abstract issues to the concrete, elaborating on these criteria and making others explicit. First, I argue that good work is historically grounded. Second, such work is focused. Third, whatever the ideals, given the focus, work must be judged in terms of what it is practical to accomplish. Fourth, a good researcher gains persuasive ability by anticipating others' counter-arguments and making the arguments for his or her own case explicit. Finally, good qualitative internet research makes its case by providing resonant interpretive frames that help us understand both what is new about new technologies and how research on new technology connects to other areas of inquiry.

❖ CONNECT TO HISTORY

Too often internet researchers take the stance that, since the internet is new, old theory and methods—even those concerning media—have nothing to offer in its exploration. But, as Christians and Carey (1989) advocate, the best internet research attends to earlier scholarship about the internet, about other media, about earlier incarnations of similar social practices, and about methodology, a point echoed by researchers in this volume. Hammersley suggests we would be better served by moving to "a situation where there is less emphasis on the investigation of new phenomena or the generation of new ideas (important as these are) and more on improving existing knowledge" (Hammersley, 1998, p. 121). For internet researchers, this can be a liberating insight. As we argued in the introduction, one can barely keep up with the internet's novelty even if one attends to it daily, let alone within the framework of academic publishing. Furthermore, connecting with historical precedents for the phenomena we study increases the sophistication with which we can think about our topic, expands the breadth of the contexts in which our work can be relevant, and provides a means for readers to integrate what the researcher has to offer into what they may already know.

In Baym (2006), I discussed how Brenda Danet's (2001a) analyses of play in online spaces benefited tremendously from the connections she found with theory and research on the history of typography, aesthetics, and folk art, among other areas. My work with understanding social organization in an online soap-opera discussion group (e.g., Baym, 2000) adapted practice theory as a methodological and analytic approach. Both Lynn Cherny, whose study of a MOO (1999) was one of the earliest internet culture monographs, and I drew on the concept of the "speech community" from the ethnography of communication to make sense of the language practices we were seeing in our online communities. As I wrote in Baym (2006),

> The theories that we have developed to explain social organization need to be able to address new media. Existing theories may not be perfect fits. This is, in fact, a way in which internet research can contribute to social theory as well as enhancing our understanding of the internet. As internet researchers find the ways in which old theory does and doesn't work, we are able to refine and improve social theory. But new technology does not reinvent the social world. Old structures have simply not collapsed and been replaced by new ones in the wake of the internet. (p. 83)

Researchers must disabuse themselves of any notion that, because a research topic involves the internet, there is no need to be grounded in existing literatures, theories, or methods. Analysts learn the most and are most persuasive when they are able to make their contribution clear by articulating the connections between what they have found and what we already know.

❖ FOCUS

Clear grounding in research from other traditions as well as the literature most germane to one's specific topic can also help one fulfill the second guideline, which is to develop a clear focus and stick to it. Projects need "key guiding principles" (see Hine in Chapter 1)—a clear sense of what it is that we are seeking to understand. Messiness is inevitable, but when one starts from a vague beginning, one will never end up with a cogent explanation of that mess. Given that we cannot do it all, we must limit our attentions to a domain small enough that we can examine it with some degree of thoroughness. A researcher's focus will inevitably shift throughout the process, but when we have a grounding in a specific inquiry from the start, it is considerably easier to note when a fascinating sideline is too much of a digression. Furthermore, our focus sets the core standard against which our work will and should be judged: Given what we wanted to know, did we make the choices with the most potential to tell us?

When we are clear on our research objects, goals, questions, and the contexts in which we will situate our interpretation of the research objects, we develop more coherent and focused tales to tell about them. For instance, in her analysis of the MOO she studied, Lori Kendall's consistent focus on the construction of masculinity kept her from veering into areas too far afield, as did Shani Orgad's emergent focus on narrative in breast cancer survivors' internet use (and nonuse). Surely neither knew that this was going to emerge as her core focus, but once both learned enough from their research fields to see the importance and value of those practices, their analyses remained centered on them.

❖ BE PRACTICAL

It is a point too often forgotten, especially by those excited about their work, that we have to work within practical constraints. The internet may make near-infinite piles of data available, and many paths may lead to fruitful and fascinating interpretations, but we have to make choices or we will never get past data collection. We can only work with what we have the time, capital, personnel, and background to observe and reasonably interpret (Lindlof & Taylor, 2002; see Hine, Chapter 1, and Bakardjieva, Chapter 2). It may be desirable, for example, to conduct face-to-face interviews with people one has studied online, but doing so may be prohibitively expensive. There may be more relevant historical material in other disciplines than we can take in and synthesize. We can only resolve tensions within the limits of our circumstances.

We therefore need to think carefully about what we can and cannot do, and plan projects in ways that make the most of the possibilities we have. This planning should happen first and foremost at the point of formulating the research question, so that what we seek to know can be found within the scope of data we can access. Beyond that, it is perfectly legitimate to acknowledge that, while it would have been ideal to, say, visit more research sites, resources precluded the ability to do so. Indeed, if it is believable that it was too onerous to make such visits, that acknowledgment can enhance credibility as it shows that a researcher understood the situation well enough to know what might have elicited better data.

❖ ANTICIPATE COUNTER-ARGUMENTS

The counter-arguments for which qualitative researchers need to be prepared are endless. Among the questions readers may legitimately ask are the following: How do I know this isn't just your opinion? How do I know that you didn't just go in and find what you expected to find? How do I know your examples are representative rather than cherry-picked? How is this different from an anecdote? These are, in essence, truth tests that are applied by lay and academic audiences alike. It is by attending to these kinds of questions throughout the research process that researchers are able to convince others of the value of their work.

Research quality can hence be seen as a rhetorical matter of persuading others by effectively addressing all their potential questions within the research and its presentation. Fortunately, there are good ways to anticipate these arguments, learn what they have to teach, and provide compelling evidence that one is not guilty of such allegations. As I discuss below, researchers can enter the field with an open mind, demonstrated by problematizing core concepts. The limits of data collection and interpretation can be pushed by collecting diverse and contradictory information from members, contexts, and one's self.

Seemingly incommensurable data can be played off against each other to push interpretation. In building interpretations and speculating on their significance, we can limit our claims. Documenting the research process provides the tools to accomplish self-reflection and to tell others precisely what we did and why we did it. Finally, framing a study in ways that consider a wide variety of readers can raise new counter-arguments for researchers to consider.

Problematize Your Core Concepts

It is both the task and responsibility of qualitative research to problematize concepts that are taken for granted. Christians and Carey (1989, p. 358) describe it as "a general task of qualitative studies—to make us aware of the categories in which we think and to analyze and critique such models." "A major part of our task," they write, "is to clarify systematically what we and others already know, or potentially know, of the social world" (p. 355). This systematic clarification begins with making "problematic the common-sense reasoning used" in how we define our variables and establish our research problems (Silverman, 1993, p. 29; see also Hammersley, 1998).

This presents a quandary since, as Silverman (1989) notes, in qualitative research "the phenomenon always escapes." In the context of internet research, one job of qualitative researchers is to problematize the meaning of "the internet" while recognizing that the more closely we look for "the internet," the less likely we are to find such a thing. Rather than predefining "the internet" (see Hine in Chapter 1), we must disaggregate it. At one level, this task means understanding the architecture of the elements of the internet we study and how it compares and contrasts to the architectures of internet media others have studied. At another level, it means we must look for and consider the interconnections among the internet and the life-worlds within which its use is situated and which it is used to construct. Much as we problematize and unpack our concepts, however, ultimately, we must break them down until we are working with a set of clearly, concretely defined concepts that we can apply consistently.

Listen to Participants

In problematizing concepts and otherwise coming to an understanding of the social context being studied, most qualitative researchers need to pay attention to how the members of those contexts see things. Qualitative research, especially ethnography, is generally concerned with understanding a social group as its members understand themselves, to articulate the concepts they know tacitly but silently. However, it is common to see studies of online materials, including interactions among people posted in public spaces, that ignore the perspectives of those who authored and consumed those texts. This is not a problem if one makes no claims regarding participant perspectives (e.g., those who study language patterns online without reference to intent, such as Herring, 1993), although even these scholars might gain insight into the most profitable ways to bound their studies if they begin from the participants' orientations. Yet, listening to participants does not mean taking their account at face value (Silverman, 1989). To the contrary, as Briggs (1986) wrote about in *Learning How to Ask*, what we hear from those we interview—and observe as well—has to be seen as situated performances rather than direct truth-dumps. Watching and listening to how they define concepts and how they frame situations can, however, provide materials for stronger interpretations of social worlds and, when well documented (see below), can create evidence to support those interpretations.

Attend to Context

Research objects come to mean in context (Christians & Carey, 1989), and one way to produce high-quality work is to make decisions that are informed by thoughtful consideration of the research contexts (see Orgad in Chapter 2). We cannot know in advance which contexts will emerge as most meaningful. Every research field has multiple possible sites that could be studied, and throughout a study we may have to make judgments about which ones are most "valuable for studying the scenes that structure the social reality of a particular group" (Lindlof & Taylor, 2002, p. 80). We must be sensitive to the boundaries that are constructed by participants to frame their activities, though we may have good reason to subsume participant perspectives within a larger framework. In the context of internet research, those boundaries may be tracked by following the online traces that are left in field sites (see Hine and boyd in Chapter 1). Perhaps most important, though, is the need to immerse one's self in a field over time while seeking to understand its many contexts. The scholars in this collection all took months, if not years, to amass data from a range of areas of online spaces or in a range of situations both online and off. The understanding of context that comes as a result enables them to explain for their readers why one analytic route made more sense than another or why a few examples should be taken to represent a larger phenomenon.

Attend to Yourself

It is almost a cliché at this point to argue that qualitative research should be reflexive. This book can be seen as a collection of exemplars of reflexivity. Reflexivity is sometimes cast as a question of identifying one's assumptions and biases up front so that readers can make independent assessments of their impact on the research process and resulting interpretations. That is, indeed, important. But these chapters demonstrate that it is not enough to engage in reflexivity only to identify biases (or, at the opposite extreme, to write autobiography). Our work is strengthened when we second-guess ourselves and think deeply about how our background and personal reactions shape our research focus, approach, and interpretation (see Hine and Kendall in Chapter 1 and Markham in Chapter 5). To do this well, researchers must not only engage in continuous honest reflection on their own experience but they must also show how those reflections lead to insights. For instance, Kendall in Chapter 4 shows how she could have used reflection on her own emotional and sexual attitudes toward the people and conversations she studied as a source of considerable insight into social formation, power, and hierarchy, had she been prepared to risk their discussion.

Seek Contrasts in the Data

When researchers examine cases that seem to contradict the patterns they are claiming, yet show how those seeming exceptions demonstrate an underlying principle able to account both for the pattern and deviations, it is hard to argue against their interpretation. Silverman argues for the principle of refutability, telling qualitative researchers to continuously argue against their initial assumptions (1993, 2005). "Interpretations need to be made explicit and full advantage should be taken of any opportunities to test their limits and to assess alternatives" (Hammersley & Atkinson, 1995, p. 19). Deviant cases are particularly important both in refuting and refining interpretations and in convincing readers that your interpretation is able to account for examples that do not seem to fit the pattern (Silverman, 2005). Shani Orgad's discussion in Chapter 2 of women who did not use the internet in handling their breast cancer offers a particularly nice example in this collection. Through talking with these women, she was able to gain insight into the limits of the online spaces on which she focused and take a more critical stance toward their claims to inclusiveness.

Limit Your Claims

An otherwise fine piece of qualitative research can be undone by overstated claims, and an important component of thinking through the arguments one might make against an interpretation is determining to what extent claims are supported by the evidence brought to bear. We need to remain focused on what we actually assessed and on what we can demonstrate to others with systematically collected examples (and counter-examples). Even as qualitative researchers recognize the local particularity of their study, most strive to produce work with significance beyond those local parameters. Rather than striving for "generalizability"—a concept that assumes a stable replicable world in which one set of meanings prevail—qualitative researchers need to focus on providing thick descriptions against which other contexts can be compared and on articulating processes and dynamics that can be used as bases for exploring other domains. As Montgomery and Baxter (1998, p. 170) write, "The purpose [of dialogic inquiry] is to elaborate the potential for coordination."

Document Your Research Process

The last two guidelines I offer regarding counter-arguments pertain to writing. It's essential to document your research project. Throughout this collection, scholars have argued that we need to make our implicit considerations explicit (Sveningsson in Chapter 3), articulate our choices (Markham in Chapter 5), and turn "tentative forays ... into defensible decisions, and retrofit research questions to emergent field sites" (Hine, Chapter 1, p. 6). Writing down what we do at the time, rereading those writings, and considering our own reactions to them are essential parts of reflexive practice and also provide the means to concretely demonstrate to readers how and why we made the choices that we did.

Such records can also enhance our claims to reliability (Silverman, 2005). We should not be in the business of promising that other people will see exactly the same things we did should they return to our field sites; indeed, they should expect change. But we should be in the business of convincing readers that had they been there when we were, looking at the things we looked at using the analytic perspectives we used, then they would have seen things that were extremely close to what we saw. Keeping copious notes makes it far easier to articulate our process to others so that they have grounds on which to make this and other judgments.

Frame the Study for Diverse Readers

Researchers who have attended to these points have probably anticipated most of the likely counter-arguments and are well positioned to write up what they have to offer. But as Markham discusses in Chapter 5, qualitative researchers need to consider how their work will be read by distant and different audiences, a rhetorical (and ethical) challenge for which we are rarely if ever trained. Every audience needs the researcher to spell out clear connections between evidence and claims it is used to support (Hammersley, 1998). "No matter the perspective, assumptions should be stated and methods should be explained in relation to the perspective's ideals of inquiry, and the reporting should be accessible to other scholars" (Montgomery & Baxter, 1998, p. 173). Researchers owe it to readers to make clear what "analytical or practical significance [they are] being asked to attach to [a] 'finding'"(Silverman, 2005, p. 70).

❖ DEVELOP COMPELLING EXPLANATIONS

Much of the discussion thus far has presented quality primarily as a matter of recognizing limitations and being preemptively defensive. However, we mustn't lose sight of the proactive power of qualitative research. What makes qualitative research valuable is its ability to offer ways of thinking that change how we understand and perhaps act in our social world. In concluding my recommendations, then, I want to consider what we should strive for in the findings we offer.

Several thinkers have argued that, at its best, qualitative analysis has an "analytic depth" (Silverman, 2005, p. 236) that achieves "poetic resonance" (Christians & Carey, 1989, p. 362) with both the people studied and those in other contexts. The "prophetic sensitizing concept" (Goffman's use of "stigma" is an excellent example), write Christians and Carey (1989, p. 373), is "the most lasting contribution qualitative research can make":

> By sensitizing concepts we mean taxonomical systems that discover an integrating scheme within the data themselves . . . the qualitative researcher maps out territories by finding seminal ideas that become permanent intellectual contributions while unveiling the inner character of events or situations. (Christians & Carey, 1989, p. 370)

In this quote, Christians and Carey note that compelling explanations offer a taxonomical system, but they also point out that these schemes are not merely lists but are "integrating schemes" that reveal "inner character."

Too often for my tastes, qualitative researchers develop lists of categories or emergent themes or generate typologies, but do not go far enough to understand the underlying dynamics that account for those categories. "Emergent grounded theory" is used to "generate themes" that are then analyzed piecemeal rather than integrated into an insightful explanation of the dynamics responsible for these patterns.

I have found Bourdieu's writings on the logic of practice (1990) particularly helpful in thinking about how categorizations are not research ends in themselves but evidence of an underlying social logic that organizes not only the list but other social phenomena (including those not observed) as well. Identifying logics lets one offer explanations that are, to quote Christians and Carey (1989, p. 367) both "well rounded and parsimonious." The practices I have outlined above for thinking about data and the research process should all help guide researchers toward logics. The key is to examine data not as cumulative but as mutual contexts for one another (see Orgad in Chapter 2). Looking to logic rather than types also keeps the focus on process. Our focus should be on the "processes through which the relations between elements are articulated" (Silverman, 1989, p. 226).

Importantly, the dialectic approach positions the understanding of difference and the interplays of difference as more important than strivings for unity. Our goal is not to find a single explanatory element (Silverman, 1989), but to reveal the complexity of our subject, in part by identifying the dialectic pulls in the field. Baxter (2007, p. 138) writes, "The vexing problem is an orientation toward unity and the intellectual problem is how to embrace difference." One measure of quality from this perspective is thus the extent to which our approaches and findings speak to the interplay among different voices rather than taking a unified path to a unitary outcome.

In my work (Baym, 2000), I identified (listed) strategies that participants in a soap-opera discussion group used to maintain the group's self-identity as "a bunch of friends." However, I was also able to use their own discursive practices to demonstrate that there was an underlying rationale for maintaining that identity—it allowed people to voice both contradictory opinions about the television show they were watching and personal self-disclosures that could enhance others' interpretations of the show. Friendliness was thus a way to mediate between the competing needs to have diverse perspectives and to have an environment safe enough that people would be willing to engage in highly personal self-disclosure.

These rich and insightful understandings that qualitative research can offer should go beyond explaining the field bounded by one's study to offer insights that can be applied outside of their contexts of origin and contribute to an enhanced understanding. There are many ways to offer insights of relevance and use beyond the specific area of inquiry. A work may generate new sensitizing constructs. It may generate new theory, or it may refine older theories. Value may be provided through novel claims or through affirmation of the applicability of old ones in other contexts.

We cannot predict the ways in which others may find our work useful. However, if we are clear in the decisions we make throughout our research practices, document our procedures and reflections well, and provide our readers with concrete thick descriptions and convincing evidence for the processes and logics we describe, then we will have given them the materials to find their own value in our work.

In closing, I return to my claim in the introduction and beginning of this chapter that we benefit from thinking of qualitative internet research as a process of managing dialectical tensions. This conclusion has argued that dialectics can be seen throughout the research process, as we make choices about how to collect, interpret, and present our data. However, dialectic thinking is also important in understanding our very understandings of quality. From a dialectical perspective, our goal is not to convert others to our own way of seeing. We are not after one true explanation. Rather, we are after a thorough, grounded, trustworthy voice that makes meaningful contributions to ongoing dialogues and on which others can build.

Finally, I note again that nothing I have written here is limited to the internet. That is as it should be. The internet is an exciting and ever-changing research focus. It is a research tool that offers unbridled access to new kinds of data and may offer exciting new ways to present research. Certainly, the internet magnifies and forces us to confront what seem like new challenges in our research. Yet when we confront those challenges, as the voices in this book have done, we find that these are challenges all researchers face, not just internet researchers. Bringing internet research into the dialogue serves to highlight questions of concern to all, but reaffirms that to do good qualitative internet research is to do good qualitative research.

Response to Nancy Baym

Annette N. Markham

❖   ❖   ❖

A trap in qualitative internet inquiry (or qualitative inquiry of any sort, not just internet related) is to believe that qualitative methods bestow a natural interpretive clarity and self-reflexive awareness on the researcher. As Nancy Baym aptly points out, the myriad approaches falling into this broad category, most of which are flexible and adaptive, can lead researchers to believe that "anything goes." This oversimplification is exacerbated when researchers new to this form of inquiry read publications in which the author buries the literature review, application of procedures, analytical processes, and theoretical development within the story and between the lines. The interpretation can seem to flow effortlessly from the writer, and the unique case can seem unlinked from any other phenomenon or case.

Add to this the fact that even among methodologists "qualitative inquiry" means very different things. Are we talking about the methods of collecting information? The application of procedures? The rigor of interpretation? The worldview of the researcher? Qualitative inquiry continues to discover and embrace its diversity, encompassing a multiplicity of worldviews, procedures, and approaches. Within this broad research context, it is difficult to know where a particular author is coming from in the research unless he or she spells out in great detail the procedures he or she followed, the inclusion of which can clash with current modes of writing and the ability to present research in flowing narrative forms. Nancy Baym's discussion of a dialectical approach to finding quality in qualitative internet research offers a useful treatment of some of these tensions. The criteria she offers are welcome starting points for identifying what might be the framework for quality in social internet research, particularly for researchers new to this form of inquiry.

I've been studying the theories and practices of qualitative research methods for more than 15 years now, first within the social sciences and, shortly thereafter, diving into interpretive, feminist, and postmodern schools of thought. A certain part of me enjoys the idea of putting together a puzzle or solving a mystery so that I can see the whole. Another, stronger part of me enjoys the disjuncture, the seams and gaps and points of connections between elements or ideas. A disruptive deconstruction allows me to see new patterns of meaning not otherwise identifiable at the placid surface of everyday taken-for-granted experience.

Nancy and I come from similar educational backgrounds, but the way we experience qualitative inquiry and think about method differs in both subtle and sharp ways. As I composed this final response of our book, I tried multiple variations on a theme: finessing Nancy's arguments, arguing about the details of dialogical and dialectical theories, making a few erudite (I hoped!) comments about quality in methods, taking the discussion to the level of epistemology and ontology, and even writing an illustrative narrative. As I listened to the voices in my head, I heard not just a dialogue but a cacophony. I found myself writing in circles.

I finally realized that, although I wanted to embrace the notion of dialectics, this image did not satisfactorily capture the complexity of qualitative inquiry as I have experienced it. I find the concept useful, yet its historical roots don't sit well with me. Early conceptions of the dialectical process hold that it will eventually yield a middle ground that is Truth. In later conceptions, the dialectical process yields a third alternative, drawing on and also stronger than both elements. The fragmented postmodernist in me resists the dualism. A dualism is certainly not what Nancy intended, but I can't stop thinking about the limits of a two- or three-sided image. Also, as I reflect on my own research, almost every moment during the course of a study illustrates yet another dialectical tension that cannot be managed or balanced. Rather than bore you and me with an elaborate explanation of the long stretches of paralysis that result during any given project because of these irresolvable tensions, I realized I needed to figure out what image of quality and qualitative inquiry made better sense in my world.

❖ CRYSTALS VERSUS TRIANGLES

On further reflection, it occurred to me that the very interplay and juxtaposition of dialectical tensions in my own research seem to yield the most interesting possibilities, particularly within the criteria for quality Nancy discusses in the second part of her essay. So while I might begin a sentence agreeing with Nancy that the phenomenological problem is irresolvable and, therefore, we should get on to the more practical issue of determining what might make a study more or less compelling, in the same breath, I find I disagree—because struggling with this problem is part of what yields reflexive research, a key to generating research that is perceived as trustworthy and compelling.

The image of a prism mentioned by Lori Kendall in Chapter 1 resonates strongly. Laurel Richardson (1994, 1997; Richardson & St. Pierre, 2005) proposes that the central image for qualitative inquiry should be the crystal. Her metaphor is worth quoting at length here:

> The central imaginary is the crystal, which combines symmetry with an infinite variety of shapers, substances, transmutations, multidimensionalities, and angles of approach. Crystals grow, change, and are altered, but they are not amorphous. Crystals are prisms that reflect externalities *and* refract within themselves, creating different colors, patterns, arrays, casting off in different directions. What we see depends on our angle of repose—not triangulation, crystallization.
>
> In a crystal, light can be both waves and particles. Crystallization, without losing structure, deconstructs the traditional idea of validity (we feel how there is no single truth, we see how texts validate themselves); and crystallization provides us with a deepened, complex, thoroughly partial understanding of the topic. Paradoxically, we know more and doubt what we know. (Richardson, 1997, p. 92)

This image is compelling because it values both interior and exterior aspects of the research process, giving credence to the fact that all research is situated and personal—a thoroughly human endeavor. Yet order and rigor are necessary to preserve the integrity of the outcome.

❖ CRITERIA VERSUS STANDARDS

To shift to a slightly different point, no matter what metaphors or principles we apply to our own research, in the academic world of knowledge production, "quality" is a state granted and recognized from the outside. One's work is assessed in context by various audiences, who have their own sets of standards and context-specific criteria for evaluation. Frankly, my own beliefs about what makes quality in social research vary widely, depending on the context within which I am making a judgment. Let's problematize this more closely.

Who is doing the research? If am teaching new researchers, I am patient but highly skeptical of their work, insisting on in-depth explanations and justifications of approach. On the other hand, if I know a researcher has previously conducted what is commonly perceived to be high-quality research, a certain level of credibility is built into my reading of all that person's work. I more readily accept experimental or narrative work from someone who has proven herself previously.

Where was the research published? If someone writes about a cultural practice in a piece labeled "fiction" and I find meaning in this work, I feel grateful that I gained added benefit from what might otherwise be "merely" a story [scare quotes to denote I understand the irony]. Sure, I might question the methods, but since he published something as fiction, I don't quibble with the details. On the other hand, if someone writes a good story and labels it "research," I am much more likely to question those methods and expect some explanation of how and on what empirical evidence that researcher derived her conclusions.

What is the goal of the research? This book takes a fairly narrow stance on the goal of research and therefore offers definitions and perspectives that align with this goal. Producing research findings for publication in academically acceptable venues for the purpose of contributing to a body of knowledge is not a universal or all-encompassing end. Research intended to build community, promote social justice, disrupt dominant patterns of power, or dismantle tidy categories of meaning requires quite different criteria for evaluation.

The three previous paragraphs may seem to paint a picture of qualitative inquiry as a perilous house of cards, where the criteria always change and determinations of quality are essentially fickle. However, I want to focus attention on the idea that criteria and standards are intertwined concepts, but they are not synonymous: A criterion specifies an attribute or behavior, which then serves as a measure for judgment. A standard can be thought of as a set of criteria or a principle on which assessments rely.

While one's criteria may change for various reasons, one's standards need not. The former necessarily morph with each specific piece of research, because each research project is a unique, situated, authored cultural product, whereas the latter can and most often do remain firmly embedded in one's ontological and axiological frameworks for understanding what it means to do "good" research within the vast umbrella we call "qualitative inquiry."

I draw attention to this distinction because it helps clarify the idea that qualitative inquiry can be wide open for the creative invention and mixing of methodological approaches, and yet, at the same time, particular criteria must inform one's work: As Nancy emphasizes, a systematic focus and consistency will build symmetry within the crystal that—even if not apparent to the reader—will have high resonance, thus marking the project as one that is credible and trustworthy.

This is why the crystalline image works well as a way of thinking about quality: Order and rigor exist in a form that exhibits multiple refracting surfaces, appears differently depending on how you look at it or what type of light is targeted at it, and reveals both processes and products (in a crystal we can see both waves and particles). The criteria Nancy describes provide a beginning point for thinking about how one might introduce order and rigor as and within crystalline forms, but are not an ending, because within this metaphor, multiplicities can emerge.

❖ IMPROVISATION AND A FULL TOOLBOX

Given the most likely audience reading this book, I think most would agree with the notion that "the more you know, the better off you are." If you want to create research reports that are respected by academics (and I'm not suggesting this as the sole or most admirable goal of research by any means; I'm just acknowledging that it is probably the most common objective held by readers of this book), you should be well trained in a range of approaches—not only so that you make good choices from the beginning but so that you also know how to explain your decisions later. Mastery of multiple methods allows one to move with ease in multiple directions. Improvisation is easier if one has a broad range of skills to begin with, because it requires the ability to be fully present and aware and to draw on any number of options in the moment as we interact with the context of study.

Of course, as we grow more aware of the multiple perspectives that inform qualitative inquiry, the choices can become daunting. Every year, I realize how much more I don't know. As I study epistemological and axiological discussions within different cultures, my methodological choices only become more bewildering. On the one hand, we want more tools and techniques to draw on, so that we don't fall prey to the axiom, "When the only tool one has is a hammer, everything looks like a nail." On the other hand, when our toolbox includes an ever-growing mix of interpretive, critical, queer, feminist, postmodernist, postcolonialist tools, nothing looks like the comfortable familiarity of a nail. The project of hammering a nail shifts to something else entirely, which can open up possibilities for political and resistive acts that cannot be ignored in the search for clarity, balance, or parsimony.

Here, I'm not so much talking about method as "application of procedure," whereby we might ask the question of whether it is better (loaded term intended) or not to use interviews or surveys to collect information. I am focused more on the issue of "interpretive rigor," a more recent discussion addressing the methods associated with framing questions, analyzing texts, and interpreting/representing Other in the process of writing and editing findings.

If we take a postmodern stance on knowledge production, we might reject such concepts as theory-building, agreeing with Tyler (1986) that the purpose of ethnography is evocation through aesthetics. If we take to heart a feminist critique of the processes of knowledge production, the search for method might become one that "interrogate[s] what the theoretical move that establishes foundations *authorizes*, and what precisely it excludes or forecloses" (Butler, 1995, p. 39, emphasis in original). With these perspectives on inquiry, the list of criteria offered by Nancy may not suffice. We might need to raise additional questions: How well do reflexivity, irony, bricolage, intertextuality, pastiche, and hyperreality fit into the master narratives that still discipline our procedural decisions during the research project? And if not at the level of dictating the precise method that ought to be used, how can we find a broader range of options within which we are authorized to call our inquiry legitimate or publishable?

Continuing, if we embrace these contemporary lenses, the goal of meeting some authority's criteria becomes increasingly difficult. Nancy's list is extremely practical—a useful and fruitful starting point. But if that list doesn't resonate with you or you seek to interrogate and dismantle those ideas, what models or concepts associated with methodological rigor would be more useful? What standards apply to your own work, if not these?

❖ ACCOUNT-ABILITY

There are innumerable possible sets of criteria, each with its particular set of delimiters. I find the ethic of accountability a compelling way to address quality because it identifies a standard and specifies underlying criteria that can guide ethical rigor. What does accountability *mean*?

As Maria Christina Gonzalez articulates beautifully in a brief essay on the ethics of a postcolonial ethnography (2003), the term "accountability" has lost its strength as an ethical guide because in the academy, it is "so familiar as to almost be cliché in our intellectual parlance" (p. 78). If we look more closely at what accountability means, we can rediscover its strength as a guide:

> From a colonialist perspective, when we think of the concept of accountability, we are concerned with the possible repercussions for not having followed "the rules" as set forth by the imperial force. Let go of this meaning. Instead, look at the word. Account-ability. The ability to account. To tell a story. (Gonzalez, 2003, p. 82)

Importantly, the ethic of accountability,[1] continues Gonzalez, "is not just the telling of the ethnographic tale. It is the telling of our story, of how we came to know the ethnographic tale. There is no natural boundary between a story and our learning of it" (p. 82). This goes beyond simple explanation, because it is an accounting of choices among various alternatives, as well as a story of missteps, shortcuts, shifts, revelations, and battles. It is only possible if we are able to articulate the beliefs underlying each choice. Since choice necessarily involves competing options, the accountability part comes into play when we are able to explain why we chose this method instead of another equally acceptable method. We can only engage in this level of reflexive analysis of our methodology when we know a lot about methods and where they come from, epistemologically and ontologically speaking. Whether or not accountability is fully expressed in every research report, it is a quality that can be called on at any point, when we should then be able to tell the story of the story. As Gonzalez notes, "It's not so easy" (p. 84).

Nancy and I steadfastly agree that questions of quality must be addressed, but that at some level, one should note a distinctive difference between the methodological level of reflexivity and the rhetorical challenge of making arguments. It is important to be able to explain oneself or preempt some of the audience's questions, but this type of improvisation requires a solid knowledge of the possible choices, a keen awareness of the criteria applied to one's own work, and a reflexive analysis of what criteria might be used by others to assess the quality of our work. Paradoxically, perhaps, I believe this process is less about finding the answers than asking good questions.

❖ RECOMMENDED READING

All three editions of the *Handbook of Qualitative Research* (Denzin & Lincoln, 1994, 2000, 2005) are a valuable resource for understanding the complexities of qualitative inquiry.

For an exhaustive and interesting discussion of paradigmatic controversies and debates over legitimacy, I recommend Guba and Lincoln's chapter, "Paradigmatic Controversies, Contradictions, and Emerging Confluences," in the third edition of that handbook (2005).

For a dense elaboration of the history of qualitative inquiry as well as an outline of the major issues being currently debated in this arena, it is worth reading carefully the introduction to the third edition by Denzin and Lincoln, "Introduction: The Discipline and Practice of Qualitative Research" (2005). For a contrasting perspective that more aligns with Nancy's perspective, I recommend Silverman's edited volume *Qualitative Research: Theory, Method, and Practice* (2004).

❖ NOTE

1. The other three ethics discussed by Gonzalez include (2) context, an open-eyed mindfulness; (3) truthfulness, which, more than a "simple consciously expressed truth . . . [is] an opening of the heart, a willingness to be absolutely existentially naked . . . ; and (4) community, a radical transformation of the separated, disengaged 'audience,' 'the field,' 'our readers,' and 'our colleagues'" (2003, p. 84). As I've oversimplified her argument in this footnote, I recommend reading her essay in its entirely.

Acknowledgments

First and foremost Nancy wants to thank Annette for her vision and persistence in spearheading this book and for her friendship. She'd also like to thank the students in her graduate seminars in Qualitative Methods at the University of Kansas who helped her think through many of the issues raised in this book; Margaret Seawell for originally taking this book on and Todd Armstrong at SAGE for seeing it through; and last but never least, Rex, Zane, and Eli.

Annette would like to thank the contributors, whose work inspired the book from the beginning. Without them, this project would not exist. It wouldn't have been finished, either, without the persistent support of her friends within the Association of Internet Researchers (AOIR), who have become the stable community in her gypsy life. Among this community, Nancy has been steady and true. She was a fantastic colleague throughout this project, proving that it can be fun to do collaborative work with good friends.

In addition, many thanks to our colleagues whose keen sensibilities in reading early versions gave strength and shape to this volume: John W. Creswell (University of Nebraska–Lincoln); Norman Denzin (University of Illinois at Urbana–Champaign); Klaus Bruhn Jensen (University of Copenhagen); Mark D. Johns (Luther College); Steve Jones (University of Illinois, Chicago); and William K. Rawlins (Ohio University).

References

Allen, C. (1996). What's wrong with the "Golden Rule"? Conundrums of conducting ethical research in cyberspace. *Information Society, 12,* 175–187.

Altork, K. (1995). Walking the fire line: The erotic dimension of the fieldwork experience. In D. Kulick & M. Willson (Eds.), *Taboo: Sex, identity, and erotic subjectivity in anthropological fieldwork* (pp. 107–139). London: Routledge.

Amit, V. (Ed.). (2000a). *Constructing the field: Ethnographic fieldwork in the contemporary world.* London: Routledge.

Amit, V. (2000b). Introduction: Constructing the field. In V. Amit (Ed.), *Constructing the field: Ethnographic fieldwork in the contemporary world* (pp. 1–18). London: Routledge.

AoIR (Association of Internet Researchers). (2002). *Ethical decision-making and Internet research. Recommendations from the AoIR ethics working committee.* Retrieved January 30, 2006, from http://www.aoir.org/reports/ethics.pdf

Appadurai, A. (1996). *Modernity at large: Cultural dimensions of globalization.* Minneapolis: University of Minnesota Press.

Ashmore, M. (1989). *The reflexive thesis: Wrighting sociology of scientific knowledge.* Chicago: University of Chicago Press.

Atran, S., Medin, D., & Ross, N. (2005, October). The cultural mind: Environmental decision making and cultural modeling within and across populations. *Psychological Review, 112*(4), 744–776.

Bagilhole, B. (2002). *Women in non-traditional occupations.* New York: Palgrave Macmillan.

Bakardjieva, M. (2005). *Internet society: The Internet in everyday life.* London: Sage.

Bakardjieva, M., & Feenberg, A. (2001). Involving the virtual subject. *Ethics and Information Technology, 2,* 233–240.

Bakardjieva, M., Feenberg, A., & Goldi, J. (2004). User-centered Internet research: The ethical challenge. In E. Buchanan (Ed.), *Readings in virtual research ethics: Issues and controversies.* Hershey, PA: Idea Group.

Bakardjieva, M., & Smith, R. (2001). The Internet in everyday life: Computer networking from the standpoint of the domestic user. *New Media & Society, 3*(1), 67–83.

Bakhtin, M. M. (1981). *The dialogic imagination: Four essays,* (M. Holquist, Ed.; C. Emerson & M. Holquist, Trans.). Austin: University of Texas Press.

Bakhtin, M. M. (1986). *Speech genres & other late essays.* Austin: University of Texas Press.

Balsamo, A. (1990). Rethinking ethnography: A work for the feminist imagination. *Studies in Symbolic Interaction, 11,* 45–57.

Baron, N. (2003). Why email looks like speech: Proofreading, pedagogy, and public face. In J. Aitchison & D. Lewis (Eds.), *New media language* (pp. 102–111). London: Routledge.

Baron, N. S., Squires, L., Tench, S., & Thompson, M. (2005). Tethered or mobile? Use of away messages in instant messaging by American college students. In R. Ling & P. Pedersen (Eds.), *Front stage–back stage: Mobile communication and the renegotiation of the social sphere.* Retrieved January 28, 2005, from http://www.american.edu/tesol/Grimstad-Baron.pdf

Bauman, Z. (2000). *Liquid modernity.* Cambridge, MA: Polity Press.

Bauman, Z. (2005). Afterthought: On writing; on writing sociology. In N. Denzin & Y. Lincoln (Eds.), *The SAGE handbook of qualitative research* (pp. 1089–1098). Thousand Oaks, CA: Sage.

Baxter, L. A. (2007). Problematizing the problem in communication: A dialogic perspective. *Communication Monographs, 74*(1), 118–124.

Baxter, L., & Montgomery, B. (2007). *Relating: Dialogues and dialectics.* New York: Guilford Press.

Baym, N. K. (2000). *Tune in, log on: Soaps, fandom, and online community.* Thousand Oaks, CA: Sage.

Baym, N. K. (2002). Interpersonal life online. In L. A. Lievrouw & S. Livingstone (Eds.), *Handbook of new media* (pp. 62–76). London: Sage.

Baym, N. K. (2006). Finding the quality in qualitative internet research. In D. Silver & A. Massanari (Eds.), *Critical cyberculture studies: Current terrains, future directions* (pp. 79–87). New York: New York University Press.

Beaulieu, A. (2004). Mediating ethnography: Objectivity and the making of ethnographies of the Internet. *Social Epistemology 18*(2–3), 139–164.

Beaulieu, A. (2005). Sociable hyperlinks. In C. Hine (Ed.), *Virtual methods: Issues in social research on the Internet* (pp. 183–197). Oxford: Berg.

Behar, R., & Gordon, D. A. (Eds.). (1995). *Women writing culture.* Berkeley: University of California Press.

Bell, D., & Valentine, G. (1995). Introduction: Orientations. In D. Bell & G. Valentine (Eds.), *Mapping desire: Geographies of sexualities.* London: Routledge.

Bhabha, H. (1994). *The location of culture.* London: Routledge.

Bijker, W. E. (1995). *Of bicycles, bakelites and bulbs: Toward a theory of sociotechnical change.* Cambridge: MIT Press.

Binik, Y., Mah, K., & Kiesler, S. (1999). Ethical issues in conducting sex research on the Internet. *Journal of Sex Research, 36*(1), 82–90.

Boast, R., Bravo, M., & Srinivasan, R. (2007, October). Return to Babel: Emergent diversity, digital resources, and local knowledge. *Information Society, 23*(5), 395–403.

Bourdieu, P. (1990). *The logic of practice.* Stanford, CA: Stanford University Press.

Bouthillette, A.-M., Retter, Y., & Ingram, G. B. (Eds.). (1997). *Queers in space: Communities, public places, sites of resistance.* Seattle, WA: Bay Press.

Bowker, G. C., & Star, S. L. (1999). *Sorting things out: Classification and its consequences.* Cambridge: MIT Press.

boyd, d. (2007). Why youth (heart) social network sites: The role of networked publics in teenage social life. In D. Buckingham (Ed.), *MacArthur Foundation Series on Digital Learning—Youth, identity, and digital media volume.* Cambridge: MIT Press.

Branwyn, G. (1994). Compu-sex: Erotica for cybernauts. In M. Dery (Ed.), *Flame wars: The discourse of cyberculture.* Durham, NC: Duke University Press.

Braziel, J. E., & LeBesco, K. (Eds.). (2001). *Bodies out of bounds: Fatness and transgression.* Berkeley: University of California Press.

Brewer, J. (2000). *Ethnography.* Buckingham: Open University Press.

Briggs, C. (1986). *Learning how to ask.* Cambridge: Cambridge University Press.

Brin, D. (1998). *The transparent society: Will technology force us to choose between privacy and freedom?* Reading, MA: Addison-Wesley.

Brown, K. M. (1991). *Mama Lola.* Berkeley: University of California Press.

Bruckman, A. (1997, January 20). *MediaMOO Symposium: The ethics of research in virtual communities.* Retrieved February 12, 2002, from http://www.cc.gatech .edu/fac/asb/MediaMOO/ethics-symposium-97.html

Buchanan, E. (Ed). (2004). *Readings in virtual research ethics: Issues and controversies.* Hershey, PA: Idea Group.

Burawoy, M. (2001). Manufacturing the global. *Ethnography, 2*(2), 147–159.

Burawoy, M., et al. (2000). *Global ethnography: Forces, connections, and imaginations in a postmodern world.* Berkeley: University of California Press.

Butler, J. (1990). *Gender trouble: Feminism and the subversion of identity.* New York: Routledge.

Butler, J. (1993). *Bodies that matter: On the discursive limits of "sex."* New York: Routledge.

Butler, J. (1995). Contingent foundations. In S. Benhabib, J. Butler, D. Cornell, & N. Fraser (Eds.), *Feminist contentions: A philosophical exchange (thinking gender)* (pp. 35–57). London: Routledge.

Califia, P. (1994). *Public sex: The culture of radical sex.* Pittsburgh, PA: Cleir Press.

Callaway, H. (1992). Ethnography and experience: Gender implications in fieldwork and texts. In J. Okely & H. Callaway (Eds.), *Anthropology and autobiography* (pp. 29–49). London: Routledge.

Callon, M. (1999). Actor-network theory—The market test. In J. Law & J. Hassard (Eds.), *Actor network theory and after* (pp. 181–195). Oxford: Blackwell.

Campbell, J. E. (2004). *Getting it on online: Cyberspace and gay male sexuality and embodied sexuality.* Binghamton, NY: Harrington Park Press.

Carey, J. W. (2005). Historical pragmatism and the Internet. *New Media and Society, 7*(4), 443–455.

Castells, M. (2000). *The rise of the network society: The information age: Economy, society and culture, Vol. 1.* Oxford: Blackwell.

Cesara, M. (1982). *Reflections of a woman anthropologist.* New York: Academic Press.

Cherny, L. (1999). *Conversation and community: Chat in a virtual world.* Stanford, CA: CSLI Publications.

Christians, C. (2000). Ethics and politics in qualitative research. In N. Denzin & Y. Lincoln (Eds.), *Handbook of qualitative research* (2nd ed., pp. 133–155). Thousand Oaks, CA: Sage.

Christians, C. G., & Carey, J. W. (1989). The logic and aims of qualitative research. In G. Stempel & B. Westley (Eds.), *Research methods in mass communication* (2nd ed., pp. 354–374). New York: Prentice Hall.

Clair, R. P. (Ed.). (2003). *Expressions of ethnography: Novel approaches to qualitative methods.* Albany: SUNY Press.

Clarke, A., & Fujimura, J. (Eds.) (1992). *The right tools for the job: At work in twentieth century life sciences.* Princeton, NJ: Princeton University Press.

Clifford, J., & Marcus, G. (Eds.). (1986). *Writing culture.* Berkeley: University of California Press.

Connell, R. W. (1995). *Masculinities.* Berkeley: University of California Press.

Consalvo, M., & Paasonen, S. (2002). *Women & everyday uses of the Internet: Agency & identity.* New York: Peter Lang.

Cooper, G. (2001). Conceptualising social life. In N. Gilbert (Ed.), *Researching social life* (2nd ed., pp. 1–13). London: Sage.

Correll, S. (1995). The ethnography of an electronic bar: The lesbian café. *Journal of Contemporary Ethnography, 24*(3), 270–298.

Crotty, M. (1998). *The foundations of social research: Meaning and perspectives in the research process.* London: Sage.

Cunningham, S., & Turner, G. (2006). *The media and communications in Australia.* Sydney: Allen and Unwin.

Dalmiya, V., & Alcoff, L. (1993). Are "old wives' tales" justified? In E. Potter & L. Alcoff (Eds.), *Feminist epistemologies* (pp. 217–244). New York: Routledge.

Daneback, K. (in press). *Love and sexuality on the Internet.* Dissertation in progress. Institution for Social Work, Gothenburg University.

Danet, B. (2001a). *Cyberplay: Communicating online.* Oxford: Berg.

Danet, B. (2001b). *Studies of cyberpl@y: Ethical and methodological aspects.* Paper prepared for the Ethics Working Committee, Association of Internet Researchers. Retrieved January 15, 2002, from http://www.cddc.vt .edu/aoir/ethics/case.html.

Danet, B., Ruedenberg-Wright, L., & Rosenbaum-Tamari, Y. (1997). "HMMM . . . WHERE'S THAT SMOKE COMING FROM?": Writing, play and performance on Internet relay chat. *Journal of Computer-Mediated Communication, 2*(4).

De Laet, M. K., & Mol, A. (2000). The Zimbabwe bush pump: Mechanics of a fluid technology. *Social Studies of Science, 30,* 225–263.

Denzin, N. (1989). *The research act* (3rd ed.). Englewood Cliffs, NJ: Prentice Hall.

Denzin, N. (2004). Prologue: Online environments and interpretive social research (pp. 1–12). In M. D. Johns, S. S. Chen, & G. J. Hall (Eds), *Online social research: Methods, issues, and ethics.* New York: Peter Lang Press.

Denzin, N., & Lincoln, Y. (Eds.). (1994). *Handbook of qualitative research.* Thousand Oaks, CA: Sage.

Denzin, N., & Lincoln, Y. (Eds.). (2000). *Handbook of qualitative research* (2nd ed.). Thousand Oaks, CA: Sage.

Denzin, N., & Lincoln, Y. (Eds.). (2003). *Collecting and interpreting qualitative materials* (2nd ed.). Thousand Oaks, CA: Sage.

Denzin, N., & Lincoln, Y. (Eds.). (2005). *The SAGE handbook of qualitative research* (3rd ed.). Thousand Oaks, CA: Sage.

Dervin, B. (1998). Sense-making theory and practice: An overview of user interests in knowledge seeking and use. *Journal of Knowledge Management, 2*(2), 36–46.

Dimitrov, V., & Hodge, B. (2002). *Social fuzziology: Study of fuzziness of social complexity.* Heidelberg: Physica-Verlag.

Dodge, M., & Kitchin, R. (2001). *Mapping cyberspace.* London: Routledge.

Donath, J. S. (1999). Identity and deception in the virtual community. In A. M. Smith & P. Kollock (Eds.), *Communities in cyberspace* (pp. 29–59). London: Routledge.

Döring, N. (2000). Feminist views of cybersex: Victimization, liberation, and empowerment. *CyberPsychology and Behavior, 3*(5), 863–884.

Eichhorn, K. (2001). Sites unseen: Ethnographic research in a textual community. *Qualitative Studies in Education, 14*(4), 565–578.

Eisenberg, E. (1984). Ambiguity as strategy in organizational communication. *Communication Monographs, 51,* 227–242.

Enslin, E. (1994). Beyond writing: Feminist practice and the limitations of ethnography. *Cultural Anthropology, 9*(4), 537–568.

Escobar, A. (1994). Welcome to Cyberia: Notes on the anthropology of cyber-culture. *Current Anthropology, 35*(3), 211–231.

Ess, C., & Jones, S. (2003). Ethical decision-making and Internet research: Recommendations from the AoIR Ethics Working Committee. In E. A. Buchanan (Ed.), *Virtual research ethics: Issues and controversies.* Hershey, PA: Idea Group.

Featherstone, M., & Venn, C. (2006). Problematizing global knowledge and the New Encyclopaedia Project: An introduction. *Theory, Culture & Society, 23*(2–3), 1–20.

Feenberg, A., & Bakardjieva, M. (2004). *Groupware for community: Between the real and the possible.* Paper presented at Public Proofs: Science, Technology and Democracy, Society for the Social Studies of Science (4S) & EASST Conference, Paris.

Fine, G. A. (1993). Ten lies of ethnography: Moral dilemmas of field research. *Journal of Contemporary Ethnography, 22*(3), 267–294.

Forte, M. (2004). Co-construction and field creation: Website development as both an instrument and relationship in action research. In E. Buchanan (Ed.), *Readings in virtual research ethics: Issues and controversies.* Hershey, PA: Idea Group.

Forte, M. (2005). Centering the links: Understanding cybernetic patterns of co-production, circulation and consumption In C. Hine (Ed.), *Virtual methods: Issues in social research on the Internet* (pp. 93–106). Oxford: Berg.

Foucault, M. (1978). *The history of sexuality: An introduction, Vol. I* (R. Hurley Trans.). New York: Random House.

Frankel, M., & Siang, S. (1999). Ethical and legal aspects of human subjects research on the Internet: A report of a workshop. *American Association for the Advancement of Science.* Retrieved February 1, 2002, from http://www.aaas.org/spp/dspp/sfrl/projects/intres/main.htm.

Gajjala, R. (2004). *Cyberselves: Feminist ethnographies of South Asian women.* Walnut Creek, CA: AltaMira Press.

Gajjala, R., Rybas, N., & Altman, M. (2007). Epistemologies of doing: E-merging selves online. *Feminist Media Studies, 7*(2).

Garfinkel, H. (1967). *Studies in ethnomethodology.* Englewood Cliffs, NJ: Prentice Hall.

Geertz, C. (1973). *The interpretation of cultures.* New York: Basic Books.

Geertz, C. (2000). *Local knowledge: Further essays in interpretive anthropology.* New York: Basic Books.

Gergen, K. (1991). *The saturated self: Dilemmas of identity in contemporary life.* New York: Basic Books.

Giddens, A. (1990). *The consequences of modernity.* Cambridge, MA: Polity Press.

Glaser, B. G., & Strauss, A. (1967). *The discovery of grounded theory: Strategies for qualitative research.* London: Weidenfeld and Nicolson.

Glennie, P. D., & Thrift, N. J. (1996). Consumers, identities, and consumption spaces in early-modern England. *Environment and Planning, A28,* 25–45.

Goffman, E. (1961). *Asylums: Essays on the social situation of mental patients and other inmates.* New York: Doubleday Anchor.

Goffman, E. (1974). *Frame analysis: An essay on the organization of experience.* Cambridge, MA: Harvard University Press.

Goggin, G. (2004). *Virtual nation: The Internet in Australia.* Sydney: University of New South Wales.

Gonzalez, M. C. (2003). An ethics for postcolonial ethnography. In R. P. Clair (Ed.), *Expressions of ethnography: Novel approaches to qualitative methods* (pp. 77–86). Albany: SUNY Press.

Goode, E. (1999). Sex with informants as deviant behavior. *Deviant Behavior, 20,* 301–324.

Green, N. (1999). Disrupting the field: Virtual reality technologies and "multi-sited" ethnographic methods. *American Behavioral Scientist, 43*(5), 409–421.

Grindstaff, L. (2002). *The money shot: Trash, class, and the marking of TV talk shows.* Chicago: University of Chicago Press.

Grint, K., & Woolgar, S. (1997). *The machine at work: Technology, work and organization.* Cambridge, MA: Polity Press.

Gross, L. (1991). Out of the mainstream: Sexual minorities and the mass media. In M. Wolf & A. Kielwasser (Eds.), *Gay people, sex, and the media.* New York: Harrington Park Press.

Guba, E. G., & Lincoln, Y. S. (2005). Paradigmatic controversies, contradictions, and emerging confluences. In N. Denzin & Y. Lincoln (Eds.), *The SAGE handbook of qualitative research* (3rd ed., pp. 191–215). Thousand Oaks, CA: Sage.

Gubrium, J. F., & Holstein, J. A. (1999). At the border of narrative and ethnography. *Journal of Contemporary Ethnography, 28*(5), 561–573.

Hacking, I. (1999). *The social construction of what?* Cambridge, MA: Harvard University Press.

Hakken, D. (1999). *Cyborgs@cyberspace.* New York: Routledge.

Hamman, R. B. (1996). *Cyborgasms: Cybersex amongst multiple-selves and cyborgs in the narrow-bandwidth space of America Online chat rooms.* MA thesis, Department of Sociology, University of Essex. Retrieved September 26, 2006, from http://www.socio.demon.co.uk/Cyborgasms_old.html

Hammersley, M. (1998). *Reading ethnographic research* (2nd ed.). London: Longman.

Hammersley, M., & Atkinson, P. (1995). *Ethnography: Principles in practice* (2nd ed.). London: Routledge.

Hannerz, U. (1992). *Cultural complexity: Studies in the social organization of meaning.* New York: Columbia University Press.

Haraway, D. (1991a). *Simians, cyborgs and women: The reinvention of nature.* New York: Routledge.

Haraway, D. (1991b). Situated knowledges: The science question in feminism and the privilege of partial perspective. In *Simians, cyborgs and women: The reinvention of nature*. New York: Routledge.

Haraway, D. (1997a). *Modest witness@second millennium: FemaleMan©_meets OncoMouse™*. New York: Routledge.

Haraway, D. (1997b). The virtual speculum in the new world order. *Feminist Review, 55*, 22–72.

Haraway, D. (2000). *How like a leaf: An interview with Thyrza Nichols Goodeve*. New York: Routledge.

Harding, S. (1991). *Whose science? Whose knowledge?* London: Open University Press.

Harding, S. (1992). After the neutrality ideal: Science, politics, and "strong objectivity." *Social Research, 59*(3), 567–587.

Haythornthwaite, C., & Wellman, B. (2002). The Internet in everyday life: An introduction. In B. Wellman & C. Haythornwaite (Eds.), *The Internet in everyday life* (pp. 3–41). London: Blackwell.

Heath, D., Koch, E., Ley, B. L., & Montoya, M. (1999). Nodes and queries: Linking locations in networked fields of inquiry. *American Behavioral Scientist, 43*(3), 450–460.

Herman, A., & Swiss, T. (2000). *The world wide web and contemporary cultural theory*. London: Routledge.

Hermes, J. (1995). *Reading women's magazines: An analysis of everyday media use*. Cambridge, MA: Polity Press.

Herring, S. (1993). Gender and democracy in computer-mediated communication. *Electronic Journal of Communication, 3*(2).

Herring, S. C. (2004). Slouching toward the ordinary: Current trends in computer-mediated communication. *New Media & Society, 6*(1), 26–36.

Hess, D. (2001). Ethnography and the development of science and technology studies. In P. Atkinson, A. Coffey, S. Delamont, J. Lofland, & L. Lofland (Eds.), *Handbook of ethnography* (pp. 234–245). London: Sage.

Hey, T., & Trefethen, A. E. (2002). The UK e-Science Core Programme and the grid. *Future Generation Computing Systems, 18*(8), 1017–1031.

Hine, C. (1995). Representations of information technology in disciplinary development: Disappearing plants and invisible networks. *Science, Technology and Human Values, 20*(1), 65–85.

Hine, C. (2000). *Virtual ethnography*. London: Sage.

Hine, C. (2001).Web pages, authors and audiences: The meaning of a mouse click. *Information, Communication & Society, 4*(2), 182–198.

Hine, C. (2002). Cyberscience and social boundaries: The implications of laboratory talk on the Internet. *Sociological Research Online, 7*(2). Retrieved from http://www.socresonline.org.uk/7/2/hine.html

Hine, C. (2005a). Introduction: Virtual methods and the sociology of cyber-social-scientific knowledge (pp. 1–16). In C. Hine (Ed.). *Virtual methods: Issues in social research on the Internet.* Oxford: Berg.

Hine, C. (Ed.). (2005b). *Virtual methods: Issues in social research on the Internet.* Oxford: Berg.

Hine, C. (2008). *Systematics as cyberscience: Computers, change and continuity in science.* Cambridge: MIT Press.

Holloway, S., & Valentine, G. (2003) *Cyberkids: Children in the information age.* London: Routledge Falmer.

Howard, P. N. (2002). Network ethnography and the hypermedia organization: New media, new organizations, new methods. *New Media & Society,* 4(4), 550–574.

Howard, P. N., & Jones, S. (Eds.). (2004). *Society online: The Internet in context.* Thousand Oaks, CA: Sage.

Howard, P. N., Rainie, L., & Jones, S. (2001). Days and nights on the Internet. *American Behavioral Scientist, 45*(3), 382–404.

HSFR. (1990/1999). *Forskningsetiska principer i humanistisk-samhällsvetenskaplig forskning. Antagna av Humanistisk-samhällsvetenskapliga forskningsrådet i mars (Ethical principles for scientific research in the humanities and Social Sciences adopted by the Swedish Council for Research in the Humanities and Social Sciences [HSFR]).* Retrieved February 11, 2002, from http://www.vr.se/download/18.6687410b37070528800029/HS%5B1%5D.pdf

IRB Guidebook. (n.d.). Office for Human Research Protections. Retrieved from http://www.hhs.gov/ohrp/irb/irb_introduction.htm

Irwin, K. (2006). Into the dark heart of ethnography: The lived ethics and inequality of intimate field relationships. *Qualitative Sociology, 29*(2), 155–175.

Jackson, S. (1986). Building a case for claims about discourse structure. In D. G. Ellis & W. A. Donohue (Eds.), *Contemporary issues in language and discourse processes* (pp. 129–147). Hillsdale, NJ: Erlbaum.

Johns, M. D., Chen, S. L. S., & Hall, G. J. (Eds.). (2004). *Online social research: Methods, issues, and ethics.* New York: Peter Lang Press.

Jones, S. G. (Ed.). (1999). *Doing Internet research: Critical issues and methods for examining the Net.* Thousand Oaks, CA: Sage.

Kanter, R. M. (1977). *Men and women of the corporation.* New York: Basic Books.

Karlsson, A. M. (2002). *Skriftbruk i förändring. En semiotisk studie av den personliga hemsidan.* Dissertation. Acta Universitatis Stockholmiensis. New series 25. Stockholm: Almquist & Wiksell.

Kauffman, B. (1992). Feminist facts: Interview strategies and political subjects in ethnography. *Communication Theory, 2*(3), 187–206.

Kendall, L. (2002). *Hanging out in the virtual pub: Masculinities and relationships online.* Berkeley: University of California Press.

Kendall, L. (2005). Diary of a networked individual. In *Internet research annual, Vol. 2*. New York: Peter Lang.

King, S. A. (1996). Researching Internet communities: Proposed ethical guidelines for the reporting of results. *Information Society, 12*(2), 119–127.

Kivits, J. (2005). Online interviewing and the research relationship. In C. Hine (Ed.), *Virtual methods: Issues in social research on the Internet* (pp. 35–50). Oxford: Berg.

Kleinman, S., & Copp, M. (1993). *Emotions and fieldwork*. Thousand Oaks, CA: Sage.

Kohler Riessman, C. (1993). *Narrative analysis: Qualitative research methods Series 30*. London: Sage.

Kraidy, M. M. (1999). The global, the local, and the hybrid: A native ethnography of glocalization. *Critical Studies in Mass Communication, 16*, 456–476.

Kulick, D. (1995). Introduction: The sexual life of anthropologists: Erotic subjectivity and ethnographic work. In D. Kulick & M. Willson (Eds), *Taboo: Sex, identity, and erotic subjectivity in anthropological fieldwork* (pp. 1–28). London: Routledge.

Kulick, D., & Willson, M. (Eds.). (1995). *Taboo: Sex, identity, and erotic subjectivity in anthropological fieldwork*. London: Routledge.

Lally, E. (2002). *At home with computers*. Oxford: Berg.

Lather, P. (2001). Postbook: Working the ruins of feminist ethnography. *Signs, 27*(1), 199–227.

Latour, B. (1987). *Science in action: How to follow scientists and engineers through society*. Cambridge, MA: Harvard University Press.

Latour, B. (1990). Drawing things together. In M. Lynch & S. Woolgar (Eds.), *Representation in scientific practice*. Cambridge: MIT Press.

Law, J. (2004). *After method: Mess in social science research*. London: Routledge.

Law, J., & Urry, J. (2004). Enacting the social. *Economy and Society, 33*(3), 390–410.

Leander, K. M., & McKim, K. K. (2003). Tracing the everyday "sitings" of adolescents on the Internet: A strategic adaptation of ethnography across online and offline spaces. *Education, Communication & Information, 3*(2), 211–240.

Lengel, L. B. (1998). Researching the "other," transforming ourselves: Methodological considerations of feminist ethnography. *Journal of Communication Inquiry, 22*(3), 229–250.

Lenhart, A. (2001, September 21). *Who's not online: 57% of those without Internet access say they do not plan to log on*. Retrieved January 28, 2005, from http://www.pewinternet.org/pdfs/Pew_Those_Not_Online_Report.pdf

Lessig, L. (1999). *Code and other laws of cyberspace*. New York: Basic Books.

Lévi-Strauss, C. (1966). *The savage mind*, trans. John Weightman and Doreen Weightman. Chicago: University of Chicago Press.

Lindlof, T. R., & Taylor, B. C. (2002). *Qualitative communication research methods* (2nd ed.). Thousand Oaks, CA: Sage.

Livingstone, S. (2002). *Young people and new media: Childhood and the changing media environment.* Thousand Oaks, CA: Sage.

Livingstone, S. (2006). Children's privacy online: Experimenting with boundaries within and beyond the family. In R. Kraut, M. Brynin, & S. Kiesler (Eds.), *Computers, phones and the Internet: Domesticating information technology.* Oxford: Oxford University Press.

Lövheim, M. (1999). *Making meaning of virtual religion: Methodological and ethical concerns.* Paper presented at the annual meeting of the Society for the Scientific Study of Religion, and the Religious Research Association, Boston.

Lull, J. (1991). *Inside family viewing.* London: Routledge.

Lynch, M. (2000). Against reflexivity as an academic virtue and source of privileged knowledge. *Theory, Culture & Society, 17*(3), 26–54.

Mackay, H. (2005). New connections, familiar settings: Issues in the ethnographic study of new media use at home. In C. Hine (Ed.), *Virtual methods: Issues in social research on the Internet* (pp. 129–140). Oxford: Berg.

Malinowski, B. (1967). *A diary in the strict sense of the term.* London: Routledge.

Mann, C., & Stewart, F. (2000). *Internet communication and qualitative research: A handbook for researching online.* London: Sage.

Månsson, S. A., & Söderlind, P. (2003). *Sexindustrin på nätet. Aktörer, innehåll, relationer och ekonomiska flöden.* Stockholm: Egalité.

Marcus, G. E. (1995) Ethnography in/of the world system: The emergence of multi-sited ethnography. *Annual Review of Anthropology, 24,* 95–117.

Marcus, G. E. (1998). *Ethnography through thick and thin.* Princeton, NJ: Princeton University Press.

Holmes, D. R., & Marcus, G. E. (2005). Refunctioning ethnography: The challenge of an anthropology of the contemporary. In N. K. Denzin & Y. S. Lincoln (Eds.), *The SAGE handbook of qualitative research* (3rd ed., pp. 1099–1113). Thousand Oaks: Sage.

Markham, A. (1995). Designing discourse: A critical analysis of strategic ambiguity and workplace control. *Management Communication Quarterly, 9*(4), 389–421.

Markham, A. (1998). *Life online: Researching real experience in virtual space.* Walnut Creek, CA: Alta Mira Press.

Markham, A. (2003, October 19). *Broadening options and raising standards for qualitative Internet research: A dialogue among scholars.* Roundtable conducted at the Association of Internet Researchers 4th annual convention, Toronto.

Markham, A. (2004a). Internet communication as a tool for qualitative research. In D. Silverman (Ed.), *Qualitative research: Theory, method and practice* (pp. 95–124). London: Sage.

Markham, A. (2005a). Disciplining the future: A critical organizational analysis of Internet Studies. *Information Society, 21,* 257–267.

Markham, A. (2005b). Go ugly early: Fragmented narrative and bricolage as interpretive method. *Qualitative Inquiry, 11*(1), 813–839.

Markham, A. (2005c). The politics, ethics, and methods of representation in online ethnography. In N. Denzin & Y. Lincoln (Eds.), The SAGE *handbook of qualitative research* (3rd ed., pp. 793–820). Thousand Oaks, CA: Sage.

Markham, A. (2006). Ethic as method, method as ethic. *Journal of Information Ethics, 15*(2), 37–54.

Marshall, J. (2003). The sexual life of cyber-savants. *Australian Journal of Anthropology, 14,* 229–248.

Martin, E. (1995). *Flexible bodies: The role of immunity in American culture from the days of polio to the age of AIDS.* Boston: Beacon Press.

Marvin, C. (1988). *When old technologies were new: Thinking about communication in the late nineteenth century.* New York: Oxford University Press.

McQuail, D. (2000). *McQuail's mass communication theory* (4th ed.). London: Sage.

McRae, S. (1996). Coming apart at the seams: Sex, text and the virtual body. In L. Cherny & E. Reba Weise (Eds.), *Wired women* (pp. 242–263). Seattle, WA: Seal Press.

McRae, S. (1997). Flesh made word: Sex, text and the virtual body. In D. Porter (Ed.), *Internet culture* (pp. 73–86). New York: Routledge.

Miller, D. (Ed.). (1995). *Worlds apart: Modernity through the prism of the local.* London: Routledge.

Miller, D., & Slater, D. (2000). *The Internet: An ethnographic approach.* Oxford: Berg.

Mitchell, E. (1985). The dynamics of family interaction around home video games. In M. B. Sussman (Ed.), *Personal computers and the family.* New York: Haworth Press.

Montgomery, B. M., & Baxter, L. A. (1998). *Dialectical approaches to studying personal relationships.* Mahwah, NJ: Erlbaum.

Moor, J. (1997). Toward a theory of privacy for the information age. *Computers and Society, 27*(3), 27–32.

Moores, S. (2000). *Media and everyday life in modern society.* Edinburgh: Edinburgh University Press

Morley, D. (1980). *The nationwide audience.* London: British Film Institute.

Morley, D. (1986). *Family television.* London: Comedia.

Mosher, J. (2001). Setting free the bears: Refiguring fat men on television. In J. E. Braziel & K. LeBesco (Eds.), *Bodies out of bounds: Fatness and transgression* (pp. 166–196). Berkeley: University of California Press.

Munt, S. R. (2001). *Technospaces: Inside the new media.* New York: Continuum.

Negus, K., & Pickering, M. (2004). *Creativity, communication and cultural value.* London: Sage.

NESH. (1999). *Forskningsetiske retningslinjer for samfunnsvitenskap, jus og humaniora. (Guidelines for research ethics in the social sciences, law and the humanities)*. Retrieved February 11, 2002, from http://www.etikkom .no/NESH/nesh.htm

Newton, E. (1993a). *Cherry Grove, Fire Island*. New York: Beacon.

Newton, E. (1993b). My best informant's dress. *Cultural Anthropology, 8,* 1–23.

Nippert-Eng, C. E. (1995). *Home and work*. Chicago: University of Chicago Press.

O'Brien, J. (1999). Writing in the body: Gender (re)production in online interaction. In M. Smith & P. Kollock (Eds.), *Communities in cyberspace*. London Routledge.

Olwig, K. F., & Hastrup, K. (Eds.). (1997). *Siting culture: The shifting anthropological object*. London: Routledge.

Orgad, S. (2005a). Moving from online to offline relationships with research participants. In C. Hine (Ed.), *Virtual methods: Issues in social research on the Internet* (pp. 51–65). Oxford: Berg.

Orgad, S. (2005b). *Storytelling online: Talking breast cancer on the Internet*. New York: Peter Lang.

Orgad, S. (2007). The interrelations between online and offline: Questions, issues and implications. In R. Mansell, C. Avgerou, D. Quah, & R. Silverstone (Eds.), *The Oxford handbook of information and communication technologies* (pp. 514–536). Oxford: Oxford University Press.

O'Reilly, T. (2005). What is Web 2.0? *IRB guidebook*. Retrieved from www .hhs.gov/ohrp/irb/irb_guidebook.htm

O'Riordan, K., & Phillips, D. (2007). *Queer online: Media, technology, & sexuality*. New York: Peter Lang.

Oudshoorn, N., & Pinch, T. (2003). *How users matter: The co-construction of users and technology*. Cambridge: MIT Press.

Park, H., & Thelwall, M. (2003). Hyperlink analyses of the world wide web: A review. *Journal of Computer-Mediated Communication, 8*(4). (http://jcmc.indiana.edu/)

Patton, M. Q. (1990). *Qualitative evaluation and research methods*. Newbury Park, CA: Sage.

Philo, G., & Berry, M. (2004). *Bad news from Israel*. London: Pluto Press.

Pinch, T. J., & Bijker, W. E. (1987). The social construction of facts and artifacts: Or how the sociology of science and the sociology of technology might benefit one another. In W. E. Bijker, T. P. Hughes, & T. Pinch (Eds.), *The social construction of technological systems* (pp. 17–50). Cambridge: MIT Press.

Pitts, V. (2004). Illness and Internet empowerment: Writing and reading breast cancer in cyberspace. *Health, 8*(1), 33–59.

Plant, S. (1998). Coming across the future. In J. Broadhurst Dixon & E. J. Cassidy (Eds.), *Virtual futures: Cyberotics, technology and post-human pragmatism* (pp. 30–36). London: Routledge.

Plummer, K. (2001). *Documents of life 2*. London: Sage.

Porter, D. (1997). *Internet culture*. London: Routledge.

Poster, J. (2002). Trouble, pleasure, and tactics: Anonymity and identity in a lesbian chat room. In M. Consalvo & S. Paasonen (Eds.), *Women & everyday uses of the Internet: Agency & identity*. New York: Peter Lang.

Potter, J., & Wetherell, M. (1987). *Discourse and social psychology: Beyond attitudes and behaviour*. London: Sage.

Rabinow, P. (1977). *Reflections on fieldwork in Morocco*. Berkeley: University of California Press.

Radway, J. (1984). *Reading the romance*. Chapel Hill: University of North Carolina Press.

Rambo-Ronai, C. (1995). Multiple reflections of child sex abuse: An argument for a layered account. *Journal of Contemporary Ethnography, 23*, 395–426.

Reid, E. (1996). Informed consent in the study of on-line communities: A reflection on the effects of computer-mediated social research. *Information Society, 12*(2), 169–174.

Reid, E. (1999). Hierarchy and power: Social control in cyberspace. In A. M. Smith & P. Kollock (Eds.), *Communities in cyberspace* (pp. 107–133). London: Routledge.

Richardson, L. (1994). Writing: A method of inquiry. In N. K. Denzin & Y. S. Lincoln (Eds.). *Handbook of qualitative research* (pp. 516–529). Thousand Oaks, CA: Sage.

Richardson, L. (1997). *Fields of play: Constructing an academic life*. New Brunswick, NJ: Rutgers University Press.

Richardson, L., & St. Pierre, E. A. (2005). Writing: A method of inquiry. In N. K. Denzin & Y. S. Lincoln (Eds.), *The SAGE handbook of qualitative research* (3rd ed., pp. 959–978). Thousand Oaks, CA: Sage.

Robins, K., & Webster, F. (1999). *Times of the technoculture: From the information society to the virtual life*. New York: Routledge.

Robinson, W. (2001). *Clicks, cliques, soaps, and posts*. Resource Center for Cyberculture Studies. Retrieved from http://rccs.usfca.edu/bookinfo .asp?ReviewID=115&BookID=103

Rogers, R., & Marres, N. (2000). Landscaping climate change: A mapping technique for understanding science and technology debates on the world wide web. *Public Understanding of Science, 9*(2), 141–163.

Rommetveit, R. (1980). On "meanings" of acts and what is meant and made known by what is said in a pluralistic social world. In M. Brenner (Ed.), *The structure of action* (pp. 108–149). Oxford: Basil Blackwell.

Rosenau, J. N. (2003). *Distant proximities: Dynamics beyond globalization*. Princeton, NJ: Princeton University Press.

Rutter, J., & Smith, G. W. H. (2005). Ethnographic presence in a nebulous setting. In C. Hine (Ed.), *Virtual methods: Issues in social research on the Internet* (pp. 81–92). Oxford: Berg.

Sanders, T. (2005). Researching the online sex work community. In C. Hine (Ed.), *Virtual methods: Issues in social research on the Internet* (pp. 67–79). Oxford: Berg.

Schaap, F. (2002). *The words that took us there: Ethnography in a virtual reality.* Edison, NJ: Transaction Publishers.

Schneider, S. M., & Foot, K. A. (2004). The web as an object of study. *New Media & Society, 6*(1), 114–122.

Schneider, S. M., & Foot, K. A. (2005). Web sphere analysis: An approach to studying online action. In C. Hine (Ed.) *Virtual methods: Issues in social research on the Internet* (pp. 157–170). Oxford: Berg.

Schrage, M. (1990). *Shared minds: The new technologies of collaboration.* New York: Random House.

Seale, C. (2005). New directions for critical Internet health studies: Representing cancer experience on the web. *Sociology of Health & Illness, 27*(4), 515–540.

Select Committee on Science and Technology (2002). *What on Earth? The threat to the science underpinning conservation.* London: House of Lords.

Selwyn, N., Gorard, S., & Furlong, J. (2005). Whose Internet is it anyway? Exploring adults' (non)use of the Internet in everyday life. *European Journal of Communication, 20*(1), 5–26

Sennett, R. (1974). *The fall of public man.* New York: W. W. Norton.

Shaw, D. (1997). Gay men and computer communication: A discourse of sex and identity in cyberspace. In S. Jones (Ed.), *Virtual culture: Identity & communication in cybersociety.* London: Sage.

Silverman, D. (1989). Six rules of qualitative research. *Symbolic Interaction, 12*(2), 215–230.

Silverman, D. (1993). *Interpreting qualitative data.* London: Sage

Silverman, D. (2004). *Qualitative research: Theory, method and practice.* London: Sage.

Silverman, D. (2005). *Doing qualitative research: A practical handbook* (2nd ed.). Thousand Oaks, CA: Sage.

Silverstone, R. (1994). *Television and everyday life.* London: Routledge.

Skeggs, B. (1994). Situating the production of feminist ethnography. In M. Maynard & J. Purvis (Eds.), *Researching women's lives* (pp. 72–93). Basingstoke: Taylor and Francis.

Skeggs, B. (2001). Feminist ethnography. In S. Delamont, P. Atkinson, & A. Coffey (Eds.), *Handbook of ethnography* (pp. 426–442). London: Sage.

Slack, J. D. (1981). Programming protection: The problem of software. *Journal of Communication, 31,* 151–163.

Slack, J. D. (1989). Contextualizing technology. In B. Dervin, L. Grossberg, B. O'Keefe, & E. Wartella (Eds.), *Rethinking communication; Vol. 2: Paradigm/ exemplars* (pp. 329–345). Newbury Park, CA: Sage.

Slack, J. D., & Allor, M. (1983). The political and epistemological constituents of critical communication research. *Journal of Communication, 33,* 208–218.

Slack, J. D., & Wise, J. M. (2005). *Culture + technology: A primer.* New York: Peter Lang.

Slater, D. (2002). Social relationships and identity online and offline. In L. Lievrouw & S. Livingstone (Eds.), *The handbook of new media* (pp. 534–547). London: Sage.

Smith, J. K., & Deemer, D. K. (2000). The problem of criteria in the age of relativism. In N. Denzin & Y. Lincoln (Eds.), *Handbook of qualitative research* (2nd ed., pp. 877–896). Thousand Oaks, CA: Sage.

Smith, M., & Kollock, P. (Eds.). (1999). *Communities in cyberspace.* London: Routledge.

Spinello, R., & Tavani, H. (2004). *Readings in cyberethics.* Boston: Jones and Bartlett.

Srinivasan, R. (2006). Indigenous, ethnic, and cultural articulations of new media. *International Journal of Cultural Studies, 9*(4).

Srinivasan, R. (2007). Ethnomethodological architectures: The convergence between an information system and the cultural landscape. *Journal of the American Society of Information Science and Technology, 58*(5).

Srinivasan, R., & Huang, J. (2005). Fluid ontologies for digital museums. *International Journal of Digital Libraries, 5,* 193–204.

Srinivasan, R., & Pyati, A. (2007). Diasporic information environments: Re-framing immigrant information focused research. *Journal of the American Society of Information Science and Technology, 58*(12), 1734–1744.

Stacey, J. (1990). *Brave new families.* New York: Basic Books.

Stern, S. (2003). Encountering distressing information in online research: A consideration of legal and ethical responsibilities. *New Media and Society, 5,* 249–266.

Stern, S. (2004). Studying youth online: A consideration of ethical issues. In E. A. Buchanan (Ed.), *Readings in virtual research ethics: Issues and controversies* (pp. 274–287). Hershey, PA: Idea Group.

Sterne, J. (2000). Bordieu, technique, and technology. *Cultural Studies 17*(3/4), 367–389.

Sterne, J. (2005). Digital media and disciplinarity. *Information Society, 21,* 249–256.

Sterne, J., & Leach, J. (2005). The point of social construction and the purpose of social critique. *Social Epistemology, 19*(2–3), 189–198.

Stone, A. R. (1996). *The war of desire and technology at the close of the mechanical age.* Cambridge: MIT Press.

Suchman, L. A. (1987). *Plans and situated actions: The problem of human-machine communication.* Cambridge: Cambridge University Press.

Sudweeks, F., & Rafaeli, S. (1995). How do you get a hundred strangers to agree? Computer-mediated communication and collaboration. In

T. M. Harrison & T. D. Stephen (Eds.), *Computer networking and scholarship in the 21st century university* (pp. 115–137). New York: SUNY Press.

Sundén, J. (2003). *Material virtualities: Approaching online textual embodiment.* New York: Peter Lang.

Sveningsson, M. (2001). *Creating a sense of community. Experiences from a Swedish web chat.* Dissertation, Linköping Studies in Art and Science.

Sveningsson, M. (2003). Ethics in Internet ethnography. In E. A. Buchanan (Ed.), *Virtual research ethics: Issues and controversies.* Hershey, PA: Idea Group.

Sveningsson, M. (2005). Ungdomars köns- och identitetsarbete på internet. In B. Axelsson & J. Fornäs (Eds.), *Kulturstudier i Sverige. Nationell forskarkonferens.* Norrköping, Sweden: Linköping University Electronic Press.

Sveningsson, M., Lövheim, M., & Bergquist, M. (Eds.). (2003). *Att fånga nätet: Kvalitativa metoder för Internetforskning.* Lund: Studentlitteratur.

Svensson, I. (2002). Maskulinitet som behag och begär. Om läderbögars självpresentation. In L. Gerholm (Ed.), *Lust, lidelse och längtan. Kulturella perspektiv på sexualitet.* Stockholm: Natur och Kultur.

Taylor, T. L. (1999). Life in virtual worlds: Plural existence, multimodalities, and other on-line research challenges. *American Behavioral Scientist, 43*(3), 436–449.

Thompson, J. B. (1994). Social theory and the media. In D. Crowley & D. Mitchell (Eds.), *Communication theory today* (pp. 27–49). Stanford, CA: Stanford University Press.

Thorne, B. (1993). *Gender play: Girls and boys in school.* New Brunswick, NJ: Rutgers University Press.

Thorseth, M. (Ed.). (2003). *Applied ethics in Internet research.* Programme for Applied Ethics, Publication Series No. 1. Trondheim: Norwegian University of Science and Technology.

Turkle, S. (1995). *Life on the screen: Identity in the age of the Internet.* New York: Simon and Schuster.

Turnbull, D. (2007). Maps, narratives and trails: Performative, hodology, distributed knowledge in complex adaptive systems—An approach to emergent mapping. *Geographical Review, 45*(2), 140–149.

Tyler, S. (1986). Postmodern ethnography: From document of the occult to occult document. In J. Clifford & G. Marcus (Eds.), *Writing culture: The poetics and politics of ethnography* (pp. 122–140). Berkeley: University of California Press.

Urry, J. (2000). *Sociology beyond societies: Mobilities for the twenty-first century.* London: Routledge.

Vanderwal, Thomas (n.d.). *Folksonomy.* Retrieved from http://www.vanderwal .net/folksonomy.html

Van Maanen, J. (1988). *Tales of the field: On writing ethnography.* Chicago: University of Chicago Press.

Van Zoonen, L. (2002). Gendering the Internet: Claims, controversies and cultures. *European Journal of Communication, 17*(1), 5–23.

Wakeford, N. (1996). Sexualized bodies in cyberspace. In W. Chernaik, M. Deegan, & A. Gibson (Eds.), *Beyond the book: Theory, culture, and the politics of cyberspace.* London: University of London.

Wakeford, N. (2000). Cyberqueer. In D. Bell & B. Kennedy (Eds.), *The cybercultures reader.* New York: Routledge.

Wakeford, N. (2003). Research note: Working with new media's cultural intermediaries. The development of collaborative projects at INCITE. *Information, Communication and Society 6*(2), 229–245.

Walker, J. (2002, June). *Making common ground: Methodological and ethical challenges in Internet research.* Presentation at Nordic Interdisciplinary Workshop at NTNU, Trondheim, Norway.

Ward, K. (2003). *An ethnographic study of Internet consumption in Ireland: Between domesticity and the public participation.* Retrieved from http://www.lse.ac.uk/collections/EMTEL/reports/ward_2003_emtel.pdf

Warren, C. A. B., & Hackney, J. K. (2000). *Gender issues in ethnography.* Thousands Oaks, CA: Sage.

Waskul, D. (2003). *Self-games and body-play: Personhood in online chat and cybersex.* New York: Peter Lang.

Waskul, D., & Douglass, M. (1996). Considering the electronic participant: Some polemical observations on the ethics of on-line research. *Information Society, 12*(2), 129–139.

Wellman, B. (2002). Little boxes, globalization, and networked individualism. In M. Tanabe, P. van den Besselar, & T. Ishida (Eds.), *Digital cities II: Computational and sociological approaches* (pp. 10–25). Berlin: Springer.

Wellman, B. (n.d.). *Little boxes, glocalization, and networked individualism.* Retrieved March 1, 2006, from http://www.chass.utoronto.ca/~wellman/netlab/PUBLICATIONS/_frames.html

Wellman, B., & Haythornthwaite, C. (Eds.). (2002). *The Internet in everyday life.* Oxford: Blackwell.

Wengle, J. (1988). *Ethnographers in the field: The psychology of research.* Tuscaloosa: University of Alabama Press.

Weston, K. (1991). *Families we choose: Lesbians, gays, kinship.* New York: Columbia University Press.

Weston, K. (1998). *Long slow burn: Sexuality and social science.* New York: Routledge.

Willis, P. (1977). *Learning to labor: How working class kids get working class jobs.* New York: Columbia University Press.

Wilson, B., & Atkinson, M. (2005). Rave and straightedge, the virtual and the real: Exploring on-line and off-line experiences in Canadian youth subcultures. *Youth & Society, 36*(3), 276–311.

Wolcott, H. (1994). *Transforming qualitative data.* Thousand Oaks, CA: Sage.

Wolcott, H. (1999). *Ethnography: A way of seeing.* Walnut Creek, CA: AltaMira Press.

Wolcott, H. (2005). *Art of fieldwork* (2nd ed.). Walnut Creek, CA: AltaMira Press.

Wolf, M. (1992). *A thrice told tale: Feminism, postmodernism, and ethnographic responsibility.* Stanford, CA: Stanford University Press.

Woodland, R. (2000). Queer spaces, modem boys and pagan statues: Gay/ lesbian identity and the construction of cyberspace. In D. Bell & B. Kennedy (Eds.), *The cybercultures reader.* New York: Routledge.

Woolgar, S. (1988). Reflexivity is the ethnographer of the text. In S. Woolgar (Ed.), *Knowledge and reflexivity: New frontiers in the sociology of knowledge* (pp. 14–34). London: Sage.

Woolgar, S. (Ed.). (2002). *Virtual society? Technology, cyberbole, reality.* Oxford: Oxford University Press.

Wright, L. K. (Ed.). (1997). *The bear book: Readings in the history and evolution of a gay male subculture.* Binghamton, NY: Harrington Park Press.

Index

Researchers:
  big picture, keeping track of,
    95–96
  criteria *vs.* standards, 193
  erotic in fieldwork, suppression
    of, 101–102
  global as manner *vs.* scope of
    research, 139–140
  global audience, location of self
    for, 147–151
  privacy, shifting duties and, 97
  privacy and research decisions, 94
  privacy and responsibility
    of, 89–92
  privacy expectations of researched
    and, 96–97
  reflexive inquiry by, 140–141
  reflexivity, creativity as part of
    research process, 161–163
  reflexivity, focus on object of
    research, 143–147
  reflexivity as analytical/rhetorical
    method, 141–142
  reflexivity for global research,
    165–166
  reflexivity of, 185
  sexual attraction to participants,
    102–105
  sexual feelings of, 99–101
  sexuality, openness about,
    127–128
  sexuality, research ethics
    and, 114–116
  sexuality of, research subjects
    and, 126–127
  situatedness, 156–157
  tensions, balance of, 174–176
  See also Qualitative Internet
    research, quality of
Retter, Y., 129
Richardson, L., 192
Riessman, C. K., 130 (n1)
Rigor:
  within crystalline forms, 194
  interpretive, 195
  quality standards for qualitative
    research, 177
  in research, 159
Risks, 176
Roberts, P., 87 (n1)

Robins, K., 163
Robinson, W., 87 (n1), 174
Rogers, R., 15
Rommetveit, R., 131
Rosenau, J. N., 8
Rosenbaum-Tamari, Y., 37
Ross, N., 170
Ruedenberg-Wright, L., 37
"RumCom" newsgroup online, 41
Rutter, J., 41
Rybas, N., 67

Sanders, T., 42
Scale, 167
"Scapes," 8
Schaap, F., 35, 129
Schneider, S. M., 15
Schrage, M., 163
Science, 12–17
Science and technology studies, 2–6
*Science in Action: How to Follow
  Scientists and Engineers through
  Society* (Latour), 19
Scope, 139–140
Seale, C., 60
Searchability, 30–31
Select Committee on Science and
  Technology of the House of
  Lords, 13
Self:
  location of for global audience,
    147–151
  production of cyberselves, 61–67
  role of in research, xviii–xix
  shifting nature of, x–xi
Self-determination, 69
Selwyn, N., 60
Semi-private environment:
  definition of, 75
  informed consent for, 76
  offline guidelines for online
    research, 79
Semi-public environment:
  definition of, 75
  informed consent for, 76
  offline guidelines for online
    research, 78–79
Sennett, R., ix–x
Sensitive content, 80–82
Sensitizing concepts, 187–189

About the Contributors

Maria Bakardjieva is an associate professor in the Faculty of Communication and Culture, University of Calgary. She is the author of *Internet Society: The Internet in Everyday Life* (2005, Sage). Her research examines how users mobilize and appropriate the internet in a variety of social contexts including the home, educational settings, and online and local communities.

Nancy Baym is an associate professor of Communication Studies at the University of Kansas. She has written many widely cited articles about online fan communities and social aspects of online interaction and is the author of the book, *Tune In, Log On: Soaps, Fandom, and Online Community* (2000, Sage). She is a co-founder and past president of the Association of Internet Researchers. She is an award-winning teacher whose courses address the use of new communication technologies in creating identities, relationships, and communities; interpersonal communication; and qualitative research methods. She serves on the editorial boards of the premier journals in the field, including *New Media & Society, Journal of Communication, Journal of Computer-Mediated Communication,* and *Information Society.* Her blog about fan activity on the internet can be found at http://www.onlinefandom.com

danah boyd is a doctoral candidate in the School of Information at the University of California-Berkeley and a fellow at the Harvard Berkman Center for Internet and Society. Her dissertation focuses on how youth engage in networked publics like MySpace, YouTube, Facebook, Xanga, and the like. In particular, she is interested in how American teens formulate a presentation of self and negotiate socialization in mediated contexts amidst invisible audiences. This work is funded by the MacArthur Foundation as part of a broader grant on digital youth and informal learning. danah also holds a bachelor's degree in computer science from Brown University and a master's degree in sociable media from MIT Media Lab.

Elizabeth Buchanan is an associate professor and director of the Center for Information Policy Research, School of Information Studies, University of Wisconsin–Milwaukee. She researches and teaches courses in the areas of information ethics and research methods. She serves as co-director of the International Society of Ethics and Information Technology (INSEIT), chair of the Association of Internet Researchers Ethics Working Group, and is chair elect of the Wisconsin Library Association Intellectual Freedom Round Table. She spends her time with her systems librarian husband, two children, five cats, numerous fish, and one lizard.

John Edward Campbell is a doctoral candidate at the Annenberg School for Communication at the University of Pennsylvania and an instructor at the University of Minnesota. He is interested in the construction of identity and community in cyberspace and how it is increasingly shaped by the commercial forces of target marketing and consumer surveillance. He is currently working on his second book, which examines the commodification of online communities. His first book, *Getting It On Online: Cyberspace, Gay Male Sexuality, and Embodied Identity,* was published by Haworth Press in 2004. John also holds a master's degree from the University of Massachusetts–Amherst.

Malin Sveningsson Elm is an assistant professor in the department of Media and Communication studies at Karlstad University, Sweden. She received her PhD from the Department of Communication Studies at Linköping University, Sweden. Her publications include *Creating a Sense of Community. Experiences from a Swedish Web Chat,* and she is a co-author of the edited collections, *Digital Borderlands: Cultural Studies of Identity and Interactivity on the Internet* and *Cyberfeminism in Northern Lights. Gender and Digital Media in a Nordic Context.* She is also a co-author of a Swedish textbook on internet research methods. Her research interests include computer-mediated communication, social interaction, youth culture, and gender and identity.

Radhika Gajjala, who received her PhD from the University of Pittsburgh, is an associate professor and graduate coordinator in the School of Communication Studies at Bowling Green State University in Ohio. Her research interests include Science and Technology Studies, ICTs and globalization, South Asians and cyberspace, and the production of race online and in virtual learning environments. Her work has appeared in *Feminist Media Studies, International and Intercultural Annual, Contemporary South Asia, Technospaces: Inside the New Media (2001),* and *Domain Errors! Cyberfeminist Practices (2003).* Her book, *Cyberselves:*

Feminist Ethnographies of South Asian Women, was published by Altamira Press in 2004. She is currently co-editing two interdisciplinary collections of essays, one on South Asian technospaces and the other on webbing cyberfeminist practice. She is also working on a book to be titled *Technocultural Agency: Production of Identity Through Presence/ Absence at the Intersection of Virtual/Real Digital Cultures* (under contract with Lexington).

Christine Hine is a senior lecturer in the Department of Sociology at the University of Surrey. Her main research centers on the sociology of science and technology, including ethnographic studies of scientific culture, information technology, and the internet. Her published work on research methods and the internet includes *Virtual Ethnography* (2000, Sage) and the edited collection *Virtual Methods* (2005, Berg). Christine is currently president of the European Association for the Study of Science and Technology.

Lori Kendall is an associate professor in the Graduate School of Library and Information Science at the University of Illinois, Urbana–Champaign. Her research focuses on information technologies and culture, including online community and identity. Her book *Hanging Out in the Virtual Pub: Masculinities and Relationships Online* (2002) was published by the University of California Press. Other writings regarding online research methods can be found in *Doing Internet Research* (1999, Sage), *Online Social Research: Methods, Issues, & Ethics* (2004, Peter Lang), and *Handbook of Research on New Literacies* (in press, Lawrence Erlbaum).

Elaine Lally is a senior research fellow and assistant director of the Centre for Cultural Research at the University of Western Sydney. She conducts research in the areas of art and technology as material culture and the role of arts and culture in regional development (especially in Western Sydney). Recent projects include the development of a digital cultural atlas to support cultural planning by local government, and she is currently undertaking a three-year Australian Research Council grant to document and evaluate an innovative contemporary arts-in-business initiative in Western Sydney. Dr. Lally is author of *At Home with Computers* (2002, Berg). She holds a PhD in Cultural Histories and Futures from the University of Western Sydney and a master's degree in Anthropology from Australian National University.

Annette Markham is a senior research fellow in the Center for Information Policy Research at the University of Wisconsin–Milwaukee, researching the connection between method and ethics and conducting research of decision-making processes in institutional review boards. She is also a senior development specialist for the State of Wisconsin, working with subject matter experts in the corrections system to design ethically grounded online training. Her primary research focuses on ethical practices in qualitative internet research and sense-making in technologically mediated spaces. Her book *Life Online: Researching Real Experience in Virtual Space* (1998, Alta Mira) has been regarded as a foundational sociological study of the internet experience. Other writing related to method can be found in the *The SAGE Handbook for Qualitative Research* (Denzin & Lincoln, 2005, 3rd ed, Sage); *Qualitative Research: Theory, Method, and Practice* (Silverman, 2004, Sage), and such journals as *Qualitative Inquiry, Information Society,* and *Journal of Information Ethics.* Annette received her PhD from Purdue University.

Shani Orgad, PhD, is a lecturer in Media and Communications at the London School of Economics and Political Science. Her first book, *Storytelling Online: Talking Breast Cancer on the Internet,* explores the online communication of breast cancer patients (2005, Peter Lang). Her work has appeared also in journals including *New Media & Society* and *Feminist Media Studies* and in these edited collections: *Oxford University Press Handbook on ICTs* (2007, Oxford University Press), *Virtual Methods* (2005, Berg), and *Web Studies* (2004, Arnold).

Ramesh Srinivasan, assistant professor of Information Studies at the University of California at Los Angeles (UCLA), has focused his research globally on the development of information systems within the context of culturally differentiated communities. He has studied how the cultural practices specific to communities can manifest themselves in an information system's architecture, particularly with respect to how it represents, categorizes, and disseminates the information it stores. His research has spanned such bounds as e-governance; public health; development informatics; and digital preservation across Asian, African, Australasian, and North American field environments. His research has received international acclaim and has appeared in top academic and international journals. For more detail, please consult his web page: http://polaris.gseis.ucla.edu/srinivasan/index.html

Susannah Stern, who received her PhD from the University of North Carolina at Chapel Hill, is currently an associate professor in the Communication Studies Department at the University of San Diego. Her research is situated at the intersection of electronic media and